STEPHEN SCHWARTZ

Stephen Schwartz is a member of the board of the Daniel Dajani, S.J., Albanian Catholic Institute, based in San Francisco. An internationally-known journalist and author, he has published major books on the Spanish and Nicaraguan civil wars and on the cultural history of California. He is a frequent contributor to the 'Wall Street Journal', the world-renowned Sarajevo daily 'Oslobodenje', and other leading newspapers and magazines around the world.

Kosovo: Background to a War
Stephen Schwartz

Editor: Mark Hegarty
Anthem Press
P.O. Box 9779
London SW19 7QA
Tel: 020 7401 8855
ISBN: 1898855 56 0

Printed in Hungary by Interpress

KOSOVO:

BACKGROUND TO A WAR

By Stephen Schwartz

Preface by Christopher Hitchens

To the Memory of Gjon Sinishta, 1930–1995

Founder of the Daniel Dajani, S.J. Albanian Catholic Institute

"The brave are not those who pull the trigger to commit a crime, but those who extend the hand of reconciliation."

– Kosovar Albanian writer and political leader Adem Demaçi,
in his 1958 novel *Gjarpinjt e Gjakut* (*Bloodthirsty Vipers*)

"Kill me, but do not insult me."

– Demaçi to Serb police during the 1999 NATO bombing,
as interviewed by Belgrade weekly *Vreme* (*Time*)

Contents

Preface

By Christopher Hitchens

All through the decades of anti-fascism, anti-Stalinism, anti-coloniaism and the battle for "self-determination", in which so many intellectuals either distinguished or disgraced themselves, there was probably no cause with fewer friends than that of the Kosovar Albanians.

There was also, in all probability, no national minority with a less favorable geopolitical locus. The Basques, the Catholics of Northern Ireland, the Kurds... these minorities at Europe's periphery at least had their partisans and defenders and advocates, and were able to communicate with the outside world. But the Kosovars labored under a double or triple indemnity. Their past was not understood or examined, their kinship with the strange and inward nation of Albania seemed tribal and bizarre, and they were considered lucky (when they were considered at all) to be enclosed within a state – that of Tito's Yugoslavia – which possessed various 'progressive' seals of approval.

It was dimly understood, by those who followed the resistible rise of Slobodan Milošević, that the Kosovo question lay at the dark heart of his "national socialist" project. He began his demagogic bid for power first by openly racist grand-standing in Prishtina and then, power having been secured, by repealing such elements of "autonomy" as the Kosovars had enjoyed hitherto. The Kosovars were actually the first people to experience, in their lives and their bodies, the nightmare of transition from Yugoslavia to Great Serbia. Nonetheless, and for some years, it was my experience in Washington that more people in the think-tank and "policy" world could tell you of Serbia's supposed 'Jerusalem' in Kosovo than could name Ibrahim Rugova, for instance, or could even guess at what was happening in what would better have been termed Serbia's Gaza Strip.

A paradox disclosed itself in this cultural and political deafness. On the one hand, the word Albanian (whether or not coupled with the word Muslim) seemed to summon free-associated terms like 'clan', 'blood feud' and 'ancient hatreds'." On the other, the Kosovar leadership steadily refused any tactics apart from civil resistance and the creation of a parallel society. Thus when I had the privilege of meeting Mr Rugova in Washington some years ago, his seminar at the Carnegie Endowment did not magnetise the sort of attention that is created by the visit of a "freedom fighter" or *guerrillero*. The very meekness of the Kosovars seemed to condemn them to obscurity, whereas any show of obduracy on their part would revive the classical stereotypes that were used to defame them.

4

During this period of what one might call suspended animation – while Bosnia was being dismembered by Milošević and Tuđman, and while Milošević was stockpiling Serbian refugees from the disaster he had helped bring upon his 'own' people in the Croatian *Krajina*, and while Richard Holbrooke was welcoming Milošević to Dayton and agreeing with him that Kosovo should be excluded from the conference agenda – the Kosovar cause depended quite largely on the work of a handful of volunteers. One of these was Stephen Schwartz, who went to considerable trouble to acquaint himself with the situation, and who decided to become a bore, a crank and a fanatic to the bargain.

He just would not shut up about the topic. I write, here, as one who benefitted from his harangues and polemics. Without such madmen, we might be even more ignorant - and even more culpable and complicit – than we are.

No mistake should be made about this, and no euphemism should be tolerated. The Milošević leadership, and its auxiliaries among the death-squad movements led by Arkan and Šešelj, intended to find an opportunity for the liquidation of Kosovo. The element of calculation and pre-arrangement was inscribed from the very beginning of the Greater Serbian project. And there was always a chance that the Great Powers would have permitted such an atrocity to occur. Not only that; there was always a chance that failure to prevent such an atrocity would have been met with relative public indifference, or even indulgence. Even now, one quakes to think of how nearly things went that way.

In these ensuing pages, those who wish can read of the time when the European conscience was not so dulled. The great Serbian socialist and anti-militarist Dimitrije Tucović, having witnessed what occurred during the initial conquest of Kosovo in the first Balkan war, wrote imperishable accounts of the business and concluded that Serbia itself would be enslaved and compromised by its own colonial rule. His descriptions – and his warnings – read as freshly and urgently today as any newspaper account of our own time, whether they are of the killing fields themselves or of the hopeless state of the internal Serbian "opposition." A nation that oppresses another nation, as was once memorably said, cannot itself be free. That this is no mere rhetoric is amply demonstrated by the events and arguments here described.

There is no more need to romanticise Kosovar nationalism than that of any other stripe, but it is important to understand that the Kosovars were fighting not for independence, or a 'Greater Albania', or for a restored autonomy (or any other conceivable or inconceivable outcome) as much as they were contending for survival. Here I think Schwartz is quite right in his impatience with – or contempt for – Western moral relativism. In their wounded or diseased psyches, the Serbian irredentists frankly wished the Kosovars dead or 'disappeared,' and in their propaganda made little secret of the fact. In practice, they would have settled for scattering them into a wretched diaspora (and thus of course metastasising their own wild chauvinism by beckoning on the birth of an intransigent "Greater Albania" movement). It was this element – of the promiscuous destabilisation of the neighboring states of Albania and Greece and Macedonia – that seems to have persuaded the NATO powers that Mr Milošević, like his forerunners Manuel Noriega and Saddam Hussein, had ceased to be useful as a "partner in peace" or "regional strongman," and become a menace in his own right.

This does not mean that, other things being unequal, there might not have been a serious attempt to eliminate the Kosovars physically. I had a most illuminating conversation, at the height of the war, with a very senior member of the Greek Foreign Ministry. He was still reeling from a conversation he had had with Mr Zoran 'Baki' Anđeljković, identified as a war criminal subject to arrest if he should leave Yugoslavia, and, one of the Serbian satraps in Kosovo. "All we want," this humanoid had said – believing himself to have a sympathetic audience of fellow-Orthodox listeners – "is to reduce the Albanian population to a manageable level." Quite evidently, the rapid Serbian deployment of cleansing forces, and the swift and massive resort to deportation, promotes this story beyond the realm of mere anecdote. Such things do not occur ad hoc, or unplanned. (Anđeljković went on to confide that Stage Two would have been the planting of settlers from the hapless Croatian *Krajina* refugee population.) And yet there are those who will themselves to believe that the mass expulsions resulted from the measures taken to counter them...

At the time, I admit, it looked as if one might have the worst of both worlds: a NATO action that hurt Serbian civilians while failing to redeem Kosovar ones. And, as it happens, I do not share Stephen Schwartz's idealistic view of NATO's character, either in this or in the earlier instances that he cites. Indeed, in his honest account and critique of the clumsiness and arbitrariness of the occupation, he may even contradict himself. However, a glance at the haphazard and improvised post-war regime in Kosovo is enough to dissolve the stupid idea that NATO wanted colonial rule in the province, let alone in Serbia, or indeed much wanted the province at all. The people of Kosovo remain the orphans of European history and of Western understanding. Our engagement with them, which should have started very much earlier than it did, has just begun.

Inconceivable indignities have been endured, and some ineffaceable resentments have resulted. That these could in large measure have been forestalled is not the fault of those who tried, in the teeth of serious discouragement, to keep the Kosovo question before our eyes. In contrast with the view held by such bizarre anti-interventionists as Henry Kissinger and Patrick J. Buchanan (to say nothing of the strangly neutral American 'anti-war' forces, some of whom spent some part of the summer of 1999 wearing the pro-Milošević "target" symbol on their vests; a pro-fascist 'first' for many comrades) we do not have too many busybody internationalists. We have too few. Stephen Schwartz's moral and scholarly seriousness has earned him a place in distinguished company. His work makes it impossible, even subconsciously, to go on regarding the Kosovars as in some way inconvenient. I hope and trust that he one day receives the recognition that he despises.

Palo Alto, California
November 25, 1999

NOTE

In addition to sources cited in the bibliography, some material in this book first appeared, as journalistic reportage and commentary by the author, in the Albanian Catholic Bulletin (San Francisco), the *San Francisco Chronicle*, the *Wall Street Journal* and the *Wall Street Journal Europe*, *Oslobođenje* (Sarajevo), *Weekly Standard* (Washington), *The American Spectator* (Arlingon, Va.) *Policy Review* (Washington), and *Illyria* (New York).

ORTHOGRAPHIC ADDENDUM

In writing this book I have utilized the Albanian versions of place names (Prishtina, Vushtrri, etc.) except for three obvious exceptions. The first involves the regions studied, for which I have used the Serbian Kosovo rather than Albanian Kosova, and Metohija rather than Albanian Dukagjini, and that of the northwestern city of Peć (Albanian Peja). In all three cases, this decision is solely based on widespread usage in Western style manuals. However, in referring to Albanian political groups such as the Kosova Liberation Army I deem it appropriate to use the Albanian spelling, even if this conflicts with foreign canons. I have based the Albanian spelling of other towns on *Harta e Kosovës, Qendra për Informim e Kosovës*, Prishtina, 1997. I have rendered the names of Serb holy sites such as the Dećani monastery in Serbian, while spelling the name of the town in which it is located in Albanian, as Deçan.

Kosovo and the surrounding area

Eastern Europe and the Balkans

Chapter I:

Albanians and Slavs

Until the Kosovo War of 1998-99, the place called Kosovo by Slavs and Kosova by its Albanian population, and Albanian culture in general, were almost completely unknown outside the Balkans, except among a handful of specialists, who themselves belonged to a neglected category of scholarship called Albanology.

What is Kosovo and who are its people? One may begin to understand Kosovo by imagining the Balkan peninsula as a woman's body, with high mountains grouped in broad ranges, suddenly opening up at a warm place from which life emerges. This green, fertile plain is flat and almost unbroken, reminiscent of the great Central Valley of California, or of 'England's green and pleasant land'. To come into it from the north, following the road out of the bleak ranges of Montenegro – literally, the Black Mountains – is to seem to have arrived at a kind of paradise.

It also seems, and is, inconceivably ancient, as a place of human habitation. Since time immemorial, it has known foreign invaders and rulers, and bloody conflicts as its people fought for their freedom. When the latest chapter in this saga of resistance began, with the Yugoslav crisis of the 1980s, Kosovo had about 2 million citizens, almost 90 percent of them Albanian. It was a center of mining, power generation, and the chemical industry. But Kosovo was also the poorest region in Yugoslavia.

This is the story of that place and its people, who, as one Christian millennium gave way to another, suddenly emerged from their timeless isolation to capture the attention of the whole world.

* * * * *

The antiquity of the Albanian presence in the Plain of Kosovo cannot be doubted. A century and a half of latter-day speculation has been concerned with this topic, much of it fuelled by the nationalistic claims of Serbian and other Slav scholars. But there is simply no reasonable basis to believe otherwise than that the people who today speak the language they call *Shqip*, or 'the speech of the eagles', are descendants of the Illyrian inhabitants of the region 2,000 years ago.

Admittedly, this presumption rests more on common sense than evidence of the usual sort. Texts in ancient Illyrian are lacking, and little, aside from the names of the Illyrian tribes and their rulers, exists to guide us. Nevertheless, the absence of unchallengeable data does not permit one to freely indulge such fancies as the argument, occasionally heard among Serbs and their sympathizers, that the Albanians were imported *en masse* from the Caucasus, by the Ottoman Turks. The overall linguistic and historical record dating from the classic period offers no sound basis for an alternative to the Illyrian hypothesis. As the modern Greeks clearly originate with the Hellenes of the past, as the Romanians evince links with the lost world of the Geto-Dacians, so must the Albanians be viewed as a remnant of a people residing, today, on territory they have inhabited from relatively soon after the arrival there of the Indo-Europeans.

Furthermore, the Albanians, in their language and culture, are clearly a Mediterranean people, having almost nothing in common with the Slavs who have ruled over them. Although they share some characteristics with the Greeks, their idiom, poetry, music, dance, i.e. virtually everything making up their identity, more resembles those of the Italians, and even the Spanish, than of the Slavs. Anybody who has seen the Catalan dance known as the *sardana*, and who then watches Albanian folk and wedding dances, cannot but recognize the similarity between them.

We may presume, however, that centuries ago the Illyrians, or the primordial Albanians, as we should prefer to understand them, dominated a much larger area than they later controlled. Roman Illyricum included present-day western Slovenia, Croatia, and Bosnia, all of Albania, and much of Serbia. Thus, in addition to the present lands of Albania proper, Kosovo, and parts of Montenegro, Macedonia, and Greece, the ancient Illyrian or proto-Albanian language was probably spoken all the way to the Danube. The Danish scholar Kristian Sandfeldt, founder of modern Balkan linguistics, traced the very name of Dardania, the Roman province that is now Kosovo, to the Albanian word *dardhë*, or pear; thus, 'the land of pear-trees'.

Numerous specialists have noted links between the Albanian and Romanian languages, indicating that they were, at some time in the past, spoken in close proximity to one another. One such example involves the word *bukur*, which is Albanian for 'pretty', and Romanian for 'happy', giving rise, ultimately, to the name of the capital city of Bucuresti. Others include the words *vatra* (hearth), and *flutur* (butterfly), which are the same in both. (*Flutur* is a fascinating lexical item for other reasons; it is clearly a very old Indo-European word, and the original term in English, 'flutterby', was transformed into its modern equivalent by the linguistic process known as metathesis.) Some scholars have assumed, therefore, that Romanian was spoken south of the Danube, and thus influenced proto-Albanian; but there seems no compelling reason to exclude the alternate possibility, that proto-Albanian once extended far to the northeast of its present boundaries. Indeed, although this book does not pretend to be a linguistic study, it is not unacceptable to argue that the Romanians originally spoke an Illyrian that was replaced among them by a form of Latin, but which survived among the Albanians.

Put bluntly, we must assume that the ancestors of the Albanians were pushed by the massive Slavic invasions of the 6th century A.D. into their present narrow homeland: Kosovo, western Macedonia, and, particularly, into the craggy mountains of southeastern Montenegro and of Albania proper, high ranges that gave these native *Shqipetar* inhabitants a belief in their relation, and that of their language, to the eagles (in Albanian, eagle is *shqiponja*). The incursions from the north were led by the Asiatic people known as Avars. They burst through the Danubian borderland, occupied by a thin Roman guard, which was allied with proto-Romanians and progenitors of the contemporary Germans, and deposited a large Slav population, including the later Slovenes, Croats, Serbs, and Slavic Macedonians, in the Balkans. But the Danubian frontier would, not long after, be reinforced with the arrival of the Hungarians, leaving the South Slavs permanently separated from their relatives, the vast majority in the Slavic heartland of Poland, Ukraine, and Russia.

The Slavs may be assumed to have inhabited the zone from the Carpathians to the Urals nearly as long as the Albanians have lived in the western Balkans. As the Albanians are the very likely descendants of the Illyrians, so are the Slavs the probable offspring of the ancient Sarmatians, whose Iranian-influenced, warlike society was known to the classical geographers and other commentators. Here, too, unfortunately, we are handicapped by the lack of linguistic records; recording the speech of the *Sarmati* was no more a priority for the Roman imperial state than documenting that of the Illyrians.

But the aggressive Slavic sweep that, a millennium and a half ago, drove the proto-Albanians into the peaks and high plateaux, left a linguistic legacy. This is as visible in the language patterns of the Balkans, as are the waves of Anglo-Saxon occupation that left the Celts in possession of no more than a fringe of Britain and Ireland, or the similar immigration and conquest that drove the native Americans off their land. The earliest Slav penetration of the Dardanian plain cannot be fixed on a timeline; but its impact continues to be felt today, as Albanians and Slavs have continued their competition for control of its fertile soil – the land, indeed, of pear-trees.

Tension between the local, rural Illyrians and Geto-Dacians, on one hand, and the raiding Sarmatians, on the other, predated the definitive Avar-Slav intrusion in the 6th century. The Roman poet Ovid described Illyria and Moesia in his *Sorrows*, written during his exile to the Black Sea town of Tomis, today's Constanza, almost two millenia ago. This is how he described a raid by the Sarmatians:

"Swift, on horseback, the barbarians ride to the attack;
an enemy with horses as numerous as their flying arrows;
and they leave the whole land depopulated.
Some flee, and with their plowed furrows
unguarded, know their fields will be despoiled.
The poor products of their labor, in creaking carts
are driven with their flocks, all the poor peasant owns.
Among the refugees, some are seized as captives
and with their arms bound, march to an unknown fate;
they cast a sad eye behind them, at their homes and farms.
Some fall in agony, pierced by barbed arrows;
for the metal head of the shaft is loaded with poison.
What the barbarians cannot steal, they destroy
and a flame rages through the innocent houses."

(Tristia, III, x.)

We must stipulate, at this point, that placing the Albanian-Serb controversy in so long a historical context forces us to confront a certain contradiction in the global policy debates over Kosovo that have taken place during the final decade of the 20th century. This may prove problematical for some; but the dramatic nature of the Balkan problem in the 1990s has made it impossible to craft a study of the phenomenon without occasionally leaving the field of pure historiography for that of the most recent headlines. Given the intention to provide a survey of the background of the violent conflict that has lately scarred the region, it is appropriate.

The discontinuity in worldwide discussion of Kosovo has had to do with a multiple paradigm about the Balkans. Such writers as Robert D. Kaplan, in his extraordinarily-influential book *Balkan Ghosts*, articulated one aspect of this paradigm, which we would call 'the ancient hatreds argument'. Put simply, that outlook, which came to extraordinarily influence such policy makers as U.S. President Bill Clinton, held that the overall region, and Yugoslavia in particular, are the site of rivalries and resentments of so long and profound a nature as to make them unresolvable, particularly by outside powers. 'Ancient hatreds' between differing Slavic groups, i.e. the Christian Orthodox Serbs, Catholic Croats, and Muslim Bosnians, thus became a pretext for inaction by the global powers to end the horrors of the Serbo-Croatian war, beginning in 1991, as well as the Bosnian war, commencing the following year.

Understandably, many foreigners who supported outside intervention to end the Bosnian agony, in particular, considered the ancient hatreds argument profoundly immoral. Indeed, an eventual reaction against this posture led Clinton to renounce it, and even stimulated author Kaplan to a virtual public apology for it. But the use of "ancient hatreds" as a pretext also led to a counter-argument, which we will call 'the multicultural Balkans theory', that was also unsound. The proponents of that position held that ancient hatreds were a myth invented by Serbian apologists as an excuse for unspeakable brutalities, and that the Balkan peoples had lived in peace and harmony until agitated by Serbian dictator Slobodan Milošević, beginning in the 1980s. Intervention was therefore deemed justifiable as a means to return the region to its previous tranquility.

In reality, however, both the ancient hatreds argument and multicultural Balkans theory were right and wrong, depending on where one applied them. In Croatia and Bosnia, violence between Serbs, Croats, and Bosnians is demonstrably of recent origin, and was clearly the product of political needs among Serb political leaders over several generations, indissoluble from Serb domination and abuse of the other nationalities in Yugoslavia. In Bosnia, the indigenous 'Bosniak' population had always sought to distinguish itself from those Serbs and Croats who believed first and foremost in Serbia and Croatia, and who desired to partition Bosnia between its two malign neighbors. But in late 20th century Bosnia, cultural differences between the three main ethnic groups were much less pronounced than outsiders later assumed, and intermarriage had become a norm, especially under Titoite Communism, which promoted Yugoslav 'brotherhood and unity'. Milošević and his cohort deliberately assaulted the tradition of Bosnian coexistence, rending it asunder. To defend Bosnia was necessarily to defend its multicultural past. In the debate over Bosnia, resort to the ancient hatreds argument was clearly inaccurate as well as unfair.

However, Kosovo presented another case. There, the Albanians have always seen themselves as a threatened indigenous community and the Slavs as invaders and oppressors. Each has hateful terms for the other: Albanians call Serbs *Shkije*, derived from the old Latin *Sclavones*, while Serbs, even in official and media usage, habitually mispronounce the Albanian name for their nation as šiptari or šiftari, an item of vocabulary comparable to 'Nigger' or 'Meskin' (i.e. Mexican) in America. These hatreds really were and are quite ancient and quite virulent. This could not serve as a pretext for a failure by Europe and the U.S. to intervene there, but that did not mean it was not apt. Of course, ancient hatreds exist in many places around the world, and are seldom subject to spontaneous combustion; rather, they typically explode as a consequence of deliberate agitation.

Recognition that hatred was authentically ancient in Kosovo also did not mean that the conflict there could not be resolved. It could be, but only by first recognizing the existence of a historical fact that most American and European policy makers failed to comprehend, or preferred to ignore: Serbian imperialism. Kosovo could not be understood without first grasping that Serbian imperialism did exist, and had been victimizing Albanians for a fairly long time. That this imperialism availed itself of nationalist myths in justifying its crimes in no way mitigated its essential character as an intruding power.

Finally, the paradigms of hatred and coexistence in the Balkans have another aspect that is paradoxical. Although they long lived together, the Bosnian Slavs, Muslim, Catholic, and Orthodox, were riven asunder on the basis of religious distinctions. By contrast, as we shall see, the Albanian nation, surrounded by alien cultures, has refused to be divided by differences in faith.

But the difficult conditions under which the Albanians defended their identity, after being swamped by the Slavic flood and then driven into the mountains, virtually guaranteed that the Albanians would be absent from the historical record in the Balkans until the end of the first millennium of the Christian era. Indeed, Illyricum was twice subjected to post-Roman ethnic submergence, first by Slavs in 570-580 A.D. and again by the Bulgars (a Turkic people who adopted Slavic speech) in 851. The Bulgars ruled Kosovo for two centuries, until ejected by the Byzantines. While documentation of Slavic governance began in the ninth century, the earliest historical reference to the Albanians as a distinct ethnicity appears two hundred years later, in 1043. Nevertheless, Albanians remained demographically predominant in Dardania. A Catholic source states that the church in Albania was separated from that in Macedonia in 877, at the Council of Dalmatia, held in Split (Spalato).

Albanians did not succeed in forming a state structure of their own at any time before the 20th century. While Byzantine, Serb and Bulgarian, Venetian, and Turkish rulers came and went, the Albanians consistently reasserted themselves as the majority in their lands, even when ruled by Slavs, and as a people without stable government. This does not reflect badly on them. It seems obviously to have been a consequence of life under pressure of much vaster populations that did not share their language or customs. The depth of their resentment of invaders should therefore come as no surprise. But the capacity of the Albanians to defend their speech and culture without a state seems remarkable, and even admirable.

Illyricum, including Dardania, was Christianized early. Under the emperor Hadrian, Saints Florin and Laurin were martyred at Ulpiana, today's Prishtina. The political division of the Roman empire between west and east, imposed by Theodosius in 395 A.D., left Albania (in which Dardania had up to seven bishoprics) within the eastern domain. The Illyrians were then brought under the Christian patriarchate of Constantinople by the eastern emperor Leo the Isaurian, in 732. At the village parish level, differences between Western and Eastern Christianity may have meant little until the Ottoman invasions centuries later. Nevertheless, the Kosovar Albanians remained oriented toward Rome, not Byzantium, if only for geographical reasons; Kosovo and northern Albania were simply more remote from the seat of the eastern empire, notwithstanding political boundaries. With the Great Schism between Catholicism and Orthodoxy in 1054, the northern Albanians cleaved to Rome while the Serbs submitted to Constantinople.

The first council of bishops from the west Balkan region of Dioclea, which was centered in today's Montenegrin capital of Podgorica, met in 1199 in Antivari (now Tivar/Bar in Montenegro), and was totally Albanian in composition, without Slav participation. Southern Albanians, known as Tosks, became Orthodox in large numbers, reflecting the continuity of Byzantine and Greek influence; there is no evidence of Albanian-Greek conflict until the 13th century. But those in the north, including Kosovo, who were called Ghegs, constituted the majority of Albanians, and, reflecting the essentially Mediterranean, rather than Eastern, nature of Albanian culture, remained mainly Catholic until the arrival of Islam. Lacking a state of their own, the Albanians could not maintain complete control over Kosovo, but the region was a center of their cultural survival. Kosovar Albanians today are almost entirely Muslim and Catholic, with no Albanian Orthodox presence.

The definitive Serbian seizure of Albanian-inhabited lands came at the end of the 12th century, when the Serb dynastic founder Stefan Nemanja, whose title was 'grand župan' or supreme district chief, led armies out of Raška, the genuine Serb heartland in the Balkans, located northwest of Kosovo in the area now known as the Sandžak of Novipazar. Nemanja swept through Kosovo, taking over its eastern half. In demographic terms, the Albanian population was largely unaffected by these events. But the conditions of the Serb occupation were severe for the Albanians, in religious as well as ethnic terms. The emperor Stefan Uroš III, known as Stefan Dečanski, during the early decades of the 14th century, so oppressed the Albanian Catholics that in 1320, encouraged by Rome, the Albanians organized a league for their self-defense – not, as we shall see, for the last time. However, it was hardly successful, for the Catholic archbishop of Antivari, Guglielmo Adam Brocardus, commented 12 years later that the Albanians and other non-Slavs suffered "under the unbearable yoke and harsh hand of the Slav ruler. The [non-Slavs] are heavily taxed, their clergy is hunted and despised, their bishops and their priests are very often bound in chains and their nobles are forced into exile."

In addition, it was the Nemanja dynasty, or Nemanjićes, that laid the basis for an enduring Serb religious identification with Kosovo. As noted by the South Slavicist Ivo Banac, Dečanski was remembered centuries afterward as a holy monarch whose body "radiated tongues of flame" against the later Turkish invaders, from his sarcophagus in the Orthodox monastery of Dečani in Kosovo. However, the son of Stefan Dečanski, the emperor Stefan Dušan, rose up and defeated his father (who was killed by strangulation), after Dušan enlisted Albanians as his supporters, and ended, if only temporarily, the suffering of the Albanian Catholics. Stefan Dušan's memory also perpetuated the sacred myth of Serbian Kosovo, as he awaited 'resurrection' from Prizren, which, according to Banac, the Slav peasants referred to as Tsarigrad or 'Imperial City,' a Serb Constantinople. In Banac's words, "Serb Zion was in Peć," a Kosovo town and the seat of Serbian patriarchs for some four hundred years, the latter also established by the Nemanjas.

But a yet brighter outcome was not far off for the Albanians, at least in the short term, for beginning in 1356, a year after Dušan's death, his empire fell apart. The Albanians won their freedom under prince Gjergj Ballsha, who affirmed his Catholicism in 1368, claiming leadership of the whole Albanian nation. The Ballshas soon recovered an area of southwest Kosovo. Nevertheless, a vast downfall awaited Serb and Albanian Christians without exception, for the Ottoman Turks had already entered the region. In 1389 came the legendary Battle of Kosovo, which we will discuss further on, and which marked the beginning of Turkish ascendance in the Balkans.

In the aftermath of the Kosovo battle, Slav power in the region disintegrated, and later Slav opposition to the new, Islamic dominion, proved, at least in military and political terms, meager. Most Serbs retained the Orthodox faith, but accepted Ottoman governance. Many Albanians, on the other hand, embraced Islam. But paradoxically, Albanian resistance to the new rulers was to prove spectacularly determined. This opposition may be summarized by a single name: Gjergj Kastrioti, or Skanderbeg.

How Albanians and other Christian populations in the Balkans became Muslims remains one of the most mythified topics in local popular consciousness as well as in political and intellectual discourse. Most observers today argue that Christians became Muslims to retain ownership of land and to avoid taxation imposed on non-Muslim citizens of the Ottoman empire. In the past, Westerners accepted as unarguable that Albanian and other Christians had been forcibly Islamized, in contradiction to *surah* 109 of *Qur'an:* "Say: 'Unbelievers, I do not worship what you worship, nor do you worship what I worship. I shall never worship what you worship, nor will you ever worship what I worship. You have your own religion, and I have mine'. " In addition, Islamic rulers are required to grant special protection to Jews and Christians, as *Ahl al-Kitab* or People of the Book. In *surah* 5, Muhammad is told, "Believers, Jews, Sabaeans and Christians – whoever believes in God and the Last Day and does what is right – shall have nothing to fear or regret." *Surah* 29 commands, "Be courteous when you argue with the People of the Book, except with those among them who do evil. Say, 'We believe in that which is revealed to us and which was revealed to you. Our God and your God is one.' "

Western historians who accept the claim that Islamic belief was imposed on the conquered Balkan nations do not cite sources as to where, when, how, and by what rulers or religious authorities such conversion was prescribed. If anything, the tax to which the People of the Book were subject was an incentive against forcible conversion by the Ottomans. Nevertheless, the tradition that Christianity was abandoned only under duress remains potent, particularly among Orthodox Serbs and Catholic Croats, but also among Albanians, including many who today identify themselves as Muslims. For those whose forebears remained Christian, the prevalence of such folk history is to be expected. But the opinion among Albanian Muslims that Islam was imposed upon their ancestors reflects something else: the continuing presence, over half a millennium, of a deep national resentment of the Turkish overlords, regardless of their religion. Thus does Albanian ethnicity, for Muslims, Catholics, Orthodox, and atheists alike, find an expression *par excellence* of anti-Turkish struggle, in the figure of Skanderbeg.

Unlike the Slav elite who sought accommodation with the Turkish overlords, the Albanian Skanderbeg, who lived from 1403 to 1468, battled the Ottomans for decades. More, he did so with a brilliance and vigor that electrified Christian Europe, winning him praise from four pontiffs. Pope Calixtus III wrote to him, in 1457, "There is no man in the world who can ignore your glorious undertaking, and who does not, with the greatest praise, hold you up to heaven, speaking of your nobility as a true athlete of and propagator of Christ's name." Offspring of a Kosovar family, Gjergj Kastrioti had been taken as a hostage to the Turkish court, accepted Islam, and was then made an Ottoman military commander and governor of the Albanian lands, under the name Iskander Beg or Lord Alexander.

At age 40, Iskander Beg led his Muslim armies to Niš in Serbia, where he was faced by Polish, Hungarian, German, and Slav Christians under the Romanian hero Iancu Hunedoara, the governor of Transylvania (in Hungarian, János Húnyadi). Skanderbeg ordered his army to retreat from Niš, handing the Christians a victory, and with 300 Albanian horsemen fled to Kruja in Albania, where he appealed for open revolt against the Turks and reverted to

Catholicism, declaring his own crusade against the Islamic power. In March 1444, at Lezha in northern Albania, Albanian leaders, supported by Montenegrin and Venetian representatives, unanimously elected Skanderbeg as leader of the struggle, and he rallied the entire Albanian people to his red banner, with the black double-headed eagle, that is still the national symbol. Marching to join Hunedoara, he arrived after the Turks had again defeated the Christians, at the second Battle of Kosovo, in 1448.

However, Skanderbeg continued fighting the Turks for 20 years more. He mastered the techniques that would later be known as *guerrilla* warfare. He humiliated Sultan Murat II and his son, Mehmed II, who would become known as *el-Fatih* or the Conqueror after taking Constantinople in 1453. Ottoman troops failed four times to subdue Skanderbeg's Kruja redoubt. The Albanian leader's exploits led the Venetians to name him the supreme leader of their forces in Albania, while King Alfons IV of Aragón offered to assist him.

Incredibly, Skanderbeg never lost a battle. Further, even after his death from malaria, while in council with his peers, Albanians as a nation, including Muslims, never gave up the sense that they were engaged in a permanent, hereditary, ethnic and racial conflict with the Turks. New, if brief rebellions exploded repeatedly in the succeeding centuries of Ottoman rule.

The extensive effort by Skanderbeg to throw off Ottoman domination may therefore be described as the birth of the Albanian nation as we now know it. Symbols attached to him include more than the flag. The first recorded text in the Albanian language, the 1462 *Baptism* of Pal Engjëll, was a one-line affirmation of Christian faith sworn by Skanderbeg's followers when a priest could not be present, and pronounced over infants born distantly from churches. Another outstanding figure of Albanian traditional culture, Lek Dukagjini (1410-1481), fought alongside Skanderbeg, and is credited with the formalization of Albanian customary law, the *Kanun*.

The *Kanun* of Lek, as it is popularly known, merits a digression, particularly in a study of Kosovo. Lek's was not the only *Kanun*; there were others, including one associated with Skanderbeg himself. But the *Kanun* of Lek, unlike the rest, became the dominant legal standard for virtually all northern Albanians, from the Montenegrin mountains across Kosovo to Macedonia. Observance of the *Kanun* was itself a form of anti-Turkish resistance, as a rejection of the *sharia* law used by the Islamic authorities.

The *Kanun* of Lek was oral law; it was transcribed and printed only in the 20th century by a great Albanian Catholic cleric, the Franciscan Father Shtjefën Gjeçovi, who was born in the Kosovo town of Janjeva and was assigned as a priest to a series of Albanian parishes. The *Kanun* specifies standards for property titling, family and village relations, marriage, labor, the taking of oaths, resolution of conflicts and rules for the pursuit of blood feuds, payment of damages, and, of course, punishment of crimes. It is amazingly detailed, as befits a code of justice developed for a rural people, living in villages without recourse to elaborate state institutions, or for whom state authority was always embodied by foreigners. It is also unarguably primitive, and some parts of it would be justifiably offensive to 21st century readers: for example, the famous (or infamous) principle, *"Grueja âsht shakull per me bajtë,"* i.e., "A woman is a sack, made to endure."

But there is an undeniable nobility in the *Kanun*, which is based, above all, on a concept of unbreakable personal honor. That such a view of individual dignity has fostered such social problems as endemic blood feuds, which persist today in north Albania (though more rarely in Kosovo), may make it objectionable for contemporary, urban Westerners. However its authenticity as a resource for endurance in times of trouble is also apparent. The heart of this principle, and of the *Kanun,* is *besa,* the "sacred promise and obligation to keep one's given word," as described by a great 20th century Albanian poet, Martin Camaj, linguist and academic. "A term rich in meaning and use," *besa* further encompasses "word of honor, faith, trust, protection, truce" and "hospitality, which involves uncompromising protection of a guest, even one with whom the host is in a state of blood-feud," wrote Camaj .

In his foreword to the Albanian-English bilingual edition of the *Kanun,* first printed in the U.S. in 1989, Camaj pointed out, "the permanence of the *Kanun* may be seen in its influence on Albanian folk literature – not only in a simple documentary form, but far more in terms of ethical and esthetic expression. Albanian customary law appears in a specific way primarily in epics and legends – in both form and content, the oldest types of Albanian folk literature." Camaj cited a characteristic stanza from a poem about the extraordinary neo-Illyrian culture hero Gjergj Elez Alia, an epical personality beloved to Bosnians (who know him as a Muslim warrior, Đerzelez Alija, particularly identified with Sarajevo) as well as Albanians. In this text, which like Albanian verse in general is of a clarity and beauty that cannot be easily rendered in other tongues, Gjergj Elez Alia, ill from injuries incurred in battle, must fight an Arab over honor:

> "You demanded my sister before the duel,
> You demanded the herdsmen surrender their herds,
> And I have come here to show you
> That our forefathers a *Kanun* gave us:
> Arms are first tested, before property is given."

The role of Fr. Shtjefën Gjeçovi as modern editor of the *Kanun* of Lek brings up the more general role of the Catholic clergy, particularly the Franciscans, but also the Jesuits and Dominicans, in Albanian cultural life through five centuries of Turkish rule. For although Islam was the state faith of the Ottoman empire, and the sultan was *khalifa* or chief Islamic authority worldwide, Christianity was granted certain institutional privileges under the *dhimma* or contract for protection of the People of the Book. Just as the Orthodox Ecumenical Patriarch never left Constantinople after the conquest of that city by Mehmed el-Fatih, so were the Serbian clergy granted or restored to control over the previously-mentioned monasteries at Dečani, Peć, etc. On the Catholic side, while no hierarchy comparable to that of the Orthodox churches was recognized, the Franciscans enjoyed a special status in Ottoman Bosnia, and also continued their pastoral and educational work in Kosovo and other Albanian territories. One of the most important archival sources on Kosovo's past consists in reports sent by Catholic missionaries back to the Congregation for the Propagation of the Faith in Rome.

Thus, a Catholic archbishop, Pjetër Bogdani, the outstanding pioneer of the Albanian vernacular literary tradition, and an apostle of popular enlightenment, established his seat at Janjeva in Kosovo in 1680. Bogdani was born in Guri of Hasi, a village near Prizren. He was educated in Rome and after accepting a series of difficult pastoral appointments, leading to conflicts with the Turkish authorities, launched an anti-Ottoman rebellion in Kosovo, in which he lost his life, in 1689, aged 58. In the foreword to his classic *Çeta e Profetënve* (Band of Prophets), the earliest known original prose work in Albanian, he declared his impassioned wish to "enlighten that impoverished land of Arbenit [Albania] and [that part of] Serbia [i.e. Kosovo], which, for the most part, speaks Albanian." This volume includes a considerable amount of scientific observation as well as religious discourse. In 1685, after his appointment as Catholic administrator of Serbia, he was praised, in Vienna, by another cleric, Dom Luka Summa of Shkodra:

> "Bogdani, may your glory endure
> As long as the turtle roams the earth,
> And may the honor of your name
> Leap above the clouds to the highest heavens,
> Enduring until the partridge
> Drinks the lake dry."

The Albanian Franciscan historian Vinçenc Malaj has chronicled the activity of his own predecessors among Albanians, as coordinated by the Franciscan province of Ragusa or Dubrovnik. Albanian-speaking priests were resident in Dubrovnik as early as 1382 to 1399, and a fairly considerable commerce, along with religious and other intellectual contacts between that city and the Albanian coastal ports, continued for centuries. Skanderbeg visited Dubrovnik with his army three times, in 1450, 1462, and 1468, and its citizens raised funds for him and served as diplomats on his behalf. About 1626, Franciscan Father Lovro Florio, from the Pelješac peninsula near Dubrovnik, a male nurse and pharmacist, journeyed through Kosovo as a missionary, and was ordained there.

In addition, Franciscans accompanied merchants from Dubrovnik and German or Sasi (i.e. Saxon) Catholics who established trading colonies in Kosovo and the Albanian-speaking areas of Montenegro, particularly in mining towns. But Slavic Franciscans were handicapped by their ignorance of the Albanian language – which led some Albanian church officials to criticize them. For example, a Catholic document notes that certain Albanian priests declared that they did not "want to accept any more bishops-strangers who do not know the language, customs, and situation" of the Albanians.

Nevertheless, in the late 16th century Franciscans from Dubrovnik ministered to Catholics in Janjeva, Novobërda, and the mining center of Trepça, the latter which is still a major area of minerals extraction today. Franciscans were also ordered to minister to Serbian Uniates, i.e. Christians of the Byzantine rite who were loyal to the Pope, and to maintain, as much as possible, good relations with the Serb Orthodox clergy. This attitude shows considerable forbearance, since the Orthodox attempted, under the Ottoman *millet* or communal system based on the Islamic *dhimma*, to tax Catholics as Christians of their own dispensation. (The historian Noel Malcolm points out that Catholics were not in fact mentioned in a particular *firman*, or decree, regulating religious taxes, and that an Ottoman governor in 1774 therefore ordered the local Greek Orthodox patriarch to desist from this abuse.)

In general, the Albanian Catholics, laity and clergy, were reluctant to remain subordinate to the temporal power of the Ottomans, and when Albanian Orthodox Christians resisted the Turks they followed the Catholic lead. The historian Selami Pulaha points out that late in the 16th and at the beginning of the 17th century, a series of assemblies brought together representatives of the Albanian regions in rebellion against the Ottomans, to better organize resistance, to coordinate with other Balkan peoples, and to petition the Christian powers for aid. These convocations came to be known as Albanian Assemblies, and were recorded. At one such Assembly, held in 1601-02 in the north Albanian village of Macukull, four Kosovar representatives participated: Pjetër Kolamari, Andrea Kolesi (Koleshi), Feta Kuka, and a Catholic priest, Mark Belaçi. This assembly declared, "We Catholics are a force of forty thousand swordsmen, valorous and brave fighters. Moreover, with us will be united all Albanians of the Greek rite [Albanians recognizing the Greek Orthodox Archbishop of Ohrid] and of the Serb rite [Albanian communicants of the Serbian Orthodox church] among our neighbors."

23

Pjetër Budi, Catholic bishop of Sappa in northern Albania (once a major town, today a mere hamlet) and translator of the catechism into Albanian, also organized an anti-Turkish revolt. In 1621, he wrote to Rome, "In these areas I stayed for 17 years and I tried as hard as I could to help and strengthen the people and those priests with my great care... with devoted books that I wrote in their languages, for the Serbs and for the Albanians." After his death by drowning, in 1623, the Albanians again protested against the naming of non-Albanian bishops.

Given their stubborn attitudes, it is unsurprising that life was less than luxurious for Catholic believers under the watchful eyes of the Ottomans. The Islamic *dhimma* calls for toleration and even protection of the People of the Book, but not for indulgence, obviously, for those whose activities were subversive. In addition, unlike the Orthodox, the Catholics and Uniates owed allegiance to the Pope, an alien prince and the declared foe of Islam. The death of Skanderbeg in 1468 led to the flight of tens of thousands of Christians from Southern Albania across the Adriatic to Calabria and Sicily, ten years later. In a foreshadowing of much later history, these Albanian refugees were rescued with the help of the Spanish and Genoese navies, then the dominant maritime forces in the Mediterranean, and with the special intervention of the great Genoese admiral Andrea Doria. They gained protection from King Ferdinand of Naples, and known as the Italo-Albanians or *Arbëresh*, their community survives in substantial numbers today, with its own robust Albanian dialect and Uniate churches, in Italy. They have played a considerable role in the development of modern Albanian political and literary culture.

It should be noted in passing that the *dhimma*, which extended to Jews as well as Christians, fostered some immigration in the other direction – specifically, the settling of Sephardic Jews, expelled from Spain and Portugal at the end of the 15th century, in Kosovo as well as elsewhere in Albania. These came in fairly significant numbers to Ottoman Bosnia and Macedonia. Their ranks were much thinner in Kosovo, but Jews were reported in Novobërda as early as 1498; a hundred years afterward, the local Jewry had its own autonomous administration, as provided for by the *dhimma*. Jews later established communities in Prishtina, Prizren, Peć, and Gjakova.

The 19th century Jewish notable Moshe ben Rafael Attias, a resident of Sarajevo where he was known as Moshe Rafajlović and as "Zeki-Effendi," wrote in his history of Bosnian Jews that some traveled regularly to Salonika in Macedonia, from whence they imported coffee, cotton, and other commodities, by way of Novipazar, and Mitrovica in Kosovo. In addition, when the great Spanish scholar of Sephardic balladry, Don Manuel Manrique de Lara, toured the Balkans in Attias' company in 1911, collecting oral texts, a trip to Kosovo turned up Castilian songs, still sung by the Jews of Prishtina and other Kosovo towns. The small Kosovar Jewry thus remained Spanish-speaking until the 20th century.

Religious life in Kosovo and north Albania proper produced another, more heterodox phenomenon, thanks to the ambiguity of the Albanian acceptance of Islam along with resentment of the Turks. This was the custom of crypto-Catholicism, in which families observed a public Islam and private Christianity. The ambivalence of the Catholics regarding the *dhimma* may have promoted this practice, since they had no officially recognized local hierarchy to protect them. Indeed, crypto-Christianity seems to have been unknown among Albanian Orthodox Christians, although Albanian Muslims shared some Orthodox festivals as well as pre-Islamic, Christian and/or pagan folk practices.

However, Catholic archives cited by Malcolm recorded the presence of five large crypto-Catholic families in a village near the Kosovo town of Gjakova in 1784, and note that some 50 years before a Catholic priest had reported administering the sacraments to "believers scattered among the homes of Muslims," apparently in defiance of Roman writ. Malcolm, treats the subject of crypto-Catholicism at some length in his *Kosovo: A Short History*. He refers to the local custom,...not unknown in Ottoman society," under which "men converted to Islam while their wives and daughters remained Christian." Malcolm cites such instances as that of Has near Gjakova, where in the late 17th century a priest identified 300 Christian women but no Christian men. The author ascribes this to the desire of the menfolk to escape the religious tax paid by non-Muslims, for which the heads of households were responsible.

Yet such a concept of mixed marriage between faiths is anything but local to Albanian culture or the Ottoman environment. Rather, we find in *surah* 5 of *Qur'an*, "Lawful to you are the believing women and the free women from among those who were given the Book before you, provided you give them their dowries and live in honor with them, neither committing fornication nor taking them as mistresses." Thus, marriage by a Muslim man to a Christian or Jewish woman does not require the conversion of the latter. Indeed, in Islam wives taken from among the People of the Book are specifically grant-ed the right to continue in their own faith. The outcome of such permission is visible in the observation of the Balkan expert Edith Durham, at the begin-ning of this century. When a resident of a Montenegrin village was asked, "Art thou Christian or Mohammedan?" wrote Durham, "He looked up lazily from the bench where he was a-sprawl, and 'By God, I know not,' was all the reply he vouchsafed."

Durham later noted that a certain north Albanian village "believes itself pre-eminently Christian. But nearly every member of the tribe drops his baptismal name and calls himself by a Turkish name – Seid, Suliman, Hussein, etc., though they hate the Turks." The discussion of Albanian crypto-Christianity also has certain pitfalls. The phenomenon has been compared by some commentators with the crypto-Judaism alleged to have been prevalent among Jewish converts to Christianity in Spain and Portugal during the period of the expulsions and Inquisition. But under the Ottomans, by contrast with the Iberian Peninsula, there was no threat of persecution of those whose adherence to one faith allegedly concealed a secret loyalty to another.

Further, Malcolm, in his discussion of Albanian crypto-Christianity, argues that such dual affiliation involved a real internal belief that Christianity was the only faith that assured salvation. But this cannot be assumed, and, more significantly, it is a subtlety that went unperceived by the authority generally conceded to best understand such matters, namely, the Vatican. In 1703 Pope Clement XI, born in the Italian town of Urbino but of Albanian descent, summoned a council of Albanian clerics to consider the problem of crypto-Catholicism in the Ottoman domains. The practice was condemned as a renunciation of faith.

However, both Christianity, which preaches conversion, and Judaism, which discourages conversion to it, demonstrate a considerably more complicated attitude toward public religious identification than Islam. Among other things, Christians and Jews are both expected to defend their faiths to the outer world, while Muslims are expressly allowed to worship alone and without disclosing their faith to others. But mass religious conversions are a complex phenomenon in any event. Nearly all those recorded and from the early Christianization of the Roman empire to the Islamic conquest of Arabia and other lands, through the case of the Turkic Khazars and similar peoples that adopted Judaism, – the conquest and Christianization of indigenous communities in Africa, the Americas and Asia – have involved political and economic as well as purely spiritual issues. Indeed, it is interesting to note that an awareness of the social impact of a new religious affirmation, generating armed conflict as well as a specific philosophy of governance over unbelievers, is a major aspect of the life of Muhammad, and in general sets Islam apart from the other major faiths.

It is also interesting to note that Jews compelled to convert in the Iberian Peninsula were not, at first, viewed compassionately by their co-religionists elsewhere. German Jews *(Ashkenazim)* long emphasized an unfavorable contrast between the northern European Jews (who, in medieval times, preferred the flames of public burning to renunciation of Judaism), and the allegedly soft and decadent Iberian Jews (who were loth to give up their pleasant homes and the shade of their orange trees). Furthermore, numerous Iberian Jewish converts, fleeing the peninsula and the Inquisition, went to Italy. There they were slow to immediately return to Judaism, and were also subject to criticism from loyal Jewish believers, who, if Spanish or Portuguese, typically went to the Ottoman empire where they could practice their faith unhindered. This negative outlook toward converts shares some of the rigor of Pope Clement XI's opinion on "crypto-Catholicism." It also has something in common with the general opinion in the Balkans that Bosnian and Albanian mass conversion to Islam was essentially motivated by economic and political opportunism.

It was only later, during the Renaissance, that the Spanish and Portuguese converts from Judaism to Christianity who fled the Iberian Peninsula were deemed to be victims of compulsion who should be welcomed back to the Mosaic communion. However, even that change was not accompanied by an attitude of mercy. The Palestinian *beth din* or religious court, revived after a millennium specifically to consider the cases of Iberian Jews who had converted, originally held that they should be flogged for having renounced Judaism before they could be reinstated as Jews, and although this stricture went unenforced, formal conversion back to Judaism was required.

But while city and village-dwelling Jews in Spain, - forced to abandon their ancient creed in favor of a religion that defamed and persecuted them, could not be expected to be lax in their attitude about conversion, the same cannot be said of Albanian peasants. There is no real evidence that Albanian crypto-Christianity involved genuine hypocrisy toward Islam, rather than a simple loyalty to folk traditions, or rather, to an earlier expression of Albanian identity. In addition, acceptance of Islam is a simpler process than conversion to Christianity, and there is almost no history of the Islamic harassment of converts. Once one has made *shehadeh,* or the profession of faith in one God and the prophecy of Muhammad, it is not permitted in Islam to inquire into the individual's allegiance, unless the person in question then renounces Islam. And although Muslims are permitted to keep their faith private, they are not allowed to publicly renounce it, even for self-protection; the punishment for such is normally death. Albanian crypto-Catholics were not harassed by the Islamic authorities until, in the 19th century, they abandoned their public Islam and reaffirmed their Christianity. But their infraction was the repudiation of the Islamic commitment, not the maintenance of an internal Christianity.

Thus, Albanians may have maintained private Christianity along with public Islam to strengthen their sense of themselves as Albanian rather than

Turkish. And. remarkably and controversially, the opinion that in returning to Catholicism from Islam, Albanians might reaffirm a primordial ethnic identity, is increasingly heard among Kosovar Albanians today. Of course, after Skanderbeg's death, many Albanians ceased to reject Turkish power, either publicly, as rebels, or privately, as 'hidden' Christians outwardly known as Muslims. Indeed, Albanians served the empire with great distinction as grand viziers (for example, the famous family known as Köprülü in Turkish and Qyprilli in Albanian), and as provincial governors and military leaders. In addition, anti-Muslim rhetoric by Christian historians should not obscure the considerable contributions made to Kosovar Albanian culture by Islamic intellectuals whose faith cannot be denied.

The historian of Balkan Islam H.T. Norris has catalogued much of this achievement. He, like many others, has described the entry into the Albanian culture area, and particularly Kosovo, of the Sufi or dervish orders, the mystical communities that have long stimulated philosophy and literature in the Islamic world, beginning only two centuries or so after the death of Muhammad. These orders are mainly known in the West as purveyors of inner enlightenment or as practitioners of picturesque forms of singing and dancing. But they were and are much more; the Sufi orders dedicate themselves to a great deal beyond meditation or performance in pursuit of mental clarity. They also fulfi a social and political role, and, as in the case of the Naqshbandi order, are known as leaders in the military defense of embattled Muslims.

In the longer historical context, the best-known Sufi expression in Kosovo, as well as among Albanians in general, is also the most heterodox and controversial: the Bektashiyya. The Bektashis, who account for up to half of all Albanian Muslims and perhaps a third of all Albanians, are a Shia grouping; they place Imam Ali, Muhammad's son-in-law, on an equal level with the founder of Islam, and, like other Shiites, venerate the 12 Imams. The Bektashiyya originate in Central Asia, where their founder, Haxhi Bektash Veli, was born in the year 648 of the Muslim calendar, or 1247-8.

Haxhi Bektash was a Turkish-language poet, and his tradition remains extremely influential in Turkey; but his order developed unusual practices in the Balkans. They conduct their rituals in Turkish, with the participation of women, who do not wear *hijab* or coverings, and, in an innovation that excites absolute horror among traditional Muslims, they consume wine or brandy; indeed, they get drunk in pursuit of mystical ecstasy. This and other novelties have led stricter Muslims to condemn the Balkan Bektashiyya as outside the Islamic 'umma', or global communion. They are also known for their openness to Christian folk traditions, including the celebration of Orthodox feast days and visits to Christian holy places, and there seems to be a demonstrable connection between the Bektashiyya and some of the more extreme variants of Kabbalah as it developed among the Sephardic Jews of Turkey. In particular, there are fascinating parallels between the Bektashiyya and the followers of the 16th century Jewish 'false messiah' Shabtai Zvi, who died in the Albanian-speaking city of Ulqin in Montenegro, after apparently embracing Islam, and whose tomb is presently honored by Muslim mystics.

The Bektashiyya are not the only Sufi order to have flourished in Kosovo; the region also welcomed the Sunni mystics of the Qadiriyya, well-known in Prizren and Gjakova, the Helvetiyya, whose influence has fluctuated, and the Rifa'i, amongst others. Sufis are especially respected in Kosovo for their role in the defense of Albanian nationhood, and for their literary works. Even before the Catholic authors Budi and Bogdani had commenced their writings, as noted by Norris, Albanian Muslims were composing works in the Oriental languages, exemplified by Mesihi of Prishtina, author of an *Ode to Spring* in Turkish, who died in 1521. Their intense mysticism even gained them some Serb converts.

Arguments over the motives of Albanians in becoming, in their majority, Muslims, or how far their Islamic enthusiasm went, are finally of little relevance or use. Albanians have long believed that a foreign state, the empire of the Ottomans, obliged them to accept its religion; whether or not such is accurate history, it is certainly an authentic expression of Albanian particularism, for, as the 19th century poet Pashko Vasa Shkodrani (a Catholic who served as Ottoman governor of Lebanon) put it, in the best-known statement on such matters, "the religion of Albanians is the Albanian cause."

As noted at the beginning of this narrative, and in contradistinction to the religious rivalries that helped undermine peace in Croatia and Bosnia, Albanians have consistently put their language and nationality ahead of religious issues. Whether out of ethnic obstinacy, a legacy of paganism, a desire to escape taxation, or a peculiarly enlightened attitude about such matters, which leads them to consider belief in God more important than the shape of the structure in which one worships or the garment worn by the prayer leader, they have always considered religious affiliations a secondary matter. In the Kosovar countryside, as Malcolm notes, it was frequently known that families included Muslim, Orthodox, and Catholic members. Thus, the legendary careers of Albanian soldiers and administrators in the service of the empire could not obliterate the memory of a time when Albanians had been free of Ottoman rule.

In 1878, the rebirth or Renaissance *(rilindja)* of Albanian nationalism, 500 years after Skanderbeg, produced the Albanian League for the Defense of the Albanian People, better known as the League of Prizren. This was the single most important event in Albanian history, until the 1990s, to be associated with Kosovo; and Prizren and Kosovo thus became the most powerful symbols of Albanian ethnicity. Catholic priests and Bektashi intellectuals joined in the formation of the League, and in directing the struggle for national reaffirmation. From then on, the attitudes of Catholic and Muslim Albanian intellectuals were broadly non-sectarian.

The League of Prizren came into existence against the background of extreme Ottoman decadence. The Congress of Berlin met in 1878 to reorganize southeast Europe, following Russia's defeat of Turkey the year before. The European powers there sought to revise the Treaty of San Stefano, which had been forced on the Ottoman sultan, and which called for the creation of a Greater Bulgaria and the division of the Albanian lands between the Bulgarians, Serbs, and Montenegrins. The League of Prizren protested the San Stefano injustice, calling for protection of the Albanian territory within the Ottoman borders, and thus gave the lie to the alleged claim of Bismarck, at that time, that no such nation as Albania existed. But the ports of Ulqin and Antivari (Tivar), long established as Albanian, and where Albanian is the majority language today, were nonetheless awarded to Montenegro. Ominously, the Montenegrins had massacred Albanians in the coastal district, burning Tivar. Although its original inspiration was to defend the empire, the League of Prizren was suppressed by the Turks in 1881.

Still, the Ottoman polity was doomed. In 1908 came the Young Turk revolution, spurred by the 1905 insurrection against the tsars of Russia, and the beginning of the most elaborate of many attempts to save the empire by reforming it. Unfortunately, the Ottoman elite that attempted to heal the 'Sick Man of Europe' merely hastened the patient's demise. They believed they could save Turkey by importing elements of a modern, rationalist model of the state, borrowed from France and emphasizing a single centralizing and unifying nationality, language, and citizenship. This, it was believed, would replace the vast and varied panorama of ethnicities ruled by ethnic Turks, including Bosnian and Albanian Muslims, Sephardic Jews, Kurds, and Arabs, to say nothing of the increasingly troublesome Christian peoples they had governed or from whom they had exacted tribute. These latter included Serbs, Romanians, Greeks, and Bulgarians, who now enjoyed independence, and the Slavic Macedonians and the Armenians, who did not. Under the Young Turks the *dhimma* was to be abolished, and all Ottoman citizens, Muslim, Christian, or Jew, were to bear equal responsibilities and enjoy equal rights. But every such attempt to do away with distinctions among these groups merely inflamed resentment among non-Turks, even among such pious folk as the

Bosnian Muslims; the latter were aggrieved at the decline of imperial authority rather than by a national feeling of opposition to it.

It is extremely significant that through the centuries of Turkish rule, Albanians and Serbs, although equally disdainful of their Ottoman rulers, seldom, if ever, united against them. Thus, the sense of the Albanians as indigenous and the Slavs as alien as invaders in the ultimate reckoning as the Turks, persisted. And as the Turkish presence waned, 19th century Albanian patriots, in promoting the national rebirth symbolized by Kosovo and Prizren, mainly acted in reaction to the yet more aggressive form of nationalism advanced by Serbia. This was inculcated in what was known to the Slavs as the Kosovo Idea: the belief that Serbia was destined to redeem its defeat at the hands of the Turks 500 years before, and to replace the modernizing Turks as the unifying and ruling power in the Balkan region. And it is for that reason that we must now digress to an examination of the Kosovo Idea as understood by Serbs, and its impact on the Balkans in the closing decades of the 19th century.

* * * * *

Chapter II:

The Battles of Kosovo, 1389 and 1689: Aftermath and Myth in Serbian History

Collective memory of the Battle of Kosovo remains alive in the consciousness of all inhabitants of the region, Slav and Albanian alike. For example, on a rainy night in September 1999, in the small and isolated refugee camp of Gladno Polje (Hungry Field) outside Sarajevo in Bosnia, the Kosovar Albanian folk composer Naim Berisha spontaneously offered the following story to the author of this book, completely unprompted:

"I know you are interested in songs and legends. Let me tell you one about Sultan Murat, the Turkish leader. It was in the time when the Turks invaded the country. Sultan Murat was in his camp and Miloš Kobilić, the knight, came to speak with him. They had some military things to talk about.

"Miloš Kobilić rode there on a horse that also had wings like an eagle. He offered the Sultan his hand, but Sultan Murat said he would not touch the hand of one who was not Muslim, and offered him his foot. Miloš Kobilić was very angry and killed Sultan Murat. Miloš Kobilić fought the soldiers there with his sword and the rest of the Turkish soldiers tried to cut him down, but his armor protected him. He rode swiftly away from the camp. He was about to escape when an old woman said, 'Put your swords under the legs of his horse, and they will cut him down' and the horse fell and he was caught. Then the Turks tried to take off the armor, and they asked, 'Where are the keys to the armor? And the old woman said,' He has the keys hidden in his moustache.

"The Turks opened the armor and took Miloš Kobilić out of it. But he asked to see the old woman, and with his teeth Miloš Kobilić grabbed that old lady and threw her a long way, 12 kilometers, through the air, to a place that today is called Babin Most, or the Old Woman's Bridge. And nearby are towns called Millosheva and Obiliq. And then the Turks cut off Miloš Kobilić's head but he walked away with his head under his arm. He went to a well, because he knew if he drank water from that well, through his mouth, he could put his head back on his body. Two girls saw him and they said, 'Look, a man without a head,' and he answered, 'I without a head, but you without eyes,' and they were blinded. And then he died. This was in the time when the battle was fought at Kosovo. I did not read this in a book, I heard it from my uncle Idriz Berisha, who told me these legends."

We shall return to this item from the storehouse of Kosovo legendry. But first we must examine the vision of Kosovo that occupies such a treasured place in Serb consciousness. The importance of Kosovo for Serbs began with the Nemanjić dynasty, which reigned over them from the mid -12th to the mid 14th - century. The Nemanjićes expanded Serbia into Macedonia, Kosovo and parts of Northern Albania, the largest span its borders have ever encompassed. The Nemanjić rulers came to be identified with the Serb state because of their achievement of a 'greater Serbia', but the most enduring contribution of the Nemanjićes to Serbdom was their creation of the autonomous Serbian Orthodox Church, cementing Serb nationhood by endowing it with a sovereign religion. As noted in the previous chapter, the last of the Nemanjićes, Stefan Dušan, is said to await 'resurrection' from Prizren in Kosovo.

An irony is that the early Nemanjić rulers also paid tribute to Catholicism in order to maintain political ties with the Adriatic coast and peace in their newly-acquired Catholic holdings, including territories in present-day Montenegro. The first Nemanjić ruler, Stefan Nemanja, was reputedly baptized in the Catholic church; one of his sons, who ruled over predominantly Catholic lands, followed the same faith while his successor married a Catholic Venetian noblewoman. However, a third son, Sava, chose instead to become an Orthodox monk, and after a period of residence in a monastery convinced the Patriarch of the Greek Orthodox Church to grant autocephaly, or virtual independence, to the Serbian Orthodox Church.

Orthodox churches in Serbia and Kosovo were traditionally subordinate to the Greek Orthodox Archbishopric of Ohrid, located in southwestern Macedonia. At the time of Sava's request, the Archbishopric of Ohrid was in revolt against the Patriarch, leading the Patriarch to grant Sava's wish in 1219, to reduce the power of the Archbishop. In addition, this decision partly arose from the weakening of the Orthodox church following the sack of Constantinople by the Catholic Crusaders in 1204. The Catholicism of Rome and Dalmatia had coexisted alongside the Orthodoxy of Greece and Bulgaria in the Central Balkans; this Crusader atrocity, however, caused great tension between the two religions and especially within the Serb kingdom, which now straddled the geographic frontier between them. The difficulties within Orthodoxy created by Constantinople's violation caused the leaders of the church to worry about the direction of divided lands like Serbia, compelling them to make concessions that would allow their church to maintain its foothold in the area.

Sava was named Archbishop of the new church, and, as pointed out by Noel Malcolm, promptly booted all Greek bishops out of Kosovo. Sava also apparently chose traditionally Catholic areas for the Serbian church's new buildings and bishoprics in order to establish Orthodoxy as the dominant sect of the area, forever associating Orthodoxy with the Serbian state. The

Nemanjićes are credited with constructing several monasteries, concentrated near the family's administrative centers to the north and west of Kosovo. In fact, the family never focused its governmental activities in Kosovo; the area only really gained significance when the Patriarchate of Peć was established there around 1300, the result, according to Malcolm, of a random attack on the monastery of Žiča, the original seat of the Serb Orthodox Church in central Serbia.

The Patriarchate of Peć was a physical testament to the new power of Serb Orthodoxy, and was to become the locus of Serb claims for Kosovo as the 'sacred cradle of Serbdom'. The Patriarchate's authority spanned Serbia and Kosovo, as well as parts of Montenegro, Bosnia after the Ottoman conquest, and beginning in the 18th century, areas of Croatia and Hungary. Indeed, its power increased after the Ottomans reinvaded Serbia in the mid-1500s, and declared the Serbian Church the head of an autonomous Serb community under the previously-described Ottoman *millet* system. The center of this new administration, predictably, was in Peć.

The melding of Serb identity with Orthodoxy was a potent and effective strategy for maintaining the continuity of Serbdom, for it ensured that even the less devout would defend Orthodoxy as a pillar of the Serb nation, and vice versa. Ivo Banac writes, "The Serbian church…was the only Balkan church organization capable of stamping its national movement with its own imprint. Far more than among the other South Slavs, religious affiliation among the Serbs helped to shape national identity. The relationship between the Serbian church and the Nemanjić state can be compared to the sensitive relationship between soul and body. When the body succumbed to the Turks, the soul kept its memory alive."

The Nemanjić lineage was finally canonized by the Serbian church, elevating them to the level of holy kings and objects of myth. Sava was made a saint, affirming his position as one of the guiding stars in the Serbian firmament of heroes. But the dynasty was destined for decline. It flared brightly again under Tsar Stefan Dušan, who conquered parts of southern Albania and northern Greece between 1330 and 1355. However, it began to disintegrate under Dušan's son Uroš, who died in 1371, when the Ottoman Empire was extending itself further into the Balkans with incursions into Albania, Bulgaria and Macedonia. Thus, the Serbian kingdom of legend only ruled Kosovo for around 250 years – less than half the length of Ottoman rule.

Around 1360, the Ottoman campaign evinced new energy with the ascension of Sultan Murat, who set his sights on Serbia and its rich fertile plains and silver mines, successfully taking the town of Niš in 1386. His ultimate goal was Bosnia; but an attempt to overrun a southern portion of that region ended in failure thanks to the might of the army of Bosnia's powerful leader, King Tvrtko. The only way open between the Ottoman holdings in Serbia and their Bosnian goal was the plain of Kosovo.

The three principal rulers in the central Balkans at that time were Tvrtko, the Serb ruler Lazar Hrebeljanović, who controlled the more prosperous mines of Kosovo and moved the Serb Orthodox Patriarchate back to Žiča, near his base in central Serbia; and Vuk Branković, Lazar's son-in-law and ruler of the rest of Kosovo, which he took from the Albanian Ballshas. When Murat's soldiers began proceeding northwest through Kosovo in 1389, the three Christian leaders contributed troops to a defensive force under Lazar, intending to head them off. The two sides faced each other's men in a large, wide field, later known as Kosovo Polje or the Field of Blackbirds, on June 15, 1389. The size and ethnic composition of the two armies would provide considerable fodder for romantic tales on both sides: each declared their opponents far more numerous than they probably were, to affirm their own skill and bravery. Some accounts of the battle from the 14th and 15th centuries describe Murat's army as being fortified by Greeks, Bulgarians, and Albanians, while Lazar's army was said to contain Germans and Hungarians. However, it is most likely that Albanians fought on the Christian side.

Unfortunately, accounts of the battle are unreliable, being composed after the fact and derived from marginal texts. Sources summarized by Malcolm include those by the Ottoman historian Nesri in the 15th century, a Serbian chronicle "probably written within a few years of the battle," two Bulgarian chronicles, and one by an anonymous Venetian or Dalmatian, all dated from the early 15th century. One of the earliest accounts is a letter recording King Tvrtko's report on the battle sent by Florentine senators to Italy four months after it was fought; another is a document by an anonymous Catalan author which Malcolm believes must have been written within 15 years of the event.

Of course, all of these sources exist within a social and political context formed by the ever-shifting religious and feudal loyalties of the times. For example, the author of one account, the Bulgarian historian Konstantin, served in the court of Lazar's son, while two Serb accounts were written by another Lazar courtier and a former member of the Ottoman *yeniceri* or janissaries, both producing strongly anti-Turkish texts. Official Ottoman reports, of course, emphasize the military prowess of the Ottoman army and how many Serbs, including Lazar's son, became Turkish vassals after the war.

The point is not only that modern historians have never had access to an impartial and thorough account of the event, but also that the methods of historical documentation of that time were by nature dramatized and localized: specifically, they belong to the epic tradition.

The epic, or a long narrative poem based on the exploits of legendary or divine characters, is an ancient form that thrived in medieval times. The preservation of epics in oral form was the principal mode of transmitting information over a wide area, including to the isolated and the illiterate. Evolving from classical epics such as the Iliad and Odyssey of Homer, medieval epics had their basis in events and history, but couched them in the cultural and moral context of a particular society or time. Conventions of the epic include dramatic recounting of a specific episode by revealing the events leading up to it in narrative flashbacks: the arming of the hero, extraordinary deeds of battle, a great journey, the fight between good and evil and divine intervention.

Medieval Serbia produced an enduring legacy of folk epic, poetry and song, and of translating events into these mythological forms immediately after they occurred, typically seasoned with a generous dash of theatre and a lacing of the popular themes of the day for entertainment value and relevance. However, the 'nationalist' myth about the Kosovo battle known today, as opposed to accounts of the conflict, is not a medieval epic; it did not emerge at the time of the events, or from the archaic Serb oral tradition, but as a later product. Indeed, the authentic hero of Serb oral poetry happened to be *Kraljević Marko* (Prince Marko), who submitted to Ottoman rule and warred against Christians.

The complicated origin of the Kosovo battle myth is visible in the perplexing tale of Lazar's two generals, one who turned traitor and one who emerged a hero by killing Murat during the battle. The subject of the former myth was Vuk Branković, Lazar's son-in-law and ruler of most of Kosovo. Oral and written evocations of this contrast – the earliest among the latter dated, according to Malcolm, nearly 200 years after the battle – describe Branković as deserting Lazar on the battlefield, possibly as part of a deal previously struck with Murat. The idea that Branković would collude with the Ottomans seems to have arisen from his becoming a Turkish vassal after the Kosovo defeat, though this theory seems unlikely in that many Serb noblemen also became vassals, including the *Kraljević Marko* of balladry, and Branković was not a particularly favoured or wealthy one.

A parallel myth that emerged alongside that of Branković identifies another general of Lazar, who fatally stabbed Murat. The deaths of both Murat and Lazar were highly dramatized, as befitting symbolic leaders in the fateful clash between East and West. Tales of Murat's demise portray a soldier gaining access to Murat either by hiding under a pile of corpses, leaping out to slay him, or by professing a desire to join the Turkish army, thereby being brought before the sultan and killing him as he kneels to kiss his foot. Some stories have foreign 'mystery' soldiers of Lazar's killing Murat, or even Lazar himself performing the deed in a dramatic standoff. The figure that has endured as the

Sultan slayer, however, is Lazar's soldier Miloš Kobilić, though there is no concrete evidence of the existence of such a person.

These motifs reproduce themes running through other epic poetry and song of that era, dealing with the duplicitous traitor – as in the French *Song of Roland*, as Malcolm notes – and the archetypal story of two brothers or lords who are revealed to be loyal and undermining, or good and evil, descendants of Cain and Abel or Judas and Matthew.

Like Murat's, Lazar's death was, of course, also given an elaborated treatment. Though several early documents describe Lazar as an ordinary battle casualty, others have him brought before Murat or facing him on the field of combat. But almost all prominently feature a crucial speech about Lazar's choice between heaven and earth, that has fed the Serb sense of divine purpose to this day. The popular Serb versions have Murat asking Lazar to either surrender or be killed. But the Serb myth about Kosovo does not exalt sacrifice for faith, or martyrdom, a Christian conception, but rather the pagan tradition of sacrifice for revenge in combat – in other words, to avenge Kosovo by dying, a notion that became especially popular with the rise of Romantic nationalism in the 19th century.

Malcolm, however, maintains that the idea of the speech originates in liturgical writings composed by church scribes a year after Lazar's death, declaring him a martyr. The writings refer to a speech Lazar gave to his troops before the battle in which he said "It is better to die in battle than to live in shame... in the end, we seek to accept the martyr's struggle and to live forever in heaven." Whatever the words and timing of the speech, what cannot be disputed is that such commentary supported the later Kosovo Idea, asserting a higher calling for the Serb nation, and the necessity of vengeance.

But Kosovo battle ballads – along with the pagan idealization of revenge -- are not limited to the Serbian language or to a Serb perspective. The persistence of a distinct Albanian oral ballad tradition based in the Kosovo events, is revealed by the discourse of Naim Berisha at the beginning of this chapter.

Naim Berisha clearly identified Miloš Kobilić as the hero of the legend. This anecdote and other data recorded by scholars of folklore demonstrate the shaky nature of the 19th century identification of the Kosovo battle exclusively with Serb nationalism, and the later presumptions that Albanians in Kosovo would not have shared such traditions. The leading scholars Milman Parry and Albert B. Lord carried out fieldwork collecting such texts in the 1930s in the Sandžak of Novipazar, an area whose eastern half has an Albanian-speaking majority, and in the Albanian-speaking areas of Montenegro. Lord, whose affection for Serbian culture led him to be decorated by the Serbian Orthodox Church with the Order of Saint Sava, did the same again in 1950 and 1960.

These scholars have noted that other Kosovar Albanian epic balladeers, including Muslims, had their own versions of the Kosovo epic that had played so crucial a role in the formulation of the Kosovo Idea among Serbs. The tale told to us by Berisha corresponds to an Albanian-language Kosovo ballad recorded by the folklorist G. Elezović in the 1920s and later commented upon anew by Lord. Indeed, Lord treats the tale of Murat and Miloš Kobilić as a mainly Albanian folk expression, tracing its major elements to Albanian oral traditions and noting their absence from the canon elaborated by the famous Serb linguist Vuk Stefanović Karadžić. Lord argues that two traditions, Slav and Albanian, developed independently but then borrowed from each other, meeting in the Sandžak region. Cultural influences went in both directions, with the story of the old woman and her advice to the Turks being considered by Lord as essentially Albanian but appearing as far north as eastern Croatia. Lord argued persuasively that this folk image emerged from ancient Albanian lore associated with the land and the origins of rivers.

But to further emphasize, these works, although sung by Albanian Muslims, and reflecting an oral tradition partially distinct from that of the Slavs, do not express hostility to the Serbs or sympathy for the Turks, even though some Albanian versions of the ballads include cultural elements that are clearly Islamic in origin. One, for example, states that the Babin Most or 'Old Woman's Bridge' was built in her honor by a sultan.

The outstanding Albanian American poet and scholar Arshi Pipa commented on the works of the great Albanian Franciscan ballad collectors Frs. Bernardin Palaj and Donat Kurti, who were disciples of the previously mentioned editor of the *Kanun* of Lek Dukagjini, Fr. Shtjefën Gjeçovi. Pipa went further than Lord in pointing out, first, the paradox that Albanian Catholic balladeers sang in praise of Muslim Slav heroes, but did not express themselves "for or against the Turks". By contrast, Muslim Bosnian singers praised the Turks, reflecting their identification with the Ottoman conquerors. Further more, according to Pipa, Muslim singers from Hercegovina "kept their distance" from the Turks while Muslim Albanians "maintained an even further distance".

Pipa pointed out that Albanian Muslim balladeers sang Slavic language versions of the texts as well, showing that they did not perceive the Kosovo tradition as an exclusively Slav or Christian one. Another leading Albanian scholar, Eqrem Çabej, viewed such oral traditions as originating with the Illyrians, before being disrupted, atomized, and Slavized during the period of Slavic invasions, and then taken back by the Albanians from their Slav enemies. Pipa stressed that the Albanian ballads were as recent in creation as the Serb texts, and were no less significant in the rise of modern nationalism in the 19th century.

It is important to understand, above all, that the symbolism of the Kosovo battle as a national catastrophe was by no means an exclusively Serb item of intellectual property – even though the Serbs translated it into a Kosovo Idea that justified their violence against non-Serbs.

Subordinate to the 1389 Battle of Kosovo in the collective Serb mythology about their 'sacred land' is the 17th century German-Turkish fighting in Kosovo and the so-called Great Migration that followed it. Like the first battle of Kosovo, Serb memory of this later conflict with the Turks emphasizes the theme of territories being brutally wrested from Christians, to be reclaimed in a fiery resurrection. As with the 1389 battle, the Great Migration has been interpreted and shaded over the years to fortify the cult of Serbian revenge.

By the mid-17th Century, the Ottoman empire's remote possessions in the Balkan and Central European regions required constant vigilance to maintain the integrity of their borders, as well as the collection of rising taxes from their subjects. The empire's size also resulted in infighting among the pashas and assumes assigned control of the sandžaks, in addition to discontent among local Orthodox authorities. The latter began seeking alliances with the neighboring Christian powers, Venice and the Holy Roman Empire, in overthrowing the Turks. These developments were particularly evident in Kosovo, described by visitors at the time as chaotic and unruly.

This Ottoman overextension induced the forces of the Germanic empire, of which the Austrians were a component, to launch a fresh campaign against the competing dominion; the Germans thus occupied Belgrade and Niš in 1688. The Germans made ample use of Orthodox recruits, which Serbs today argue were the deciding factor in the army's victories. Albanians, however, angue that the soldiers that aided in the victories against the Turks consisted nearly exclusively of Albanian Catholics,

In 1689, a Germanic regiment led by Eneo Piccolomini advanced into Kosovo, aided by an army that consisted, by his own account, of many locally recruited Serbs. After taking Prishtina, Kaçanik and Skopje (he set a fire to the latter to he set afire because his army was too small to control it), Piccolomini headed to Prizren, where he was met by a Christian archbishop. The identity of this cleric is a subject of debate: Serbs claim it was Patriarch Arsenije III Čarnojević of Peć; Albanians claim it was the Albanian Catholic archbishop Pjetër Bogdani. In any case, thanks to the activity of this religious figure, 20,000 men were recruited to strengthen the Christian army. The ethnicity of these new troops, like that of the man who represented them, is also a subject of controversy: Serb history portrays them as Serbian, while Austrian records identify them as being primarily Albanian.

Soon afterward, Piccolomini died of plague, and control of the Kosovo operation was assumed by a dictatorial commander, Duke Christian of Holstein, prompting many of the new recruits to flee. With weakened forces, the new general saw his forces overwhelmed in battle with the Ottomans at Kaçanik; Serb history attributes the loss to Christian Albanian soldiers who deserted on the eve of the battle. In the wake of the Austrian retreat northwards, the Ottomans exacted retribution on their disloyal subjects throughout Kosovo by burning houses, massacring residents, attacking Orthodox monasteries, and slaying their clergy, including those at Peć.

This violence prompted thousands of Orthodox Serbs to flee north towards Belgrade, including patriarch Arsenije. However, when the Germans made an attempt under a different military leader to retake some of the Kosovo lands they had lost, they contacted Arsenije to ask that he rally his subjects to the fight. This message has historically been represented within Serbian mythology as an invitation for Arsenije to lead his flock into Hungary, where they would be granted special religious and political freedoms. The popular image is of Arsenjie on horseback leading a Serbian exodus of thousands across the green plains, like Moses leading the Jews across the desert, but, in the Serb case, terrorized out of their homeland, and reduced to refugees. Malcolm extends the biblical parallel by suggesting that the Serbian myth has been drawn in the likeness of the Passion of Christ, equating the loss at the 1389 Battle of Kosovo as his crucifixion, the Great Migration as his burial and the reconquest of Kosovo by the Serbs in 1912 as his resurrection.

The truth of the exodus, of course, is likely a bit less romantic. In keeping with the church's integral role in national affairs, Arsenije was active in Serbian movements to oust the Turks, but initially cast his lot with the Venetians as allies, out of anxiety over how much freedom Orthodoxy would gain under Germandom. Certainly, however, as the Germans made stronger inroads into the Balkans, Arsenije agreed to contribute to their effort by rallying volunteers for Orthodox regiments. Accounts cited by Malcolm have Arsenije returning to Kosovo to negotiate with the Germans only because they threatened his removal; the 'invitation' to him was simply a request for recruitment of Serb troops in return for religious freedom under the German rule that would follow.

But it is disputed how many families – up to 500,000 people, by Serb claims, though modern historians number them as far fewer - made the journey from Serbia into Hungary, during which they endured a brutal winter.

The Great Migration was a justifiably traumatic chapter in Serb history. Whole towns and villages were emptied either by flight, Ottoman tyranny or plague. The relentless brutality with which the Turks slaughtered thousands, razed Orthodox monasteries and churches and looted their religious and historical treasures would scar the memory of any nation. Yet the principal significance of the Great Migration for Serb historical myth is not the event itself, but its presumed consequence: the allegedly overwhelming influx of Albanians onto Kosovo soil in the Serbs' wake, supposedly altering forever the ethnic balance of the land.

According to this view, Islamized Albanian tribes flooded into the plains of Kosovo after the Serb departure, driving out most of the remaining residents by force. Increased conversion of Catholic Albanians to Islam meant more Albanians in the Ottoman army, more Albanians in positions of administrative power and, therefore, more Albanians with the power to seize Serb land. The Serb author Dušan Bataković, offering the favorite Serb image of Albanians inundating Kosovo in an inhuman swarm, wrote: "In the decade following the Great Migration of Serbs, ethnic Albanian tribes (given their incredible powers of reproduction) was [sic] posing a grave threat to the biological survival of the Serbs in Kosovo and Metohija. Supported by the Turks and the Roman Curia, ethnic Albanians, abiding by their tribal customs and hajduk [Balkan bandit] insubordination to the law, in the coming centuries turned the entire region of Kosovo and Metohija into a bloody battleground marked by tribal and feudal anarchy. The period following the Great Migration marked the commencement of three centuries of ethnic Albanian genocide against Serbs in their native land."

Yet modern research reveals that a minority, perhaps a quarter, of the refugees in the Great Migration were from Kosovo, and not all of them were even Serbs: various Austrian and Hungarian accounts refer to Catholic Albanians and Muslims in describing the populace that arrived on their land. It does appear that the majority of the pre-exodus population was Slavic in origin, according to the Turkish property registers or *defterler*, contradicting recent claims by some Albanian historians that Kosovo actually had an Albanian majority before the 1689 battle. But the chief Serbian argument, that the size of the migration itself testifies to the fact that Kosovo was inhabited almost exclusively by Serbs before the battle, cannot be sustained.

Demographic data on Kosovo are mainly important because of a distinction that must be made between two issues in Serbian history, but which is typically ignored by both Serbian and Western commentators. That is, we must separate the matter of Serbian rule over Kosovo with that of a possible Serbian demographic dominance in Kosovo. Serbian advocates argue not only that medieval Kosovo was ruled by Serbs, but that they were also the local majority, and that through various wiles they were supplanted by Albanians from elsewhere. Nobody can deny that the Nemanjić dynasty had ruled over Kosovo. But did Kosovo ever truly have a Serb majority? Clearly, the answer to this since the 17th century flight northward is no. But before?

According to Ivo Banac and others, who are no apologists for Serbia, Albanian historians have argued falsely that Serbs were a colonizing minority even in the middle 15th century. The Ottoman *defterler* for 1455, well after the Turkish occupation, show that Kosovo, which was still ruled by the Serbian Brankovićes as Turkish vassals, had a pronounced Serb majority. This does not, however, make the Kosovo Serbs an indigenous populace, any more than the rapid replacement of Native Americans in Massachusetts made the English settlers there indigenous. It simply indicates the temporary effectiveness of the Serbs in driving Albanians off the land; thus, the efficiency of imperialist expulsions becomes a third issue in addition to those of political rule and eventual demographic weight.

On the other hand, ecclesiastical reports to Rome, by Catholic missionaries and priests who considered Kosovo a part of Serbia, show differing ethnic patterns. For example, Prizren in 1623-24, 65 years before the Great Migration, was reported to have 12,000 Muslim residents, almost all Albanian, with only 600 Serbs and 200 Catholics (the latter also probably Albanian.) In 1638, Prizren had only 34 Orthodox (i.e. Serb) households, along with 3,000 Muslim and 22 Catholic households. By 1641-42, the number of Serb families in Prizren had more than doubled, to 80, while the Muslim families remained stable at 3,000 and Catholics had risen to 40. Gjakova in 1638 had 320 Muslim and 30 Catholic households along with 20 that were Orthodox.

Janjeva, well-known for its Albanian and Slav Catholic communities, seems to have had an outsized Serb population in 1610, with 200 Orthodox families, alongside 180 Muslim and 120 Catholic; the latter two groups, if both Albanian, still outnumbered the Serbs. However, the Orthodox population of Janjeva declined to 140 in 1638-39, along with the Muslims, whose number of households fell to 120. Three years later, in 1641-42, the Orthodox had recovered their numbers, counting 180 households, while the Muslims remained at 120. Trepça saw a continuing fall in Orthodox inhabitants over the 17th century, with 200 Orthodox households in 1610, 80 in 1638-39, and 40 in 1641-42. This compared with a Muslim rise from none, apparently, in 1610 (although 40 Catholic families, which may have been Albanian, were recorded) to 20 Muslim families in Trepça in 1638-39 and 100 Muslim households only three years later. Novobërda, with its notable Jewish presence, also saw a consistent Muslim majority and fluctuation of its Serb population.

The best we may say, then, is that the issue of a Serb or Albanian major-ity on the ground in Kosovo remains unresolved, at least until the great Serb migration at the end of the 17th century. Among the communities described in the Catholic reports from that period to the mid-19th century, Prizren and Gjakova were overwhelmingly Albanian and Muslim, while Peć, Novobërda, and Trepça had Albanian Muslim majorities. Only Janjeva had a Serb major-ity. In 1671, the Catholic priest Pjetër Mazrreku wrote, "The Catholics in Prizren speak the Albanian and the Serb language, while those in the villages speak only Albanian. In the poor district of Prizren five priests are needed, but these priests must speak the Albanian language. Like other people, Albanians want priests to speak their own language," a point previously noted.

But to emphasize, Serb demographic dominance throughout Kosovo, if and when it did exist, reflected Serb political rule, rather than vice versa. And to paraphrase the historian Selami Pulaha, past Serbian rule and the presence of Serb monasteries in Kosovo no more prove Serbian claims to an ethnic majority in the region than Turkish rule and the presence of mosques during the Ottoman period made Serbia, a country mainly inhabited by ethnic Turks.

In any event, a Serb socialist, Kosta Novaković, who was an eyewitness to the 20th century reconquest of Kosovo as a soldier in the Serbian army, wrote contemptuously of the ideological uses of the Great Migration: "When the Turkish army in the Middle Ages reached the borders of Austria, the Serbian patriarch Arsenije Čarnojević and the Serbian landowners went to fight for Austria and to defend the Danube and Sava Rivers. The patriarch and the landowners took with them from Kosovo 170,000 Serbian households, mostly unmarried youth and serfs, and settled them in Banat and Bačka, which Austria gave them. The land of Kosovo remained abandoned and was gradually taken up by the Albanians who lived nearby; together with the few remaining Serbs, Albanians worked it and made it fertile again. Now, hun-dreds of years later, the pan-Serbian imperialists claim they have 'historical rights' in Bačka and Banat where the Serbs of Kosovo were settled, as well as in the Kosovo they gave up at that time. This they call historical justice!"

The frontier between the two great empires remained fluid. Austria joined the Venetians in a new war against the Ottomans in 1716, and in the follow-ing year Habsburg troops took Belgrade. Later, they contacted the Patriarch of Peć, Arsenije IV Sakabenta, who had assumed his position after the Ottomans allowed it to be filled anew. Both Sakabenta and the Catholic Archbishop of Skopje, tired of relentless taxation by the Turks, began con-spiring with the Austrians. Serb uprisings in the eastern Kosovo town of Vushtrri and in Metohija barely registered in Ottoman records but are por-trayed as bloody sprees of Turkish oppression by the Serbs. The Austrians took

Novi Pazar and Niš in 1737, but were driven back by Ottoman forces, and the Serb regiments organized by Sakabenta were forced to flee with them to escape Turkish recrimination. Many, however, were captured and killed, and several towns were destroyed in reprisals similar to the earlier Austrian loss, leading Serbs to call the debacle the second migration.

The novelist Miloš Crnjanski, who many consider the best modern Serb author, brilliantly evoked the situation of 18th century Serb mercenaries serving the Austrians, in his novel *Seobe* (Migrations), the first volume of which was written in 1929. Serb refugees were settled by the Habsburgs in the imperial borderlands, originally to ward off new Turkish intrusions, but they came to be employed as troops elsewhere in Europe. Crnjanski tells the story of Slav soldiers from the Danubian-Slavonian regiments, loyal to the Austrian empress Maria Theresa, sent to fight the French in the German lands in the mid-18th century. The venture of these warriors (who were Croats as well as Serbs), excites heroic rumors among the villagers they have left behind. They heard "the widely spread report that the body of Prince Đurađ Branković [who died three centuries before] had been brought back from abroad and buried at Fruška Gora, writes Crnjanski.

The Slav troops are led, in Crnjanski's novel, by the attractively romantic hero Vuk Isakovič, who maintains an intense loyalty to Serbian Orthodoxy in the face of Austrian Catholic attempts at his conversion. "Just as my sweet Orthodoxy did reside forever within my mother, so shall it reside forever within me and those who come after me," he insists at one point in the narrative.

Serb history recalls the succeeding period as a dark one in which strains on the Ottoman empire allowed bellicose Albanian mountain clans to terrorize Kosovo with rapes, murders and robberies. The Patriarchate of Peć was dissolved in 1766 by the Ottomans, by force, according to Serb histories. Other reports, however, describe the decision as a response to corruption in the church after Greek priests were placed in control of, among other things, excessive taxation of Catholics and heads of smaller church regions. The Serb diaspora in the Habsburg lands had already established its own Metropolitanate in Karlovci in 1713, shifting the focus of the Serb Orthodox church northwards.

Serb popular history blames these events for a high rate of Serb conversions to Islam during this time, claiming that Ottoman pressure combined with the disappearance of their religious and national lifelines forced many Serbs to surrender to Islam in order to survive. One figure places 30 percent of the present Albanian population of Kosovo as Serb in origin. The alleged Islamization and Albanization of Kosovo Serbs is ruefully viewed as a sort of degenerative disease, corrupting Serb souls for generations after. As Bataković wrote, "Albanization began only when Islamized Serbs, who were devoid of national feeling, married girls from ethnic Albanian tribal community [sic]. For a long time Orthodox Serbs called their Albanized compatriots Arnautaši, until the memory of their Serbian origin waned completely... for a long time. the Arnautaši felt neither like Turks nor ethnic Albanians, because their customs and traditions set them apart, and yet they did not feel like Serbs either, who considered Orthodoxy to be their prime national trait." Some Serb historians have extended this idea to claim that the Albanian speakers, which a 19th century census declared a majority in Kosovo, should generally be classified as Albanized Serbs who simply lost the Slavic language.

Though the 18th and 19th centuries in Kosovo produced only minor anti-Ottoman uprisings, the region continued to play a leading role in the drama of Serbian nationalism as it evolved through the 19th century. It was thus that the myths both of the Battle of Kosovo and of the Great Migration became the prime scenery of this drama.

The dawn of the 19th century saw Kosovo riddled with rivalries between Albanians and Serbs, some of the latter having returned from Hungary after tiring of the low standard of living and prejudice they experienced there. During this period, the Ottomans attempted to tighten up the loose ends of the empire by centralizing administration in Istanbul and eliminating some of the wayward pashas who had assumed increasingly autonomous and often tyrannical rulership over districts such as Kosovo. Resistance to these efforts resulted in a major battle in which Albanians enlisted in Bosnian forces fought the grand vizier's army; the Ottomans were defeated in southern Kosovo in 1831, though the Bosnians ended up negotiating with the Ottomans instead of pursuing the victory.

Some of the Ottoman reforms, such as new taxes and military service laws, provoked uprisings in Kosovo and elsewhere that were quickly (and brutally, by some accounts) suppressed. Others, such as an expansion of the educational system, resulted in an increase of Serb-language schools and related cultural institutions, which offered a window through which the gales of an emerging Serbian nationalism could enter.

Beginning in the 18th century with the scholar Dositej Obradović, pan-Serbianism, or the concept of uniting all of the South Slav peoples under the umbrella of the Serb nation, began to take shape in Serbia. Obradović advocated modernity and a turn away from the past, holding that religious and cultural differences were impediments to unification. But while movements like Obradović's drew on the rationalist ideals of the Enlightenment, the school of thought that played the biggest role in forming the modern Serb nationalism was the Romantic movement.

The precepts of Romanticism resounded strongly with 19th Century nationalists, particularly those that trumpeted tribalism, or the identification of folk culture - including language and poetry - as the pillars of ethnic identity. Romanticism dovetailed nicely with existing Serb traditions of emotionalism, ennobling tragedy, and vengeance, and stimulated the use of oral epic to rouse nationalist sentiment.

The linguistic aspect of Romanticism found a vessel in Vuk Stefanović Karadžić, who popularized use of the common South Slavic štokavian dialect as Serbia's national language in place of existing conventions. Proposing the watchword 'Serbs All and Everywhere', Karadžić asserted that all Slavs who used the štokavian dialect – i.e., most Croats, all Bosnians and all Montenegrins, in addition to Serbs in the narrowest sense – were also essentially Serbs by virtue of their use of the Serb language. This marked a profound departure from the traditional definitions of Serbdom, i.e. Orthodoxy and residence in historical lands, which still found support in several schemes for a single Orthodox state backed by Russia.

Vuk Karadžić was a collector of folk music, tales and poetry, as was his contemporary and co-founder of the Serb Romantic nationalism of the era, the Montenegrin ruler, Vladika (Prince-Bishop) Petar Petrović Njegoš. Njegoš authored the 1847 epic poem *Gorski Vijenac* (the Mountain Wreath), which has been described as equal to the Battle of Kosovo in its contribution to modern Serb nationalism and compared to the *Bible* or *Qur'an* for Serbs. The poem tells of a sanguinary massacre of Muslims at a Montenegrin hilltop on Christmas Eve, and is remarkable for its anti-Muslim epithets, marriage of religion with nationalist aggression and exaltation of violence as the path to national integrity. The Christian warrior heroes of the poem, one of which is Miloš Obilić – i.e. Kobilić – of the Kosovo Battle myth, declare that their efforts will not cease until either they or the "Turks" are exterminated, and news of their gory exploits move ecclesiastical leaders to "weep for joy".

Though many scholars have since criticized *GorskiVijenac* as a call to genocide, others still defend it as an expression of noble struggle for a just cause. The work of Njegoš was celebrated ecstatically in our own time by the Montenegrin intellectual Milovan Djilas, who progressed from fanatical and violent Stalinism in the 1930s to world renown as an anti-Stalinist and Yugoslav dissident beginning in the 1950s. Djilas was also a passionate Serb nationalist for most of his life, and he wrote about the conception of the Kosovo defeat in Njegoš' work: "(His leitmotif is the tragic destiny that overtook the Serbian people at the Battle of Kosovo… [For Njegoš] Kosovo as an event hardly exists, but its tragedy permeates every act, every thought, and the national being; it is felt from verse to verse throughout the entire work as a fateful misfortune imposed on the Serbs from on high... Kosovo is the height of misfortune, but neither the beginning nor the end, rather, the constant destiny of the Serbs... Supreme and immutable laws are at work under which our misfortune was conceived long before Kosovo, because our [elite] departed from the higher eternal order."

Djilas, taken with extraordinary seriousness in the West as a critical sociologist of Stalinism, went on to quote the novelist Ivo Andrić, a Bosnian Croat by birth who transformed himself into a Serb nationalist and who was awarded the Nobel Prize for literature in 1961. Andrić, who we shall encounter again, claimed of Njegoš, "All who were born in those mountains came into the world with the reflection of the blood of Kosovo in their glance," an intimidating idea to say the least. Djilas added, "Kosovo is for [Njegoš] a world, though not entire, and the main element in his world outlook... Evil and misfortune are our lot, as well as the struggle against them... Our national existence is permeated with our principal calamity; it was our own leaders who opened the gates of our woe to an alien faith and rule. Our unhappy people drag and shake off their chains, but always alone and weak, disunited and irresolute." That the Ottomans, who conquered a vast part of Asia and Europe, enjoyed far greater resources than the Serbian empire, never seems to enter into this discourse. The materialist and Marxist Djilas, incredibly, identified with "the concrete terms of Montenegrin reality!" The bathos of this outlook apparently went unnoticed by Djilas, although it must be admitted that even he, in the early 1990s, drew back from the dreadful implications of such delirium, as embodied in Milošević's assault on Croatia and Bosnia.

Though it was the folk or peasant culture that supplied the oral tradition, it was the Serbian intellectual circles that turned the tales of the Kosovo battle, the Great Migration and the massacres depicted in *The Mountain Wreath* into the foundation of a modern nationalist ideology.

The 19th century Serbian Pan-Slavists fell into two camps: those, such as Karadžić, who claimed that all South Slavs were actually Serb in origin, and therefore rightfully comprised an ideal Greater Serbia that needed only to be liberated; and those who believed that all South Slavs should simply put aside their cultural peculiarities and coalesce to form a stronger whole -- dominated, of course, by Serbia. Centuries of Ottoman negation of Serb statehood had prevented Serbs from cleaving to a specific political organism as a mark of a nation, forcing them to depend on cultural indicators, even as they yearned for a state of their own. But the time had seemingly come for the absence to be redressed.

Serb national romanticism differed from its Croatian counterpart, which also emerged at this time. The early 19th century Croat Romantics believed

47

ethnic or national groups should surrender localisms in the name of a single, unified, South Slav or Yugoslav cultural identity, but did not envision domination of the South Slavs by a Greater Croatia. But the rise of Yugoslavism in the later 19th and early 20th centuries led to the overwhelming of its Croat component by Serbism, including the virtual triumph of the Kosovo battle myth, which was adopted by both Serb nationalists and South Slav unifiers, the latter reframing it as a symbol of Yugoslav identity. This is illustrated in the work of the Croat sculptor Ivan Meštrović, who produced images of characters from the 1389 battle.

Meanwhile, the handy use of the myth by Serb integralists is exemplified by the outlook of the Radical Party (*Narodna Radikalna Stranka* or NRS.) The NRS was founded in 1880 on a platform of quasi-Marxist populism, rallying rural peasants with calls to the power of the plow. The NRS saw its constituency as morally and spiritually superior to the Croats and Slovenes and advocated dividing a Kingdom of Greater Serbia into a series of districts according to nationality and dialect. They did not recognize Kosovar Albanians as possessing a separate nationality, however, on the grounds that Kosovo was historically Serb because of the Serb domination centuries earlier.

Regarding a yet darker aspect of Serbian historical Romanticism, the historical critic Branimir Anzulović has commented provocatively on the accession to the Serbian traditional calendar, during the late 19th century, of celebrations honoring Vid, which he identifies as a Slavic pagan war deity. According to him, Vid was also a solar god and was honored in pre-Christian times on the summer solstice - the very day the Battle of Kosovo was fought in 1389. Though the Ottoman and Serb armies had obviously not planned to meet on such an occasion, Anzulović argues that the coincidence lent a sheen of significance to the event, elevating it beyond other conflicts in the history of Kosovo, and supporting the concept of a fiery war that would assure salvation of the Serbs.

Previous to the 19th century resurrection of Vid's Day, June 15 (by Julian reckoning; June 28 on the modern calendar) was observed by the Orthodox Serbs as the day of St. Amos, though at the monastery of Ravenica, where the cult of Lazar Hrebeljanović was centered after his death, it was celebrated as St. Lazar's day. While Vid's name at first made an innocuous appearance on the calendar alongside the names of Amos and Lazar, Serbs, likely influenced by the then-current Romantic exaltation of tribal identity, increasingly called for the installment of Vid's Day as a religious feast, around the 500th anniversary of the Battle of Kosovo in 1889. It became a permanent fixture on calendars early in the 20th century.

Thus was cemented a fresh link between nation and religion in Serb life. The day also marked several later and often violent events in Serb and Yugoslav history, including the 1914 assassination in Sarajevo of Archduke Franz Ferdinand by a Serbian nationalist conspiracy that ignited the first world war; the 1921 signature of the Vid's Day Constitution which established the political structure for a new state of Serbs, Croats and Slovenes under Serbian rule, later renamed Yugoslavia; the 1928 assassination of the Croat political leader Stjepan Radić, in the national parliament of the same state; the official announcement of the Stalin–Tito split, in 1948; and the 1989 pledge by Slobodan Milošević to "liberate" the Kosovo Serbs by any means necessary.

The most significant, for Kosovo itself, of the schemes for a Greater Serbia came relatively early, from Serb interior minister Ilija Garašanin, a correspondent of Njegoš and author of a secret Načertanie or Sketch of a Serbian national program, written in 1844. Garašanin borrowed from several texts circulating at the time, exhorting South Slavs to prepare for the breakup of the Ottoman Empire by unifying as an autonomous state, rather than being incorporated by the Russians or Austrians. Garašanin, however, took the extra step of specifying, in the spirit of Vuk Karadžić, that all South Slavs should be united under a Serb state. He provided step-by-step instructions on how to win the favor of the Catholic Croats, Muslim Bosnians, and Montenegrins.

The northern Albanians also gained his attention, revealing one of the primary motivations for all the Greater Serbia schemes: obtaining access to the sea, thereby acquiring the trading power Serbia had always lacked, and which was integral to it becoming a regional power. Garašanin wrote, "Serbia's complete foreign trade is in the hands of Austria…. Therefore Serbia must take care and provide for a new trading route which would bring Serbia to the sea coast and secure a port there. The only possible route now is the one leading through Shkodra to Ulcinj… Therefore, it is necessary to establish a Serbian trading agency there and place under its defense and protection the sale of Serbian products and the purchase of French and English goods… This opportunity would strengthen the Serbian influence on the northern Albanians and on Montenegro, and it is exactly those nations who hold the keys of the doors to Bosnia and Herzegovina and to the Adriatic Sea itself."

This geographical and economic conception was the real basis for the emergence of a Kosovo Idea that inflamed Serb minds as the 19th century drew to a close: the fantasy that Serbia could refight the Battle of Kosovo, regain the territory in which it lay, revive its past imperial glory, expel the Turks from Europe, and thus triumph as a dominant contender among the Slavic and even the southern European nations. The opportunity to realize this conception came in 1912.

* * * * *

Chapter III:

The Serbian Reconquest of Kosovo, 1912-13

The reconquest of Kosovo by Serbia came about during the original series of 20th century conflicts known as the Balkan Wars, and was made possible, in the first instance, by a treaty signed on March 13, 1912, between the kingdoms of Serbia and Bulgaria. The treaty created an alliance, the Balkan League and, in secret sections of the document, provided for the division of any territories gained in an anticipated assault on the Ottoman empire. The latter, under the title 'Turkey-in-Europe,' still controlled Rumelia, between Bulgaria and Greece, Macedonia, the Albanian lands including Kosovo, and the Sandžak of Novipazar.

The inaugural treaty was supplemented by a military convention of the two powers, consummated on May 12 of the same year. At the end of May, Bulgaria signed a treaty with Greece, bringing that country into the League, and in September, Serbia did the same with Montenegro. Bulgaria then entered into a military convention with Greece and made an informal agreement with Montenegro. Montenegro mobilized its troops on its border with Albania.

The formation of the Balkan League had behind it several recent developments of importance. First, the Young Turk revolution in 1908 had increased Ottoman vulnerability to aggression, in that its leaders' attempts to stimulate modernizing and centralizing reforms had aggravated the complaints of the non-Turkish nations within the empire. The decision by Austria-Hungary, the same year, to annex Bosnia-Hercegovina, which had been under de facto Habsburg rule since 1878, infuriated Serbian nationalists. In 1909, the 'Ottomanization' policies of the Young Turks provoked the first of an annual series of rebellions in the Albanian lands, including in Kosovo. Meanwhile, tsarist Russia in 1910 proposed a Balkan bloc be formed by Serbia, Montenegro, and Bulgaria, as an obstacle to Austria-Hungary's advance southward. And, most important of all from the practical standpoint, in 1911-12, Italy, the best-situated new candidate, in terms of its economic advantages, for imperialist expansion in southern Europe, beat Turkey in war and seized Libya.

The Albanian nation was caught between Austro-Hungarian, Italian, Serbian, Montenegrin and Greek ambitions, but in the broader regional, geographical and political context the victory of Italy over the Ottomans certainly contributed most significantly to the Turkish willingness to grant the Albanians autonomy, only two months before the commencement of the Balkan War of 1912. In addition, Italian imperialist opinion dreamed of a protectorate over the Albanians; the Habsburgs and Slavs viewed such competition in the area with considerable alarm.

The Balkan War of 1912 began on October 8 when tiny Montenegro, under King Nikola Petrović, jumped the gun and launched hostilities against Turkey. The Montenegrin action was publicly justified as necessary to defend the Albanians against the Turks. On October 13, the other League members delivered an ultimatum to the Ottomans, which was rejected the next day. Serbia, Bulgaria, and Greece then declared war on Turkey. Serbian King Petar issued a fulsome manifesto to his people, proclaiming, among other things, "I have ordered my brave army, in God's name, to wage a holy war, for the sake of the freedom of our brethren and for a better life. My army will meet in Old Serbia [Kosovo] with both Christian and Muslim Serbs, who are equally beloved to Us, but also with Christian and Muslim Albanians with whom our nation has shared, for thirteen centuries without interruption, both joys and sorrows. We shall bring freedom, brotherhood, and equality to all of them."

Notwithstanding these fine words, Serbian and Montenegrin ambitions in Kosovo and north Albania reflected something other than fraternal love for Albanians; rather, they were an expression of a strategic drive for control of a substantial Adriatic littoral. This, a main goal of Serbian nationalists from the middle of the 19th century, was made more urgent by the fear of Italian preemption. Serb nationalist intellectuals and journalists had insistently referred to Kosovo as *Stara Srbija* or Old Serbia, a construction they and their foreign admirers (the latter whose numbers were destined to grow dramatically) would repeat incessantly for at least two generations.

Serbian armies pressed through Kosovo and northern Albania, poorly outfitted and armed, but proclaiming the liberation of the region in delirious scenes and songs. Prishtina fell to the Serbs on October 22, after little more than a week. The Turkish army withdrew in disarray from Kosovo, but Albanians reacted with resistance, as was predictable. They were led by a group of Kosovars whose names impressed themselves in the Albanian consciousness, and struck fear among Slavs, for two generations: Hasan beg Prishtina (believed to be a Serb renegade from Vushtrri, born as Šišković, according to Ivo Banac), Isa Boletini from Mitrovica, who had been armed by the Serbs with new rifles as early as 1909, to fight the Turks, and Bajram Curri.

Where the prominent Albanian nationalists outside Kosovo were by and large intellectuals, these men were tough, resourceful warriors who had conspired for years against the Ottoman authorities, and had risen in arms, yet again, to challenge the Young Turk regime, earlier in 1912. They came to be known as *kaçaks*, or outlaws; in Albanian-English dictionaries the example

51

cited to define the term is often that of Robin Hood. Their combat, had, on the ground, facilitated the previously mentioned granting of Albanian autonomy. Yet this latest and most successful Kosovar uprising against the Turks had also provided the pretext for Serbian intervention and soon, Serbian mass terror; King Petar's army, which on paper promised solidarity, responded to Albanian opposition with atrocities on a scale not seen in Europe for centuries. The regular troops were aided in these activities by Serb irregulars, or četniks, typically drawn from the most ignorant and desperate poor peasants, and even more unrestrained in their cruelty. The term četnik derives from četa, a band of warriors, and was widely used to refer to Slav *guerrillas* who, with Bulgarian and Serbian assistance, harried the Ottoman authorities in Macedonia beginning in the last decade of the 19th century. Its meaning was originally positive, referring to patriotic heroes, but in the 20th century it became associated with bloodthirsty extremism.

One of the first public figures to sound the alarm about the brutality of the Serb invasion was a leader of the Serbian Social Democrats, Dimitrije Tucović. Tucović had volunteered for service in the Serbian army, and had marched in its ranks into Kosovo, on the belief that socialists needed to be with their people wherever they were. He had been won to socialism as a middle-school student, a characteristic East European phenomenon of the time, and his internationalist beliefs were sincere and profound. Almost immediately, he began writing about the horrific character of the Serbian conquest in the Belgrade socialist journal *Radničke Novine* (Workers' Journal). His statements were extraordinary for their candor and their author's authentic solidarity with the Albanians, in contrast with official rhetoric, and, therefore, the strength of his protest.

On October 22, the day Prishtina was occupied, *Radničke Novine* printed the following as a letter from a soldier: "My dear friend, I have no time to write to you at length, but I can tell you that appalling things are going on here. I am terrified by them, and constantly ask myself how men can be so barbarous as to commit such cruelties. It is horrible. I dare not (even if I had time, which I have not) tell you more, but I may say that Luma [an Albanian region along the river of the same name], no longer exists. There is nothing but corpses, dust, ashes. There are villages of 100, 150, 200 houses, where there is no longer a single man, literally not one. We collect them in bodies of forty to fifty, and then we pierce them with our bayonets to the last man. Pillage is going on everywhere. The officers told the soldiers to go to Prizren and sell the things they had stolen." The *Radničke Novine* editor added, "Our friend tells us of things even more appalling than this, but they are so horrible and so heartrending that we prefer not to publish them."

52

In later articles published by *Radničke Novine,* summarizing the Balkan Wars, the acquisition of Kosovo, and particularly the suppression of the Albanians, Tucović wrote: "We have carried out the attempted premeditated murder of an entire nation. We were caught in that criminal act and have been obstructed. Now we have to suffer the punishment... In the Balkan Wars, Serbia not only doubled its territory but also its external enemies.

"Our lordly people dreamed of foreign lands and foreign freedoms, but we who had been heralds of national liberation brought with us, instead, the banner of national enslavement... The basis for all of the misfortunes we now suffer and which we will continue to suffer in the future lies in the fact that we invaded a foreign land.

"Voltaire said the poor always like to speak of their past... This is clearly true of the tiny Balkan states, which wanted to create their future on the basis of the past. Some recall the rule of Tsar Dušan, they dream of a Greater Serbian state... The memory of that 'illustrious' past is inseparably linked to territorial expansion by the ruling classes„

"Serbian overlords are trying to turn a national minority [Kosovo Serbs] into a majority by means of a police state, and they are preparing their subjects not to be free citizens but submissive subjects. The regime of extraordinary police measures... is inspired by the reactionary desire to advance one nation and subdue another... On the other hand, it gives rise to new urges... provoking intolerance and hatred between peoples.

"The Serbian bourgeoisie desires freedom for its own nation at the price of freedom for other nations... We want freedom for our nation without denying the freedom of others. This goal can be achieved in the Balkans only by the formation of a political entity in which all nations would be completely equal... without regard to who ruled what region centuries ago."

Tucović was an extraordinary figure. A capable soldier, although he was a firm antimilitarist, he remained a reserve officer in the Serbian army, and was killed in action in the first months of World War I. He was not only an enemy of Serbian imperialism, he was also a real friend of the Albanian people. For that reason, his memory has been perpetuated as much and perhaps more among Albanians than Serbs. He believed, in effect, and with considerable reason, that the Serb, Montenegrin, and Albanian inhabitants of north Albania formed a single, interrelated regional community, embracing two nations, Serbo-Montenegrin and Albanian, and three religions, Catholic, Orthodox, and Muslim.

But he saw this in a way completely different from those Serb chauvinists who declared that population to be no more than Albanized Serbs. In reality, Tucović argued, it was the other way around: Karađorđe, leader of the Serb national uprising of 1804 and progenitor of a Serb monarchical house, the Karađorđevići, was, Tucović said, of Albanian origin. Above all, Tucović defended Albania's right to independence, and the Albanian-majority character of Kosovo, while calling for a federation of Balkan nations, a socialist item of faith at the time.

Tucović wrote, "Relations with foreign nations, and therefore with the Albanians, must be built on a democratic, civil, and humane foundation of tolerance, co-operative existence, and labour... The battle being waged today by the Albanians is a natural, inevitable, historic struggle for a different political life... The free Serb nation must respect that struggle... and deny any government the means to conduct a warmongering policy."

Alone in its uncompromising rejection of Greater Serbia, the Serbian Social Democratic Party which Tucović led was a tiny political formation, founded in 1903. Other notable internationalists in the party included Kosta Novaković, who also served as a combat soldier in the Serbian army, Dušan Popović, Dragiša Lapčević, and Triša Kaclerović. Novaković, Lapčević and Kaclerović were all elected to the Serb parliament. Their party had links with the Russian Bolsheviks and with the similar Bulgarian left socialist tendency known as *Tesnyaki* or 'Narrows', as well as with Leon Trotsky, then affiliated to no party, and other independent Russian Marxists. Tucović and Lapčević were Serbian delegates to the 1910 congress of the Tesnyaki, a major regional political event of the time.

Popović, editor of *Radničke Novine*, wrote of the 1912 Albanian campaign, "The details concerning the operations of the Serb armies are frightful. They plunder, lay waste, burn, plow up, massacre, and destroy everything, down to the roots... It is no wonder that our peasant masses have such barbaric instincts since this state never saw to it that they were educated and civilized; nor should we be shocked at the narrow and meagre political and spiritual horizons of our military commanders who are trained to regard the brutal and cold-blooded murder of tens and hundreds of Albanians, their wives and children, as heroic... The slogans in which such ideas and views are expressed come from the highest social and political strata in Serbia. It is not merely a question of a protest by Serbian workers against the Albanian policy of the Serbian bourgeoisie; we must rescue the image of the Serbian people in the eyes of cultured and democratic Europeans. We must show that there are people in Serbia, many people, who oppose this, and that at the head of this opinion stands the working class and Social Democracy."

Dragiša Lapčević wrote at the same time, with great prescience and in words that are pregnant with meaning decades later, "Through the politics of our government conditions have been created so that for a great many years (perhaps even decades!), there will be repeated clashes and suffering between two unfortunate nations... Serbia has ordered its armies to subdue and enslave... Our soldiers have marched with guns and cannons but have not only created dishonor for their land, which once had a tradition of revolution and liberation, but they have also created conditions for eternal discord. We shall constantly have conflict and misfortune if Serbia does not change its policies."

By the end of October the Serbs reached Prizren, which surrendered within days, Peć was taken by the Montenegrins, and a combined Serb and Montenegrin force overcame the Albanian defenders of Gjakova. The Serbs continued their rapid advance, heading for the sea. Nearly 20 years later Kosta Novaković recalled, "The invasion of Albania by the Serbian army was a Serbian imperialist attempt to capture the ports of Shkodra, Durrës and Shen-Gjin... The Serbian imperialist government left nothing undone against Albanians during its occupation. It issued orders for scaffolds to be erected in a dozen parts. It massacred, killed and plundered the impoverished Albanian population. And it persecuted only the poor.

"When they invaded Kosovo, the Serbian imperialists proclaimed that they were going to regain the historical rights they had in 1389. Basing themselves on these 'historical rights,' Italy or France, Greece or Turkey, could demand half of Europe, because they had held those parts at one time. Indeed, France could demand a piece of Russia, because once in 1812 Napoleon went as far as Moscow.

"Kosovo is a purely Albanian territory; it has only 10-15 per cent Serbs. The Serbian imperialists employed the tactics and methods of medieval warriors or colonial invaders: the annihilation of the population under the pretext of military operations, the disarming of people, and the suppression of the armed resistance. Thus... 120,000 Albanians -- men, women, boys, old folk and children, were wiped out; hundreds of villages, more in Kosovo and fewer in Macedonia, were bombarded and most of them completely destroyed. It should be pointed out that the representative of the Tsarist Russian imperialist policy, Hartwig, the minister of Russia to Belgrade, blessed Belgrade's policy of annihilation. The Orthodox Russian Tsar urged his Orthodox Serbian brothers, King Petar and his son Aleksandar, to kill a whole people and to spread the Orthodox faith in the Balkans. At least 50,000 Albanians were forced to become refugees and flee to Turkey and Albania to save their lives. This annihilation thinned out the Albanian nation in Kosovo, but in no way changed the Albanian character there. The objective of these massacres of Albanians in Kosovo was to replace them with Serbs and to colonize and Serbianize it. However, until the end of 1912, when there was resistance on the part of the Albanians, the colonization progressed rather slowly. Only a few Serbs settled in the Kosovo region at the start."

Serb atrocities in Kosovo were also reported on by none other than Leon Trotsky himself, who had gone to the Balkans as a war correspondent, for the liberal Russian dailies *Kievskaya Mysl'* (Kiev Thought), *Dyen'* (The Day), and *Luch* (Ray). It is probable that Tucović, his friend and comrade, was the source of one of Trotsky's most shocking dispatches. In 'Behind the Curtain's Edge', published by *Kievskaya Mysl'*, Trotsky quotes a first-hand account of Serbian military atrocities: " 'The horrors actually began as soon as we crossed the old frontier... The sun had set, it was starting to get dark. But the darker the sky became, the more brightly the fearful illumination of the fires stood out against it. Burning was going on all around us. Entire Albanian villages had been turned into pillars of fire -- far and near, right up to the railway line... Dwellings, possessions accumulated by fathers, grandfathers, and great-grandfathers, were going up in flames. In all its monotony this picture was repeated the whole way to Skopje.' " The remainder of this long account consisted of an unforgettable series of murders, tortures, massacres, and thefts committed by Serbian soldiers and officers.

The issue of tsarist Russian encouragement to Serbian aggression was a preoccupation of many commentators, and radical criticism of the Russian role was extremely sharp. Trotsky lashed at examples of 'ethnic cleansing' *avant la lettre,* and the complicity in it of Russian tsarist and democratic nationalist politicians including the liberal Pavel Milyukov, in two extraordinary texts, published in *Dyen'* in January 1913: 'An Extraparliamentary Question to Mr. P. Milyukov', and 'Results of the 'Question About the Balkans."

In the former, Trotsky wrote: "Mr. Deputy! ...You have frequently, both in the columns of the press and at the tribune of the Duma, assured the Balkan allies... of the unaltered sympathies of so-called Russian society for their campaign of 'liberation'. Recently, during the period of the armistice, you made a political journey to the Balkans... Did you not hear during your travels... about the monstrous acts of brutality that were committed by the triumphant soldiery of the allies all along their line of march, not only on unarmed Turkish soldiers, wounded or taken prisoner, but also on the peaceful Muslim inhabitants, on old men and women, on defenseless children? ...Did not the facts, undeniable and irrefutable, force you to come to the conclusion that the Bulgars in Macedonia, the Serbs in Old Serbia (Kosovo), in their national endeavor to correct data in the ethnographical statistics that are not quite favorable to them, are engaged quite simply in systematic extermination of the Muslim population? ...Is it not clear to you that the silent connivance of the 'leading' Russian parties and their press... make it much easier for the (Bulgarians and Serbs) to engage in their Cain's work of further massacres of the people of the Crescent in the interests of the 'culture' of the Cross?"

In the succeeding text, 'Results of the "Question About the Balkans"'. Trotsky's polemic reached an intensity rare even for him. Addressing himself again to Milyukov, he wrote, "Since the 'leading' newspapers of Russia... either hushed up or denied the exposures published in the democratic press, a certain number of murdered Albanian babies must be put down, Mr. Deputy, to your Slavophile account. Get your senior doorman to look for them in your editorial office, Mr. Milyukov!"

He continued, "Indignant protest against unbridled behavior by men armed with machine guns, rifles, and bayonets was required for our own moral self-defense. An individual, a group, a party, or a class that is capable of 'objectively' picking its nose while it watches men drunk with blood, and incited from above, massacring defenseless people is condemned by history to rot and become worm-eaten while it is still alive."

Turkish resistance collapsed altogether, and, after five centuries, the Ottomans controlled only Shkodra in north Albania, Janina on the frontiers of the Albanian-Greek-Macedonian culture area, and Thrace. Amid this storm of blood, on November 28, 1912, Albania declaration of independence, 1912. But Kosovo was already in Serb hands, and would remain so, an Albanian-majority area separate from Albania proper, for the foreseeable future.

Meanwhile, the chorus of international protest against Serb violence in Kosovo did not end. An Austrian Jewish writer and publisher, Leo Freundlich, produced a shocking pamphlet, *The Albanian Golgotha*. What Tucović and his comrades had denounced before native Serb opinion, what Trotsky had revealed to the liberal Russian public, Freundlich exposed to readers of German. Freundlich wrote, "In the massive convulsions produced by the Balkan war, [the Albanian] nation's age-old dream of freedom and independence was at last going to be realized... However, the Serbs, prompted by their greed for conquest, devised a method of destroying the beautiful dream of a brave and freedom-loving nation shortly before it came true... 'Since we are not allowed to have Albania itself', so the Serbs thought, 'we should exterminate the Albanians'. " How, he asked, had the Serbs fulfilled the promise of fraternal assistance held out by their king? *"People were murdered in thousands, men, women, children, the elderly, tortured to death, villages burned down or looted, women and young girls raped; a whole land, devastated and ransacked, has been immersed in blood."* (itals in distracting.)

Freundlich was especially horrified by the passivity of the rest of Europe, aside from individuals, at this spectacle. "Where a modest home had been created for the poor Albanians, thanks to the diligence of generations, there now lie heaps of smoking ruins. A whole nation is bleeding on the cross – and Europe does not say a word," he wrote in anguish." A reporter from the Italian daily *Il Messaggero*, had, he noted, described "frightful massacres perpetrated by the Serbs against the Albanians in Kosovo… such towns as Ferizaj, Lipjan, Babusha, and others were completely destroyed and most of their inhabitants killed…

In all of Ferizaj, only half a dozen Muslim households remained alive. Less well-off Serbian families settled quickly in the homes of the well-to-do fugitives."

"The Serbian soldiery boasts about its hunting of human beings," Freundlich wrote. In the Kosovo town of Gjilan, he reported, "The entire population perished by arson and murder. The only survivors were a few fugitives. At present, merely ruins are left to tell about the massacres and the fall of Gjilan." The number of Albanian dead in Prishtina was reported at 5,000. Prizren, as previously stated, had surrendered after negotiations, but "blood flowed in streams," and the Albanians called the city the kingdom of death. There "the greatest havoc was wreaked by Serbian gangs. They broke into houses and massacred those who stood in their way, regardless of age and sex. For days the corpses of the murdered lay on the streets unburied, because the Serb conquerors were busy elsewhere, and the surviving Albanians were not allowed to leave their homes. The attacks were repeated every night in the city and its environs."

Individual cases were repulsive in their details. An Albanian woman who had gone to Prizren with her son, another male relative, and two male friends to purchase a wedding dress for her daughter, were on their way back home, in possession of a pass from the Serbian occupation forces. Four hours from Prizren they were robbed and the four men were bound and thrown into a pit, then shot to death. The mother, seeing her son murdered, begged the Serbs to kill her as well, but she was tied to a tree and left, in the presence of her dead son, for three days. The Serb soldiers displayed a loaf of bread in which they had placed two bullets, claiming that the victims were concealing ammunition. When the woman escaped, she went back to Prizren, but was first imprisoned by the military and then held in the house of a Serbian bishop. Finally, she was released in the custody of some Catholics.

According to Freundlich, women and children had been wrapped in bundles of straw and burned alive in front of their shackled menfolk; pregnant women had been eviscerated and fetuses bayoneted. One of his sources, "a highly responsible and absolutely trustworthy gentleman," commented, "All of this seems unbelievable, but is nonetheless true." The chronicle of criminal behavior seems endless, in a text of no more than 26 printed pages. In addition to murder and rape, the Serb troops stole whatever they wanted, killing merchants for the contents of their stores and peasants for their sandals. One Serb officer looted eighty carts full of furniture and rugs. The Serb forces did not simply requisition necessary items for their maintenance; "whatever provisions [they] could lay their hands on were taken away and destroyed." Centuries-old olive groves were cut down. Livestock were killed and grain plundered. Personal scores were settled, with Serbs who owed money to Albanians denouncing their creditors to the troops to procure their execution, then gaining control of the victims' homes. Possession of a hunting knife was sufficient grounds for a death sentence for bearing arms. Albanians who surrendered and turned in their arms were mowed down by firing squads.

Freundlich quoted a Sufi, Dervish Hilmi, who declared months after the invasion, "A large number of the Albanians may die of starvation... the corn seed has been taken away by the Serbs. Yet even if the Albanians had seed corn, they would not be able to cultivate the land. For as people say, 'should something grow, the Serb will destroy it.' "

Such accounts of the Serb assault on Kosovo and north Albania record the psychological impact of the atrocities on observers as a distinct phenomenon. A Romanian doctor named Leonte had written in the Bucuresti daily *Adevarul*, for January 6, 1913, that the horrors inflicted by the Serb army "were much more frightening than one could imagine," Freundlich pointed out. Leonte described hundreds of Albanian Muslim prisoners being pursued in a column for up to 60 miles, with those who fell by the wayside in hunger and exhaustion bayoneted on the spot. In Macedonia, where the Serbs encountered their Bulgarian rivals, "even foreign banks were robbed," and a Bulgarian professor was kidnapped and disappeared after he toasted the health of the Bulgarian monarch, King Ferdinand, at a party. Of Kosovo a Red Cross doctor reported, "Frightful things have happened over there. I do not know how many villages have been burned by the Serb troops."

Freundlich described an unnamed Serb veteran who had fled to Austria-Hungary after the fighting, and who, although a subject of King Petar, preferred "to live under Austrian 'oppression,' as far away as possible from his fatherland." This individual described with relish the massacre of Albanian peasants who, following the customs of their culture, had weapons on their homes, but were charged with no crimes. Observing Freundlich's surprise at his candor, the informant calmly added, "We were not going to waste our time escorting these people to some faraway barracks. What we did was much simpler. Then we were free again and could quietly go for drinks."

But Freundlich also elaborated on an aspect of the horrors that Tucović and Trotsky had left untouched: wholesale murder and plunder of Albanian Catholics, as well as Muslims. A published letter from a priest in Kosovo described how Catholic shrines had been looted of cash, clerics threatened with murder and imprisonment, and the Catholic faithful jailed for attending mass or going to confession. At Janjeva, Slav Catholics whose community had survived for hundreds of years were pressured to convert to Orthodoxy, while the Albanian crypto-Catholics were told they could not now come out in public with their faith. "Either Muslim or Orthodox, but not Catholic," the Serb authorities decreed. Albanian Catholic men were tied up while women were raped, houses sacked, and livestock driven off. In Kosovo so many sheep were confiscated the Serbs and Montenegrins did not know what to do with them. Whole families of Albanian Catholics from the mountains, who had come to Prizren to purchase supplies, were killed along the roads. The priest's letter ended, "may God have mercy on us, and May Europe rescue us, or we shall perish." The Vienna *Neue Freie Presse* reported that at Gjakova, on March 7, 1913, an Albanian Franciscan had been publicly beaten with rifle butts, and then bayoneted to death, in the presence of an Orthodox priest who had demanded his conversion. This incident occurred after a group of three hundred people had already been forced to renounce Catholicism, and the crowd begged the priest to do the same. He refused.

Of course, as Freundlich also indicated, the Serbian authorities employed journalists who routinely denied any such accusations. On February 8, 1913, the royal Serbian press bureau declared, "Atrocities allegedly committed by the Serbian army are simply impossible nowadays, especially among a people who are intensely religious and tolerant." These blandishments had led Tucović to write, "We have the right to save our nation from chauvinist propaganda and prevent the rule of nationalist lies... Belgrade journalists are malevolent and reactionary. They serve the regime, agitate for mass violence, and prepare their readers to more easily accept the stifling of freedom... May readers beware of the shameful role played by the Belgrade journalists."

Trotsky had written similarly, in an article titled 'The Serbian Press,' "A whole stratum of semi-intellectuals has come into being in the towns; although not highly educated and totally without ideological merits, it is filled with conviction that the future of Serbia lies in its hands. These declassed elements, standing on the fringe of the *lumpenproletariat*, and in any case permeated through and through with a *lumpen* outlook, are in absolute command of Serbia's press. They have little knowledge of Serbia's history and still less of the geography of the Balkan Peninsula... What they need, above all, is Greater Serbia... The press, whose attitude of opposition is merely another aspect of its greedy cynicism, has behind it the reactionary petty bourgeoisie of the towns; the officials, who here have a big grievance about their low salaries; a considerable portion of the officers; half-educated people of various kinds; professional intriguers; and the leftovers of the old, worn-out parties, the careerist failures and careerist heroes of yesterday. Undermining everything that is formed and well defined...; supporting every dissension and quarrel...; this press is, however, organically incapable of promoting to power any new political party, because it is itself lacking in any program or definite political mission... Talentless, semiliterate, base, the Serbian press infects the country's mental life with rottenness, and constitutes an extremely pernicious factor in Serbian society... What is to be done against the poison that the newspapers pour every day into the minds of the people? ... In the end, freedom of the press itself and it alone will heal the wounds that it inflicts. Not legislative restriction from above, but repulse from below; the education of the masses, this is the only way of countering the influence of the corrupt press."

Trotsky singled out the well-established Belgrade daily *Politika* for special criticism, describing it as "not a responsible semi-official mouthpiece on questions of foreign policy, but the organ of the moderate but persistent opposition from the Right on internal questions. Personal intrigue is the most effective weapon it wields, and poisonous innuendo its favorite literary form."

The protests of Serbs like Tucović were recorded by Freundlich and other foreigners, in addition to Trotsky. The Viennese publisher pointed out that Serb nationalists living in Vojvodina, then under Hungary, had expressed indignation at the massacre of the Albanians. But one of the most significant traces of Tucović and his work may be found in the *Report of the International Commission to Inquire into the Causes and Conduct of the Balkan Wars,* issued in 1914 by the Carnegie Endowment for International Peace. The Carnegie Commission Report, issued under the directorship of the famous American educator Nicholas Murray Butler, began with this anodyne statement: "The circumstances which attended the Balkan Wars of 1912 and 1913 were of such character as to fix upon them the attention of the civilized world." The conclusions of the report, however, were harsh enough. Tucović was cited under the heading, 'Extermination, Emigration, Assimilation'. The report declared, "The object of these armed conflicts, overt and covert, clearly conceived or vaguely felt, but always and everywhere the same, was the complete extermination of an alien population." However, the Carnegie Commission Report also stipulated to a characteristically American posture of what today is called "moral equivalence," backed up by the shibboleth, also prevalent nowadays and previously noted, of ancient hatreds. It opined, "We have repeatedly been able to show that the worst atrocities were not due to the excesses of the regular soldiery, nor can they always be laid to the charge of the volunteers... The populations mutually slaughtered and pursued [one another] with a ferocity heightened by mutual knowledge and the old hatreds and resentments they cherished."

Edith Durham was not so sure. Eight years later, in 1920, she recalled, "I packed up the Golden Medal given me by King Nikola [of Montenegro] and returned it to him, stating that I had often expressed surprise at persons who accepted decorations from [Ottoman Sultan] Abdul Hamid, and that now I knew that he and his subjects were even more cruel than the Turk, I would not keep his bloodstained medal any longer. I communicated this to the English and Austrian press. The Order of Saint Sava given to me by King Petar of Serbia I decided to keep a little longer, 'till some peculiarly flagrant case."

But the Carnegie Commission Report, the impassioned journalism of Trotsky, the eloquent pamphleteering of Freundlich, and the protests of other prominent personalities were destined soon to be swept out of the awareness of the global public by another, and yet more colossal sequence of atrocities, not least in Kosovo. On December 5, 1912, Turkey agreed to an armistice and the forfeiture of the conquered territories. On January 28, 1913, however, fighting broke out anew after Turkey refused to surrender Edirne, in the small scrap of Thrace that today remains known as European Turkey, to Bulgaria. For their part, Serb and Montenegrin troops seized Shkodra, in northern Albania. In peace negotiations held in London after the December cease-fire, Austria-Hungary, which had mobilized its armies late in 1912 to prevent Serbia from reaching the Adriatic, united with Italy to defend independent Albania, emphasizing the denial of the maritime outlet the Serbs had coveted for decades. Again, Serbian forces slaughtered Albanians; this time, Serb arguments that Albanians were mercenaries for the Turks were supplemented by the claim that they deserved death for serving the Habsburgs.

The Serb Social Democrat Kosta Novaković reminisced with cutting wit, "At the beginning of April 1913, I was in Durrës [Albania] when the Serbian armies boarded ships and sailed for Serbia. Little Albanian boys ran after the columns of Serbian soldiers singing the well-known national song: '*Si jemi serbe a s'bullgare, jemi trima shqipetare*' – 'We are not Serbian, nor Bulgarian, we are brave Albanians'. The boys put the word 'Serbian' in place of 'Greek.' The Serbian peasants, who composed the Serbian army, left for home cheerfully, because the expedition against Albania was at last over, an expedition they did not understand.

"The insulting words of the Albanian boys they did not mind at all, because they knew they deserved them; these songs hardly avenged the terrible barbarities they had committed against the Albanian people during the six months of occupation. But behind the Serbian peasants, worn out by war and diseases, stood official Serbia which ground its teeth with indignation, because it was compelled to leave Albania by the ultimatum of the Great Powers and the guns the Austro-Hungarian and Italian warships had aimed at them."

The suffering of the Albanians further engaged the attention of certain outsiders, in addition to outraged witnesses like Trotsky and Freundlich and the chancelleries of Vienna and Rome, at least for a while. Along with them and the others previously cited, the French novelist Pierre Loti and the American eccentric Raymond Duncan, brother of the famous dancer Isadora Duncan, tried to do something for the victims. Raymond Duncan, born in San Francisco, had moved to Greece where he posed as an ancient Athenian in classical dress; indeed, he was one of the champion exhibitionists of all time. In April 1913, Duncan, with his wife Penelope Sikelianos and his son, journeyed to the site of the carnage in an effort to develop a relief project for the Albanians. He even attempted to take advantage of the suffering to enlist Albanian followers in a scheme to establish something close to an independent 'state' on their territory.

But then the rules of the game changed again, and bad intentions proved weightier than good, or even merely frivolous ones. In June 1913, the Serbs, incensed at Bulgaria's territorial gains, as embodied in a peace agreement proposed in London, secretly joined with Romania and Greece against its former ally. Bulgaria attempted to gain the advantage, attacking Serbia on June 29 without formal notice. And in this second Balkan War, Serbia prevailed with Greek and Romanian help. Bulgaria emerged from the contest the loser; Serbia and Montenegro split the Sandžak of Novipazar between them, and the rest of the former Turkish possessions were divided between the Serbs, who retained Kosovo and northern Macedonia, and the Greeks, who got what was left. Romania acquired the rich Black Sea territory of the Dobrudja from Bulgaria by these methods. The pattern of Balkan borders had been set for a generation.

The Serb leadership was encouraged by these events to believe that Austria-Hungary, like Turkey, represented a weak empire ripe for amputation of its more attractive parts, particularly those inhabited by Slavs, such as Bosnia-Hercegovina, Croatia, and Slovenia. On June 28, 1914, the Bosnian Serb extremist Gavrilo Princip, as part of a Belgradesponsored terrorist conspiracy, killed the Habsburg archduke Franz Ferdinand, a liberal who favored Slavic autonomy within the empire, in Sarajevo. Vienna presented Belgrade with an ultimatum, demanding an investigation into the circumstances of the act, which was rejected. By August, a world war was in the offing.

It was a time of increasing immorality, it seemed, on all sides of the European political spectrum. Yet the Serbian Social Democrats took a firm anti-war position in the face of hostilities between Serbia and Austria-Hungary. Dragiša Lapšević and Triša Kaclerović, the party's deputies in the Serbian national assembly or Skupština, voted against war credits in August -- a position shared in the international Socialist movement, at that early moment, only by such British Labourites as Keir Hardie and John Burns. (In the German Reichstag, the left Socialist Karl Liebknecht did not vote against the war until December 1914; he was not joined by his comrade Otto Rühle, later a distinguished Marx biographer and critic of Bolshevism, until March 1915.)

In his 1918 book *The Bolsheviki and World Peace*, which opens with a chapter on 'The Balkan Question,' Trotsky provided an eyewitness account of the vote in the Skupština. "From the moment Austria-Hungary carried the question of her own fate and that of Serbia to the battlefield," he wrote, "Socialists could no longer have the slightest doubt that social and national progress would be hit much harder in Southeastern Europe by a Habsburg victory than by a Serbian victory. To be sure, there was still no reason for us Socialists to identify our cause with the aims of the Serbian army. This was the idea that animated the Serbian Socialists, Lapšević and Kaclerović, when they took the courageous stand of voting against the war credits."

In a footnote, he added, "To appreciate fully this action of the Serbian Socialists we must bear in mind the political situation by which they were confronted. A group of Serbian conspirators had murdered a member of the Habsburg family, the mainstay of Austro-Hungarian clericalism, militarism, and imperialism. Using this as a welcome pretext, the military party in Vienna sent an ultimatum to Serbia, which, for sheer audacity, has scarcely ever been paralleled in diplomatic history. In reply, the Serbian government made extraordinary concessions, and suggested that the solution of the question in dispute be turned over to the Hague tribunal. Thereupon Austria declared war upon Serbia. If the idea of a 'war of defense' has any meaning at all, it certainly applied to Serbia in this instance. Nevertheless, our friends, Lapšević and Kaclerović, unshaken in their conviction of the course of action that they as Socialists must pursue, refused the government a vote of confidence. The writer [Trotsky] was in Serbia at the beginning of the War. In the Skupština, in an atmosphere of indescribable national enthusiasm, a vote was taken on the war credits... Two hundred members all answered 'Yes.' Then in a moment of deathlike silence came the voice of the Socialist Lapšević: 'No.' Every one felt the moral force of this protest, and the scene has remained indelibly impressed upon my memory."

It was too late. The "indescribable national enthusiasm" that had shown itself in the Balkan Wars, and which was inspired by the Kosovo Idea, would dominate the Serb consciousness, and would determine the Serb relationship with Albanians in Kosovo itself, for years to come. Kosovo had been 'redeemed', in the vocabulary of Serbian ultranationalism. But at what price? As Novaković wrote, the democratic and populist culture long identified with peasant Serbia "...no longer exists. It dwindled away gradually in the course of several decades and in 1912 it disappeared completely. In place of it appeared an imperialist Serbia, with the pan-Serbian imperialists, the pan-Serbian dynasty, and pan-Serbian militarism. This new, crude, brutal and cruel imperialism dreams of reviving King Stefan Dušan's empire and is striving to catch up in the course of 10 years with the imperialist powers that have existed for centuries. The Serbian peasant has been a blind tool of pan-Serbian imperialism, cannon fodder, an animal without a tail, as the Serbian officers called him, who was driven by the whips of officers to hurl himself into the fire and to burn and devastate the places he captured.

"Although obliged by stronger imperialists to give up the coast of Albania, the pan-Serbian imperialists retained the most fertile territory – Kosovo. We call Kosovo all the region inhabited by Albanians: the Plain of Kosovo, Metohija and the southern part of the former Sandžak up to Novipazar. More than 500,000 Albanians became slaves of the new invaders." A fatal pattern in modern Serbian policy toward Albanians had been set, in imitation of the imperial excesses of the past, as Serbian intellectuals claimed to emulate the heroism of their nobles in the battles fought five centuries before.

* * * * *

Chapter IV:

Kosovo and Modern Serb Monarchs, 1914-1943

Serbia won Kosovo in 1912, but with immense and negative consequences for the political and moral health of the Serb nation, according to Kosta Novaković and the other Serb socialists. Serbia would emerge from the first world war a victor, maintaining its hold on Kosovo and Macedonia, and achieving another long-sought goal, the creation of a Greater Serbia, disguised as a single 'state of the South Slavs', or Yugoslavia. But that conquest, also, would involve enormous costs.

The bill for Serbia's entry into the first world war would be paid, and precisely in the Albanian lands, by those who had put Serb plans in the first cycle of Balkan Wars into effect: the rank and file of its army, who by the time mobilization against the Austro-Hungarian forces came, in 1914, had in many cases served continuously for two years. But Serbian ambitions in the world war would also exact a high price from the Kosovar Albanians.

The first year of the world war, from late summer 1914 to autumn 1915, blessed the Serbian army with good fortune. With the support of their British and French allies, who held Salonika in Greek Macedonia, and the prayers of their Russian backers to encourage them, King Petar's forces defended their country from the Austro-Hungarians to the north while Serb armies, in turn, invaded Albania yet again. In war, Serbia was clearly fixated on partitioning or otherwise subdividing the latter. But in October 1915 Bulgaria joined the hostilities as one of the central powers, alongside Austria-Hungary, Germany, and Turkey. The Bulgarians quickly conquered the Serb-held portion of Macedonia, where they were viewed as liberators by their Slav Macedonian cousins. These folk, speaking a dialect close to Bulgarian, had never liked the Serbs very much, even as comrades in the anti-Turkish struggle.

The Serb southern armies then retreated in disorder into Kosovo, looting and shooting as they went. Pursued by the Bulgarians, they had to contend, as well, with the anger of the Albanian populace, which they had so recently mistreated on a mass scale. The *kaçaks* or Albanian guerrilla fighters, here and there, taught them the lesson eloquently evoked decades after by Ivo Banac; in the words of an Albanian ballad, '*Shtatë krajlat kanë thanë, se shqiptaret gjakun s'lânë*' – 'Seven kingdoms have said that the Albanians do not forgive blood.' The Austro-Hungarian and German forces now pressed into Serbia proper. King Petar's government evacuated southward, adding to the confusion.

The Austro-Hungarians entered Kosovo and, with the Bulgarians, took thousands of Serb prisoners. Serb intentions to withdraw toward Salonika were blocked by the Bulgarian lines, and the Serbs soon chose to add to their existing and formidable problems by attempting to withdraw their whole army, and the retinue of the 76-year old King Petar (who had abdicated in favor of his son Aleksandar), through Montenegro and northern Albania – that is, through high mountains, in the unforgiving Balkan winter. Prevented from reaching Salonika, they were promised aid by the Allies if they got to Shkodra.

Here again was an apparent Serbian lust for martyrdom, which others might consider a form of madness. As the pro-Serb writer R.G.D. Laffan put it only two years after the events, "The Serbian General Staff called on the army to leave the fatherland and face starvation and exile rather than make terms with the invaders. The cup of bitterness must be drunk to the dregs. There were no illusions as to what a retreat through Albania would mean. It would be a disaster." The horror that ensued came to be known to Serb veterans, with justice, as their Golgotha. And certainly, they underwent cold, hunger and sleeplessness, dying along the trails, consuming their horses, even eating each other. They were tortured by dysentery; they heard the cries of wolves following their path.

But they did not suffer alone, for they forced thousands of Austro-Hungarian, German, and Bulgarian prisoners to accompany them, and they also died in great numbers. With the Serb rank and file, old King Petar often walked, spurning a horse while his soldiers went on foot, some of them bare-foot, as their boots fell apart or eventually were eaten, and their bandaged feet festered. Vojvoda Rade Putnik, a Serbian war leader for two generations, was prostrated with illness, and was carried in a sedan-chair. Other Serb aristocrats and politicians rode ahead, with good horses, and avoided the torment.

Still, one must wonder at the presumption of the Serb leaders, who apparently believed that Serb soldiers, having wreaked deadly terror against the Albanians only three years before, need not fear their former victims might not greet them hospitably. In addition, the Serb commanders did not anticipate that the Montenegrins inhabiting the high peaks would view them as prey rather than as brethren, selling them provisions in exchange for their miserable, ragged uniforms. When the Serbs finally arrived in Shkodra, there was not enough food for them, and they continued to die of starvation, as the Austro-Hungarians and Bulgarians approached. Finally, a part of the Serb forces was shipped to Tunisia, while the rest were ordered to march anew, to the Albanian port of Vlora, for transshipment to Greek territory. By the time they reached Vlora some had gone insane, but many more had died still more died in Vlora while waiting for allied ships. In the end, 150,000 of them reached Corfu.

Perhaps the most amazing aspect of this incredible tale was that the Albanians from the mountains of the north to Vlora, whose villages the Serbs passed through, did not take revenge on them. Edith Durham praised the Albanians for their quality of mercy, considering the violence they had so recently experienced at Serb hands. At worst, some local Albanians, imitating their Montenegrin neighbors, fleeced the Serb forces; even Laffan, an extreme Serbophile, accuses the Albanians of nothing worse than demanding gold in payment for transportation and goods. And back in Kosovo, the Albanian *kaçak* fighters had discovered that the Bulgarian occupiers were no better as Slav overlords than the Serbs, something their ancestors knew long, long before them.

Rebellious tendencies also appeared among the Albanians in that part of Kosovo where the Austrians held sway, and Noel Malcolm has put it well: "Particularly active here was a charismatic young Albanian from north-central Kosovo, Azem Bejta [also known as Azem Galica, from the name of his village]... Azem Bejta co-operated with the local Serbs against the Austrian army." Azem Bejta's two brothers were executed by the Austrians. His village, Galica, is located in an area called Drenica; together his name, and that of his village, and that of Drenica, would have loud echoes for generations afterward, creating a patriotic symbolism above all others, for the Kosovar Albanians unto our own time.

Once they were in Greece, the Serb forces reformed, and in the end, fortune again smiled upon them. The central powers, particularly Austria-Hungary and Germany, cut off from commerce by a British naval blockade, could not sustain their temporary advantage. In the spring of 1917, America entered the war on the side of the Allies, and although Russia left the war in November, after the Bolshevik Revolution, the latter development did not serve the Germans and Austro-Hungarians as well as their leaders believed it might. Russia's capitulation temporarily heartened the central powers, but Russia under Bolshevism offered a far more destructive weapon against the emperors who ruled in Berlin and Vienna, than any military asset held by the allies, for the internationalist, anti-war message preached by the Bolsheviks from Moscow swept through Germany and Austria-Hungary irresistibly. The German navy rebelled, which was the beginning of the end; then the Austrian navy mutinied, at the Croatian port of Kotor (today in Montenegro).

The military machine of the central powers began crumbling, as thousands and eventually millions of soldiers deserted, and an armistice with the allies was proposed by the Austro-Hungarians in September 1918. Within weeks Serbian and allied troops had retaken Kosovo. Germany and the Habsburg lands were in upheaval; the German, Austrian and Hungarian factory workers lay down their tools, and the people came into the streets. The political leaders of the Slavic nations – Poles, Czechs, Slovaks, South Slavs, and others who had been ruled by Germans, Austrians and Hungarians – demanded independence. As the outstanding Croatian and South Slav author Miroslav Krleža recalled, cited by Banac, "Austria… disappeared so silently from our little town, that none of our respected and dear fellow townsmen even noticed that Austria was in fact no longer among us."

Even before an official armistice between the allies and the central powers was declared on November 11, 1918, the German and Hungarian-ruled empires, which had endured for centuries, lay in ruins, and at the end of October, in the former Habsburg possessions, a 'State of the Slovenes, Croats, and Serbs' had been proclaimed. This was absorbed by Serbia into a 'Kingdom of Serbs, Croats, and Slovenes', ruled by the Serbian monarch, a month later; this new dominion also comprised Bosnia-Hercegovina, Montenegro, Slavic Macedonia, and Vojvodina, the latter with a mixed population of Hungarians, Serbs, Croats, Germans, and Romanians. Thus Yugoslavia, 'the country of South Slavs,' was born, also including Kosovo, which in its majority remained Albanian, rather than South Slav. This outcome benefited from misunderstanding in many places. For example, the American radical writer John Reed, in *The war in Eastern Europe*, had acclaimed a greater Serbia including Slovenes and Croats, and repeated, among other fantasies, the claims that Albanians were imported from the Caucasus by the Ottamans.

The Vid's Day (Vidovdan) Constitution of 1921 described the South Slavs as a single people with three names – Serbs, Croats, and Slovenes. Bosnian Muslims, Montenegrins, and Macedonians were viewed as Serbs by the Serbs, and the Kosovar Albanians were still widely described as Albanized Serb Muslims. The title 'Yugoslavia' would be conferred officially eight years later; but the new country was unquestionably a patchwork of ethnic groups. According to a statistical profile developed by Banac, at the foundation of the state in 1918 the Albanians were the sixth largest 'indigenous' nation on Yugoslav territory, i.e. if one excluded Germans and Hungarians. The Albanians of Kosovo and Montenegro numbered at least 440,000, or about 60 percent as many as the Bosnian Muslims, who counted 730,000, and only 25 percent below the Macedonian population, at 585,000. It was the Serb socialist Kosta Novaković who best described how matters stood on the ground in Kosovo, citing "official statistics of the Serbian Government, which demonstrate the Albanian character of Kosovo. In the district of Prizren, in 1921, there were

17 per cent Serbs; this proportion was the same also in the districts of Prishtina, Mitrovica, Gjilan, Peć and Gjakova. In some other regions there were even fewer Serbs. In 1921, the whole of Kosovo had at the most 17 per cent Serbs," Novaković concluded.

Novaković also explained with precision the response of the Yugoslav monarchist regime to this problem: "The pan-Serbian regime is well aware of this. Therefore, it has decided to denationalize Kosovo completely, by savagely suppressing the resistance of the Albanians and especially by seizing their land and colonizing it with Serbs." Ultimately, Pan-Serbism, or Serbian national Romanticism, in elaborating a style of governance, most reflected the impact of the French revolutionary-rationalist, centralist and unitary state on Europe. Jacobin and Bonapartist France fostered the widespread 19th century belief, which accompanied and occasionally conflicted with Romanticism, that large nation-states based on one 'people' could be forged out of varying local identities, by compulsory unification. French-style unitarism spread to Hungary, Germany, and Italy, and it was inevitable that it would profoundly affect the South Slavic region.

As described in chapter II of this book, Serb national ideologists of 150 years ago adopted the slogan of folk scholar Vuk Stefanović Karadžić: 'Serbs All and Everywhere'. An inclusive Serbism might have succeeded in uniting the 'Yugoslavs', and might even have assimilated some Kosovar Albanians, had it been based on the essentially tolerant, melting-pot mentality that produced an American national identity. But it was not. Rather, it was based on unitarist ethnic narcissism and eventually, only Orthodox Serbs, including Montenegrins and those Bosnian Muslims and Macedonians willing to accept a Serb identity, were deserving of the exercise of power in the South Slavic state, which had been created in 1918, it was said, by Serbs alone.

Long before France refined the concept of a single national identity defined by a centralist state, the Castilian monarchy in Spain spent at least 400 years attempting to assimilate the Basques and Catalans, with little success. Germany, although united in the late 19th century, had never seen a serious attempt to force the abandonment of local cultural identity; nor had Italy. And even in neo-Jacobin France, Brittany and other regions proved extraordinarily resistant to forcible cultural homogenization; one could hardly imagine Albanians being easier to subdue. Serbia's leaders should have learned from these examples, but they ignored them. Instead, during monarchist Yugoslavia, until its downfall in 1941, they chose as a model Greece, which imposed a unitary national identity by expelling and killing Turks and forcibly suppressing its own Albanian and Macedonian minorities. In France itself, a reactionary Romanticism had tended to exalt local identity against rationalist centralism, but in a fateful irony of history, Serbian imperialism, generations later, and in a predictable development, merged national Romantic mythification with ruthless centralism.

For two decades after its foundation monarchist Yugoslavia saw repeated attempts to achieve the total Serbification of Croats, Bosnian Muslims, and Macedonians, along with efforts to expel the Kosovar Albanians. The two former nations were dealt with politically, while the latter two faced, as Novaković so eloquently explained, aggressive Serb colonization of their territories. Yet each responded differently; the Croats through parliamentary politics, the Bosnian Muslims with an attempt at conformity, the Macedonians by way of revolutionary nationalist terrorism on a broad scale, and the Kosovars in guerrilla resistance. One observes a north-south difference as well as an economic disparity, as the richer Croats and Bosnians preferred recourse to petitioning and pressure, while the poorer Macedonians and Albanians chose direct action.

The Croats had a thorough advantage in that their political life was then dominated by a great Slavic populist and enlightener, Stjepan Radić, the main leader of the Croat Peasant Party. Radić had warned the Croats that they had wandered into the new South Slav state "like drunken geese in a fog." In 1918, addressing himself to the political élite in Belgrade he declared, "Gentlemen, your mouths are full of words like *narodno jedinstvo* [popular unity], one unitary state, one kingdom under the Karađorđević dynasty.' And you think that it is enough to say we Croats, Serbs, and Slovenes are one people because we speak one language and that on account of this we must also have a unitary centralist state, moreover a kingdom, and that only such a linguistic and state unity can make us happy... Gentlemen, you evidently do not care a whit that our peasant in general, and especially our Croat peasant, does not wish to hear one more thing about kings or emperors, nor about a state which you are imposing on him by force... Maybe you will win the Slovenes, I do not know. Maybe you will also win the Serbs. But I am certain you will never win the Croats... because the whole Croat people are equally against your centralism as against militarism, equally for a republic as for a popular agreement with the Serbs."

The period directly after the First World War was marked by great social upheaval in Croatia, including major peasant rebellions. Until the founding of the new South Slav state, Radić was the charismatic but isolated voice of a politically dispossessed peasantry, yet after 1920, with the introduction of a universal vote for male citizens, his People's Peasant Party became the leading social movement in Croatia. It was something more than a party, and Radić himself was something more than a politician. Banac has written with

71

theatrical but justifiable exaggeration, "There was never anybody quite like him in Croat history. A romantic, and yet a pragmatist, Stjepan Radić illuminated the Croat skies like the luminous flash of a meteor. His age was the decade of 1918-1928… It ended with his lying near death on the floor of the National Assembly [in Belgrade] on June 28, 1928, his body riddled with bullets."

Radić, called the 'Croat Gandhi' as an apostle of non-violence, was assassinated in a session of the national parliament by a Montenegrin, Puniša Račić. It has often been observed that the shots that killed Radić on the infamous Vid's Day – also, killed monarchist Yugoslavia, a little more than 12 years later. For some Croats soon began drifting away from the pacifist tradition of Radić to examine a more extreme, and eventually terrorist solution, which would be identified with a small and eccentric movement known as the Insurrectionaries or *Ustaša*. But most significantly, the murder of Radić dramatically illustrated the insecurity of parliamentary institutions in the South Slav monarchy, which remained Serb in its origins and outlook. And it was not an isolated event; rather, it was the culmination of a series of attempts by the Belgrade regime to rid itself of Croat disaffection, which finally had recourse to the most brutal means. The death of Radić became a pretext for the establishment of a royal dictatorship in the South Slav state, which was officially renamed Yugoslavia. Soon the atrocities committed by the Yugoslav monarchist secret police, against the non-Serbs in general, and the Croat intellectuals in particular, had gained Yugoslavia the hatred of liberal and left opinion throughout Europe, which ranked the Belgrade regime alongside Mussolini's Italy as fascist.

Through the 1920s, Radić had sought allies within the South Slav state and without, some of them fairly remarkable, given his non-ideological reformism. He, like various revolutionaries and nationalists from around the world, journeyed to Russia in search of aid; and certain Bolsheviks believed they could absorb Radić and his followers into the Communist International, or Comintern. But he ended up in a coalition with Serbian populists; Leon Trotsky wrote, a bit cruelly, that Radić had travelled from 'Green Zagreb', the Croatian capital identified as a Mecca of peasant radicalism, to 'Red Moscow', only to finally land in a ministry in 'White', i.e. counter-revolutionary, Belgrade. But Radić's temporary affection for Soviet Communism also strengthened the presence in Zagreb of the Yugoslav Communists, for Zagreb was not only 'green'; it was also the center of the South Slav labor movement and the most sophisticated city in the South Slav state. A then obscure figure who would emerge from the Zagreb left milieu of the 1920s was a metalworker named Josip Broz, destined for fame as Marshal Tito.

The Bosnian Muslims, although by no means beloved by Serbs, did not share Croat dissatisfaction with the South Slav state; nor did they, in the 1920s and '30s, experience Serb repression. Croat nationalists agitated the Bosnian Muslims to view themselves as essentially Croat, an appeal that was given weight by Bosnian Muslim memories of Serb anti-Muslim atrocities through the 19th century and in the first Balkan Wars. But many other Croat leaders also embraced national-religious pluralism, viewing Catholics and Muslims alike as members of their nation, in terms not unlike those maintained by Albanians. In a memorable declaration cited by Banac, Croat Franciscans in Bosnia argued that religion was an individual matter, and that the survival of Catholicism did not depend on the Croats, just as the Croats would continue to exist whether they were Catholic or not!

But, in a development that seems amazing to observers at the end of the present century, given the ferocity of the Bosnian War of 1992-95, some prominent Bosnian Muslims, over two generations, tended to identify themselves as Serbs of Muslim faith. Such sympathy typically reflected appreciation for the energy with which Serbia had attempted to keep Bosnia out of Austro-Hungarian hands and had then sought to pry Bosnia away from the Habsburgs after 1878. In turn, Serbs, applying the now familiar concept of "Serbs all and everywhere," claimed that Bosnian Muslims were merely Islamized Serbs who yearned to return to the fold. Finally, most Bosnian Muslims were suspicious of Serb traditions of peasant rebellion against Muslim landlords, and Bosnia-Hercegovina, like Croatia, had remained loyal to the central powers during the first world war. In the new South Slav state, the Serbs, as representatives of the victorious allied coalition, were clearly out to wreak reprisal on all who had sided with Austria-Hungary.

The Slav Macedonians exceeded the Croats in discontent with the monarchist South Slav state, but they availed themselves of mass, armed resistance long before the arrival of the Croat *Ustaša* on the scene. Their national revolutionary movement, the Internal Macedonian Revolutionary Organization (IMRO), had a long and fascinating history, becoming the most feared and the most intellectually sophisticated nationalist grouping in Europe. Somewhat like the Irish Republican Army, the IMRO would eventually generate pro-Communist and pro-fascist wings. IMRO also produced a significant tendency that repudiated Slav Macedonian separatism in favor of a federal solution for Macedonia, uniting Slavs, Turks, Sephardic Jews (then a sizeable community in the region), Greeks, and Albanians in an 'internationalist' Macedonia. Of the nationalist trends in Yugoslavia, IMRO also developed the strongest links with the Communist Party.

A Croat Communist, Ante Ciliga, later recalled that in 1923 the Bulgarian

Communists, a leading party in the Comintern, launched a campaign within the Comintern apparatus, condemning that body's alleged policy of ignoring the national struggle of the minority peoples, above all the Macedonians and Croats, in Yugoslavia. This was unsurprising in that Macedonian nationalism had long been associated with Bulgarian interests. The anti-Belgrade elements in the Comintern argued that in neglecting Macedonian and Croat grievances the Communists gave *de facto* support to Serbian imperialism. Within Yugoslav Communist ranks, then allowed to pursue factional debate under the Lenin-Trotsky regime, the party's right wing argued for a limited and lukewarm autonomy for the non-Serb masses, while the left merely affirmed that socialist revolution would resolve all national claims.

Ciliga, a member of the Yugoslav Communist leadership, proposed a more audacious solution: a federated Yugoslavia made up of seven republics, i.e. Slovenia, Croatia, Serbia, Montenegro, and Macedonia, which would be recognized as nationally homogeneous, and two mixed units, Bosnia-Hercegovina and Vojvodina. His position overlooked the problem of Kosovo and its Albanian majority, but it stood in distinct opposition to the centralist, pro-Serb posture of then-party leader Sima Marković. Moscow responded to this controversy by calling for the complete independence and sovereignty of Slovenia, Croatia, and Macedonia, while ignoring the mixed territories and Montenegro – a fatal error, according to Ciliga. From 1923 to 1926 the Yugoslav Communists officially supported independence for the Slovenes, Croats, and Macedonians while their organizations in Bosnia-Hercegovina, Montenegro, and Vojvodina, without authorization, also called for those territories' independence. For their part, a significant faction of Green' Montenegrins accepted a Serbian cultural identification but rejected the hegemony of the Karađorđević dynasty and the dissolution of the Montenegrin throne, which had been held by the Petrovićes.

But what of Kosovo? Monarchist Yugoslavia, in activities well-described by Noel Malcolm as well as Kosta Novaković, attempted to change the ethnic makeup of the province by extensive subsidies for Serb colonists in Kosovo, who were granted free land – expropriated from Albanian and Turkish landlords, in a manner intended to justify colonization as agrarian reform. Transportation costs, basic supplies, and even some homes were supplied free, the latter, often seized from Albanians. In addition, the colonists were provided cheap loans. But colonization failed. Serbs from outside Kosovo did not take to their new environment, which they found unfamiliar and unwelcoming.

The Albanians, of course, fought back. Many favored a political movement, the *Cemiyet*, or Society for the Preservation of Muslim Rights, which was linked to Bosnian Muslim politicians and advocated for Slav Muslims and Albanians throughout southern Yugoslavia, i.e. in the Sandžak, Kosovo, and Macedonia. But there were also the *kaçaks*; the movement had never really died down. They retained their arms, functioning under the umbrella of the Committee for the National Defense of Kosovo, usually known as the Kosovo Committee or K.K., founded in 1918 in Shkodra, by Hasan Beg Prishtina. The K.K. and the *kaçaks* in general fought hard to maintain their historic occupancy of the land.

The K.K. produced a *Program for the Albanian General Uprising on the Dukagjin* Plateau in spring 1919. Limited to 10 principles, it clearly demonstrated the intelligent and disciplined nature of the movement:

I. No insurgent may harm the local Slavs apart from those who put up armed resistance to the Albanian cause.

II. No insurgent may burn houses or damage churches.

III. Robbery of property is forbidden to insurgents.

IV. No insurgent may mutilate enemy corpses or strip clothes from dead, wounded, or captured enemies.

V. Most vigorous action must be taken against the army, police, and irregular forces of the enemy who fight with arms; but even when the enemy commits atrocities against unarmed Albanians, clauses I, II, III, and IV must be adhered to strictly and completely.

VI. Traitors who oppose our cause, by siding with the enemy or as individuals, must be considered enemies of the Albanian cause, and are to be killed immediately, wherever they may be found. However, an unarmed traitor must be tried by a revolutionary tribunal and sentenced on the basis of evidence and not mere hearsay.

VII. Local Slavs and markets must be guarded by trustworthy people, while loyal insurgents must pursue the enemy continuously and without hesitation through the cities and villages.

VIII. Neither the blood of our people nor of our opponents should be needlessly shed. But when necessary, insurgents must not spare their own blood nor that of their kin.

IX. European citizens, consuls, and their property must be protected by loyal and obedient people.

X. Albanian dead may not be buried until the arrival of a foreign investigative commission. Atrocities committed by the enemy must be recorded and reported in Europe and America.

According to Kosta Novaković, "The Serbian Government tried to label the Albanian *kaçaks* as bandits and outlawed them, giving any government agent and any Serbian fascist the right to kill them.

"In reality, the *kaçaks* are no robbers at all, but patriotic Albanian rebels. They have given up everything, their homes and belongings and taken to the mountains; they have formed *çetas* of freedom fighters and are fighting against the injustices and barbarous acts of the Serbian army and police. The freedom fighters believe that, in this way, they can drive the Serbian regime away from Kosovo.

"These national fighters have waged a stern war, a war which has to be admired, against much larger forces of the Serbian gendarmerie and army. The names of Bajram Curri, Azem Bejta and hundreds of other brave fighters, who have fallen martyrs in this war, are engraved on the hearts of the Albanians of Kosovo. Since 1920, more than 10,000 freedom fighters moved to the mountains of Kosovo. There were 2,000 in the Lab district alone. In 1920, at the time of the uprising at Lab, the Serbian army, under the command of colonel Radovan Radović, bombarded the large Albanian village of Prapaçica and left not a single house standing.

"As in Lab, Albanian national movements arose in many other parts of Kosovo, and large Serbian forces put them down in 1919 and 1924. Here we mention the uprisings in Plava, Gusinje and Rugova in 1919, Prishtina in 1921, Drenica in 1923, Mitrovica in 1924, and Drenica again in 1924. In suppressing these rebellions, the Serbian army killed 2,600 Albanians.

"Thus the national resistance was restricted to the actions of *guerrilla* units of freedom fighters. According to an official Serbian Government report, in 1924, 1,200 patriots had organized themselves in *guerrilla* units. In 1927, the Serbian police drew up a balance [too low to have applied to a period longer than that year]: 310 Albanian insurgents killed, 175 captured, and 626 surrendered. In 1927, the freedom-fighters ceased their operations, but their spirit lives in every village and will not die out until Kosovo is free," Novaković affirmed.

The *kaçak* insurgency of the 1920s was the most extensive Kosovar Albanian resistance movement until very recent years, and its memory is indelible in the consciousness of Albanians everywhere. The *Cemiyet* was eventually suppressed by the monarchist Yugoslav government on the pretext of its alleged service as a legal front for the *kaçaks*. But the latter were no politicians. Their greatest exemplar was Azem Bejta, who may be called a Kosovar equivalent of Emiliano Zapata or Augusto C. Sandino in the Hispanic world; and like Sandino in the Nueva Segovia department of Nicaragua, Azem Bejta became indissolubly identified with the Drenica district and his village, Galica.

But Azem Bejta, who died in 1924 after a Yugoslav attack on his forces, had something to his legend lacking in the cases of Zapata and Sandino. Azem Bejta had a loyal and resourceful second-in-command, Qerim Galica. And unknown to most of the *kaçak* combatants and their supporters, at least at the beginning, Qerim Galica had a remarkable secret. Qerim was not merely Azem Bejta's lieutenant, skilled with weapons and brave in battle; Qerim was Azem Bejta's young wife Shota, in male dress. For the highly patriarchal Albanian society, the daring of a woman warrior, fighting in arms alongside, and sometimes better than, men, constituted an extraordinary innovation. Today many songs, and even a ballet, celebrate Shota Galica as the outstanding heroine of Albanian women. Tales are retold of how the menfolk tried to get her to return to the traditional duties of Albanian women, dedicating herself to home and hearth according to the prescription of the *Kanun:* "A woman is a sack, made to endure."

Shota Galica was made to endure, but was no sack. She refused to abandon her martial calling, telling the Albanian men she was needed in war because they were too weak and trusting of the *Shkije.* After her husband's death she continued in battle for three years until 1927, when she died of combat injuries at 33. Her cult, for that is what it is, evokes the desperation of Albanian resistance, since hostilities in which women participated would be a matter of life and death, of pure survival, with the only alternative the utter destruction of the nation. As a patriotic symbol Shota Galica was even more compelling, for the Albanians, than Radić for the Croats. As Banac has written, "*Shota and Azem Galica* is not a ballet of divertissement."

Shota Galica defied one principle of the *Kanun*, the better to honor its overall conception of justice and honor. For the monarchist Yugoslav authorities, of course, the *Kanun* was an irrelevant, folkloric trifle; with the onset of full-blown anti-Albanian terror in Kosovo, one of its noblest victims was none other than Fr. Shtjefën Gjeçovi, the outstanding Albanian Franciscan scholar and compiler of the printed *Kanun.* Fr. Gjeçovi was murdered in ambush on October 14, 1929, near Zym, a village in the vicinity of Prizren, where he had been assigned as a Catholic parish priest. At his death he was only 55; he had spent most of his adult years serving the Albanian national movement. A document from 1906, attached as an appendix to the printed *Kanun*, provides evidence of his passionate dedication to the Albanian cause. Therein, above the signature of "Father Shtjefën Gjeçovi, Franciscan, witness," we read: "Anyone who joins the [Ottoman] police will have his house burned down and will be exiled for life."

The martyrdom of Shtjefën Gjeçovi underscores the most important aspect of Kosovar Albanian resistance to monarchist Yugoslavia that is neglected by outside observers: the major role played by Catholic clerics, even though the majority of Kosovars, then as now, were Muslim. However, among Albanians, recollection of the Muslim-Catholic alliance remains extremely vivid. An

Albanian scholar, Aurel Plasari recently wrote, of Catholic priest Dom Nikollë Kaçorri co-signer of the anti-Turkish resolution to which Gjeçovi was witness: "When [he] stood by the side of Ismail Bey [Qemali] to demand the independence of the homeland, he did not calculate the percentages of the religions in Albania! When Father Anton Harapi drafted the famous memorandum addressed to the great powers in 1918, he did not calculate that among the 44 signatures of the chiefs of Hoti and Gruda there were 40 Muslims and four Christians! When Monsignor Luigj Bumçi fought for the borders of Albania at Versailles, he did not have percentages on his mind! When he fell on his knees in front of the Pope to rescue the provinces of Korça and Gjirokastra, he did not consider that there was not a single Catholic soul in these districts! When Faik Konica [a Muslim beg and distinguished author and statesman], Fan Noli, [Orthodox bishop] and Gjergj Fishta [a Catholic and the national poet of Albanian resistance to the Slavs] strove for their country's recognition by the United States, I do not believe they boasted to the American senators about the balance among the religions in Albania! When Monsignor [Jak] Serreqi wrote to the League of Nations that in Albania, which was in danger of being obliterated, Christians and Muslims are brothers and want to live in the same state, he did not base his arguments on percentages!"

But the Franciscans and other Albanian Catholics were progressive as well as patriotic. In Albania proper, Franciscans like Fr. Harapi supported the short-lived government of Fan Noli, who had been the effective creator of the autocephalous Albanian Orthodox Church, and who took power in June 1924, adopting a reform program. One of Noli's first acts was to establish diplomatic relations with the Soviet Union; for his part, Fr. Harapi later commented, "These were times when we thought the Albanians had turned their backs on the Orient and were looking toward progress."

Noli's movement had emerged in revulsion of the domination of Albanian politics by an army officer, Ahmet Zogu. After the first world war, Zogu, a graduate of a Turkish military academy, had risen to prominence during an unsuccessful Yugoslav seizure of Shkodra, and later during the successful opposition to Italian annexation of Vlora. In 1922, after becoming Albanian minister of the interior, then of communications, and commander-in-chief of the army, he replaced the Kosovar patriot Hasan Beg Prishtina as prime minister of Albania; Hasan Beg Prishtina and Bajram Curri, another prominent leader of the *kaçaks*, briefly and unsuccessfully opposed Zogu.

Although Zogu was chased out of Albania by Noli, he returned to power on Christmas Day 1924, after only six months, backed by Yugoslav and 'White Russian' troops. Zogu then dedicated himself, at Yugoslavia's insistence, to liquidating the remaining *kaçaks*; it was during Noli's rule that Yugoslavia, alarmed at the modernizing character of his regime, and the possibility that it would support the Kosovo Committee, hunted down Azem Bejta. Zogu had Bajram Curri, who had supported Noli, killed within months; for nine years thereafter Hasan Beg Prishtina eluded the agents of Zogu, who proclaimed himself King in 1928. But Hasan Beg Prishtina was also finally murdered. Thus the great Kosovar rebel movement of the *kaçaks* vanished from the scene, at least temporarily.

The victims of Yugoslav intrigue during this period included others besides Croats killed for Croatia, like Stjepan Radić, and Kosovars dead in the name of Kosovo, like Azem Bejta, Bajram Curri, and Hasan Beg Prishtina. One of the worst such cases was the fatal street assault in Zagreb on the historian Milan Šufflay, in 1931. Šufflay was killed by an agent of the monarchist Yugoslav secret police, who split his head open with an iron club, and the incident elicited a major outcry from liberal intellectuals in Europe and America, including Albert Einstein and Thomas Mann. Einstein and Mann signed a letter describing the murder at length, and denouncing the Belgrade authorities for an attempt to suppress the facts in the case. They assailed the "despotic regime" governing Yugoslavia and, particularly, the "reign of terror" in Croatia. Similarly, in 1933, a group of 41 American writers, including Theodore Dreiser, John Dos Passos, and Upton Sinclair, protested publicly against repression in Yugoslavia.

A descendant of minor German-Croatian nobility, Šufflay was a prodigy who received his doctorate in history, as a Balkanist, at 22. He became a leading expert on Montenegrin and Albanian history, and has been described by Banac as "the greatest Albanologist of his generation, unsurpassed, in some respects, even today". He remains an object of profound respect among Albanian intellectuals.

Šufflay was a historian of considerable brilliance. He wrote in opposition to South Slavic unification, "The Yugoslav idea is not sufficiently dynamic. This idea is young and fragmentary. It is as nothing in comparison with the mighty Serb national consciousness, steeled in a century-long struggle for liberation." Politically, although he identified humorously with Sinn Fein, the political party of the Irish Republicans, Šufflay was a right-wing supporter of Croat independence, as a member of the small and despised Croat Party of Right *(Hrvatska Stranka Pravo)*, founded by a converted Jew, Josip Frank. The Frankists, as they were known, were progenitors of the extremist *Ustaša*, but, according to Banac, Šufflay never made the transition from classic Frankism to the fascist-tinged attitudes of the *Ustaša*. Although such rightist tendencies burgeoned among the Croat and Macedonian opponents of the Yugoslav monarchy, as the 1930s wore on they never took hold among Albanians.

Indeed, and by contrast, fascist and national-socialist ideology became increasingly fashionable among Serbs.

The year 1937 saw the presentation at the Serb Cultural Club in Niš, on March 7, of one of the most repulsive public statements of this century. Its author was Vasa Čubrilović, Ph.D., a member of the Serb network that had organized the murder of Austrian archduke Franz Ferdinand in Sarajevo in 1914. Its title was 'Iseljavanje Arnauta (Expulsion of the Albanians)', and it was quickly submitted as an advisory memorandum to the royal Yugoslav government. Four years after the accession of Adolf Hitler to power in Germany, Dr. Čubrilović stated the Serb position on the Kosovar Albanians bluntly – they must be expelled to Turkey. Further, he declared, "There is no doubt that the whole matter will arouse international reaction, inevitable in such cases. Whenever a similar affair took place in the Balkans in the last hundred years, there was always someone who protested against it... There will be some international protest... However, the modern world is accustomed to even worse. It has its own concerns so we should not be too afraid of the reactions from abroad. If Germany can evict hundreds of thousands of Jews, if Russia can transport millions of people from one part of the continent to the other, a few hundred thousand evicted Albanians will not provoke a world war. The deciding bodies must know what they want in order to carry through with their plan and not worry about world opinion." The philosophy of Dr. Čubrilović, with an occasional hiatus, would dominate Serbo-Albanian relations in Kosovo until the year 1999.

Dr. Čubrilović set out his proposals in detail. He defined Albanians as 'anarchist elements', a rather picturesque comparison when one considers that he had joined the semi-anarchist Gavrilo Princip in the assassination at Sarajevo, which touched off a world war. He restated the legends about Albanian occupation of Kosovo after the Great Migration, and blamed Albanian intrusion northward for limiting Serb influence in Macedonia. But he noted that Serbs had begun expelling Albanians in modern times, with the first Serbian anti-Turkish uprising in 1804. He warned that the Albanians were "supposed to be crushed by our present state starting in 1918". This had not been done, he lamented. Population exchanges in which Greeks had been forced out of Turkey, and Turks out of Greece, Romania, and Bulgaria, had become the norm in the Balkans, but Yugoslavia had instead sought recourse to "the slow and inefficient methods of gradual colonization", which had manifestly failed. Finally, the Albanians continued to out-breed the Serbs. And in an extraordinarily revealing remark, Dr. Čubrilović complained that the Albanians were "accustomed to the western European notions of private property" and that, "It is obvious what harm this attitude has caused our nation and state." Here we see that Dr. Čubrilović was far more an anarchist than any anti-statist Albanian.

But his vision was, of course statist for his project would require the resources of a goverment: "The only solution is to use brute force. We have always been superior to [Albanians] in its use." To effect the eviction of the indigenous population of Kosovo, he called for the application of a range of techniques: bribes and threats to the Albanian Muslim clergy and secular elites; promotion of Turkey as a place where a better life could be achieved; propaganda acclaiming the successful removal of Turks from Dobrudja on the Black Sea, held by Romania. In addition, all legal means would be brought to bear, including fines; arrests, ruthless application of all police sanctions; punishment for smuggling, uncontrolled wood cutting and letting dogs run loose; compulsory labor. Old land deeds would be cancelled, registration of land transfers would be suspended, while taxes would be increased and, along with public and private debts, collected with the utmost severity. The use of state and communal pasturage should be forbidden to Albanians; licensing of trades, coffeehouses, and small businesses would be abolished, and Albanians should be dismissed from state, private, and even self-employment! 'Health measures' would include forcible inspection of homes, destruction of walls and fences, and rigid veterinary rules against the sale of cattle.

And finally, this paragon of the Serb intellect suggested, "Albanians are most sensitive in religious matters. That is where we should hit hardest. It can be done by molesting their clergy [and] ploughing up their cemeteries." In addition, in application of a thoroughly modern and Western outlook, Islamic plural marriage would be forbidden and female children would be obliged to attend primary school. In a paragraph laden with horrific consequences, Dr. Čubrilović argued, "Our colonists should be given arms... The traditional *četnik* method should be used... A horde of Montenegrins from the mountains should be sent down to provoke massive clashes with the Albanians... With the help of our secret forces the conflict should be prepared in advance. It should be encouraged even, which will not be difficult if the Albanian resistance is fierce... In extreme cases, some local uprisings can be provoked which would later be put down by blood – the most effective means. This should not be done directly by the army, but rather by our colonists, i.e. *četniks* and Montenegrin tribes. There is one more method which Serbia used very effectively after 1878, the secret burning of Albanian villages and town quarters."

In offering his blueprint for what Dimitrije Tucović, 25 years before, had called "the attempted premeditated murder of an entire nation", Dr. Čubrilović had a virtue absent in the case of his noted contemporary, Adolf Hitler: his intentions were stated publicly and candidly. But that boldness,

81

like the murders of men like Radić, in the Belgrade parliament, and Sufflay, in city streets, doubtless had more to do with Serbian political culture, or the lack thereof, than with sincerity or openness. Indeed, Dr. Čubrilović was not alone in his outlook; similar conceptions were advanced, notably, by a then-civil servant in the Ministry of External Affairs of Royal Yugoslavia, Dr. Ivo Andrić, who would win the Nobel Prize for Literature in 1961.

Dr. Andrić authored a report in 1939, two years after the speech by Dr. Čubrilović, with an attached supplement. He was, like Dr. Čubrilović, an acolyte of the 1914 Sarajevo assassination conspiracy. In the supplement, Dr. Andrić reaffirmed the old Great Serbian principle of dividing Albania and annexing its north; but he agreed with Dr. Čubrilović that deportation of Muslim Albanians to Turkey would be made easier by the global prevalence of totalitarian methods of statecraft exemplified by Hitler and Stalin. Thousands of Albanians, under the lash of Serb chauvinism, and with the complicity of the Zog regime, departed Kosovo for Turkey during the 1930s. Accurately fixing their numbers is an impossibility, but the decade left Turkey with a considerable Albanian population, which some have estimated as high as a million in recent years.

The mass removal of the Albanians from Kosovo did not go unresisted, and the protestors against it were not limited to the victims and their ethnic compatriots. In 1938, news of a secret agreement between Yugoslavia and Turkey to expel 400,000 Albanians to Anatolia stimulated 65 students from Kosovo, of whom 56 were Serbs and Montenegrin, one a Turk, and only 8 Albanians, to circulate an illegal statement denouncing the plan throughout Kosovo and Macedonia, as well as to foreign embassies in Belgrade.

In any event, with Hitler crowding the center stage of European politics, Drs. Čubrilović and Andrić were temporarily preempted in the area of such experiments. Nevertheless, with the coming of a second world war, Serbia and its *četniks* would attempt, in a limited way, to fulfil the yearnings of both these men. For Albania proper, the war may be said to have begun with its annexation by fascist Italy in 1939. In Kosovo, the human catastrophe was delayed until April 1941, when Yugoslavia was conquered by the Germans. Riven by unresolved national grievances, and above all by the permanent unrest among Croats, Yugoslavia collapsed almost as soon as Axis troops crossed its borders. In one of the most bizarre and criminal adventures to be seen during a war filled with such events, the Yugoslav army command chose to send troops into Albania. It is therefore understandable that the Axis powers were welcomed by the Albanians of Kosovo, as well as those in western Macedonia, as liberators. Kosovo was partitioned between Germany and Bulgaria, which controlled small occupation zones, and Italian-ruled Albania, which received, in addition to the bulk of the territory, a section of western Macedonia with an Albanian majority.

The German occupation zone in Kosovo was at first administered as part of Serbia, by Nazi puppet authorities in Belgrade. The Germans granted the Albanians autonomy within this zone, but then abrogated that concession to local feelings, after protests by the Serb puppet rulers. Serbia soon came under the control of General Milan Nedić, author of a memoir of the 'Serb Golgotha' during the first world war that revealed anything but affection for Albanians. But German policies were inconsistent, and some local education in Albanian was eventually restored. As pointed out by Malcolm, the Germans also sought to suppress blood feuds among Kosovar Albanians and approved the expulsion of Serb and Montenegrin colonists. By contrast, the Italian occupiers defended local Serbs from Albanian attacks. Both the Germans and Italians recruited Serbs, Albanians, and Muslim Slavs as auxiliary troops, police, and, in the German case, members of the *Waffen-SS*. A small and ineffective SS Division Skanderbeg was recruited from among Albanians.

Still, as elsewhere in Axis Europe, Nazi and fascist rule was unpopular with Kosovar Albanians. As in Croatia, which had been united with Bosnia-Hercegovina to form an Independent State of Croatia under the *Ustaša*, the fundamentally imperialist aims of the occupiers could not be denied. Croat and Albanian collaborators tended to favor the Germans over the Italians, since the intention of the latter was clearly to replace the local populace. Thus, in Dalmatia, the section of Croatia handed over to the Italians, the expressed wish of Mussolini's government to remove the indigenous Slavs and colonize the region with Italians drove the overwhelming majority of Croats to join the Communist Partisans, for reasons that were basically non-ideological. However, it should also be recalled that Croatia traditionally possessed a significant Communist movement, from which the supreme commander of the Partisans, the former Zagreb metalworker Josip Broz, now known as Tito, emerged. But the hard-headed Albanians of Kosovo were even more impossible to convince of any long-term benefits accruing from the substitution of Italian for Yugoslav rule. Either way, foreigners treated the Albanians as colonial dependents, although the Italian construction of roads and public buildings, particularly schools, in Albania proper, was appreciated.

Yet the Kosovar Albanians were in no hurry to imitate the Dalmatian Croats in massively joining the Partisans. Communism had long been viewed among Albanians as yet another Serb scheme to maintain their oppression, and Albanian-speaking Communists were extremely thin on the ground. We have previously noted that even during its period of firm opposition to Serbian imperialism, in the 1920s, the Yugoslav Communist Party largely ignored

Kosovar Albanians. According to Banac, even though the Yugoslav Communists, after 1928, had declared their support for Kosovar Albanian rights, including that of unification with Albania, the party "had no following in the Albanian [population]". Banac further declares that after 1935, the Yugoslav Communists abandoned any pretense of supporting Albanian claims in Kosovo. The party's Kosovo cadre consisted overwhelmingly of Serbs and Montenegrins, whom Banac defines mainly as colonists; of 270 party members in Kosovo at the time of the German invasion, in April 1941, only 20 were Albanian. Once the Communists had launched the Partisan movement as a serious contender for power in the region, after the German attack on Russia in June 1941, they tended to treat the Albanians as a counterrevolutionary nation.

Thus, the Albanian Communist movement, in Albania proper as well as Kosovo, remained a marginal force through most of the second world war. When a full-fledged Albanian Communist Party was founded late in 1941, its inspiration, and even its guiding spirits, were Yugoslav; it was established in Tirana, the Albanian capital, by two Slav representatives of the Yugoslav Communist section in Kosovo, Dušan Mugoša and Miladin Popović. The intention was obvious: to recruit auxiliaries for the Yugoslav Partisans, in a manner not very different from that pursued by the Germans and Italians; Albanians remained historical objects rather than subjects. Banac emphasizes that even after an Albanian Communist Party was formed, it had to affirm on paper its support for an ethnic Albania including Kosovo and the Çameria region of northern Greece, which also has an Albanian majority. But the Yugoslav Partisan leadership sternly rebuked their Albanian 'comrades' for expressing such a desire.

One aspect of Communist organization on which Yugoslav and Albanian adherents agreed from the beginning, was insistence on the Stalinist concept of discipline from the top down. Because no indigenous Albanian Communism existed, the first Albanian Marxists originated in the ranks of an anti-Stalinist political tendency that today is virtually forgotten, These are the Greek Archeio-Marxists, so named because they published a periodical titled *Archives of Marxism*. The Archeio-Marxists fostered a youth group called *Zjarri* (The Flame) among Albanian students in Athens. With the official creation of the Albanian party by Mugoša and Popović, virtually all the pioneers of Communism in Albania were labeled Trotskyites and expelled from the movement. At least two of them, Llazër Fundo and Anastas Lula, were murdered at the behest of the Yugoslav-installed Communist chief, a former Albanian student and police agent in France named Enver Hoxha, while another among them, Sadik Premte, escaped to France where he lived in exile from 1947 until his death in 1991. According to Premte, many more were assassinated afterward.

Premte and Lula had been thrown out of the party after a purge trial in Tirana in mid-1942. The murder of such dissidents was later celebrated by the Albanian writer Ismail Kadare as a heroic instance of Partisan justice. But Premte was clear-sighted about the nature of the party that had ejected him; he castigated Miladin Popović as "a crafty Serb chauvinist who, under the mask of Communism, wanted to form a clique for the sake of better serving the interests of his country," i.e. Yugoslavia. The Yugoslavs returned the favor, with Tito's comrade, the historian Vladimir Dedijer, branding Premte an "anti-Yugoslav element."

The Communist Partisans were not the only resistance movement functioning in Kosovo. Among Serbs, četnik units sprang up in the wake of Yugoslavia's collapse, but they wavered between conflict and collaboration with the Axis occupiers. While the četniks were notably weak in Kosovo, they engaged in skirmishing with Albanians as well as combat against the Partisans, their main interest. During this period, the četniks first began to gain a broader attention from worldwide media, particularly in the democratic countries, where they were long granted the benefit of the doubt as ostensible antifascist rivals to the Communists. They seemed picturesque, with long hair and beards, which they insisted they wore because, at home in the mountains during their struggle, they had no time to shave or get their hair cut. The image of the wild-haired and bearded četnik, which reappeared in the Yugoslav wars of the 1990s, was supplemented by their devotion to the knife as the chosen weapon. Both characteristics may have had more in common with the frightful aspect of the ancient Sarmatians, as described by Ovid:

"Voices bestial, stolid faces, are the truest image of their minds,
hair uncombed, beards uncut by practised hand,
right fists never slow to inflict a wound with the knife,
that close by his side every barbarian carries."

(Tristia, V, vii.)

In such conditions it should come as no surprise that, as the Albanian Communist Koço Tashko wrote to Moscow in late 1942, in a letter cited by Malcolm, "The hatred and fear of the Kosovars for the Serbs and Montenegrins is very great." But the brunt of Tashko's letter involved a complaint that Miladin Popović had rejected proposals for a separate Communist organization to be set up in Kosovo. For, Tashko added, "Let us not forget that [Kosovars] also have a great hatred for the fascist Italians, whom they call 'weaklings' and 'infidels.' " Popović very briefly called for the party in Metohija to be placed under the authority of the Albanian rather than the Yugoslav

Communist leadership, and for the Partisans in the same area to report to the Albanian Partisan staff. But he soon abandoned that proposal.

Only once did the Albanian Communists seem to seriously dissent from their Yugoslav masters on these matters; at the end of 1943, a conference of Communists, in northeast Albania, at which only a seventh of the attendees were non-Albanian, created a Kosovo People's Committee. The Committee declared that only the common Partisan struggle with the rest of the Yugoslav nations would allow the Kosovar Albanians "to decide their own future through the right of self-determination, up to the point of secession". This formulation was almost immediately rejected by the supreme Yugoslav Partisan leaders. However, Ivo Banac has shown that Albanian Communists had attempted to break through this system of control on other occasions. The party organization within Albania proper had unsuccessfully sought to assume command over Albanian Partisans in Kosovo and western Macedonia, and to bring Metohija under its jurisdiction, in line with the original proposal of Popović. At least one obscure manifesto, very early on, had seemed to grant Kosovo and its Albanians equal standing with Montenegro, Serbia, and Greece.

But Tashko had it right: even among collaborators with the Axis occupiers discontent was visible. One of the most fascinating issues on which Albanian puppet functionaries refused to serve the Germans involved the tiny Jewish community of Kosovo. Amazingly, although Kosovo had the third-smallest Jewry in Yugoslavia, at only 550 members, it produced the second-highest rate of survival of the Nazi holocaust – 62 percent, compared with only 10 percent alive in Macedonia after the war, 12 percent in the rest of Serbia, 20 percent in Croatia, and 29 percent in Bosnia-Hercegovina. Dalmatia, with a survival rate of 63 percent, exceeded Kosovo in protecting its Jews, largely because the Italians, who did not share Nazi racial obsessions, were the occupiers there. But Kosovars sheltered their neighbors for another reason: the ancient Albanian custom of *besa*, as prescribed by the *Kanun*. Even the pro-Nazi Xhafer Deva, a political figure from Mitrovica favored by the Germans in Kosovo affairs, and then installed in power in Tirana, was reputed to have indignantly refused to hand over lists of Albanian Jews.

In September 1943 Italy withdrew from the Axis alliance. The stage was now set for an Allied victory in Europe, and the triumph of the Communist Partisans in a restored Yugoslavia whose Serbian monarchy was defunct.

* * * * *

86

Chapter V:

Kosovo and Communism
In Yugoslavia and Albania, 1944-1985

The Second World War had produced a conflict of 'all against all' in Yugoslavia. With the support of the Axis occupiers, Croat and Serb ultranationalists competed in killing one another, typically with the pretext that they were fighting against the Communist Partisans under Tito. In this situation, only the Partisans were viewed as serving the war aims of the Western allies, concentrating on combat against the Germans and struggling for the reunification of the sundered South Slav state. Notwithstanding special pleading for the Serb *četniks* advanced after the war by certain intellectuals in the West, it is undeniable that Tito and his cadres struggled for a South Slav federation, while the *četniks* frequently collaborated with the Nazis, seeking the reimposition, under German or Western auspices, of a royalist Great Serbia in which Croats would again be relegated to a second class status, with Bosnian Muslims marked for extermination and Kosovar Albanians for deportation to Turkey at best.

It is also unarguable that among Croats and Slovenes, in contrast with Serbs, no competing faction emerged to challenge the Partisans, as the *četniks* did, for Western support. Indeed, one may say in general that Slovenia and Croatia were clearly polarized between collaborators who favored the Nazis and anti-fascists who supported the Partisans, while Serbia remained ambivalent about both sides until the approach of the war's end, when thousands of *četniks*, having dedicated themselves to horrific atrocities against Partisans and Muslims, were granted an amnesty by Tito, which allowed them to join Partisan ranks.

This sequence of historical events, particularly in Serbia, is both confusing for most Western readers, and novel to them in its collision with Serb legendry, which has portrayed all Croats and Bosnian Muslims as Axis collaborators and all Serbs as supporters of the Allies. But in reality, the greater part of the Partisan war in Yugoslavia was fought on Croatian and Bosnian territory, and Croats and Bosnian Muslims were found on both sides; many Serbs in Croatia and Bosnia supported the Partisans but many did not, and little or no real Partisan activity transpired in Serbia proper. After all, Tito, the Partisan chief, considered himself a Croat in culture, demonstrating that at least one such Croat was not a Nazi collaborator. While Serbs suffered ghastly cruelties at the hands of the *Ustaša*, those within Serbia proper persisted in viewing the Communist Partisans, rather than either the *Ustaša* or the Germans, as their main enemies. Nevertheless, Serb nationalism in the higher levels of Tito's leadership structure would influence ethnic politics within the Yugoslav Communist state created by the Partisan (and Allied) victory.

Although little perceived abroad, during and immediately after the war, those citizens of Yugoslavia, monarchist or Communist, whose ethnic status was most dramatically affected by this state of affairs were neither Croats nor Serbs, but Kosovar Albanians. For notwithstanding the commitment on paper to national equality on the part of Marxist theoreticians of the past, and the very occasional blandishments by earlier Yugoslav Communist functionaries in favor of Albanian rights, the Yugoslavia conceived of by the Partisans remained a South Slav entity in intention and realization. As previously noted, Kosovar Albanians distrusted Communism as a 'pan–Slavic' conspiracy, and did not rally to the Partisans, although they evinced little depth of commitment to the ideology of the Nazi occupiers. Ironically, their response to the Allied Partisan stuggle against the Axis resembled, in its ambivalence, that of most Serbs. Serbs and Albanians alike, especially in Kosovo, were more interested in the competing claims of outsiders than in their own striving for local control, the Serbs as colonialists and the Albanians as an indigenous population. In addition, Ivo Banac has pointed out that the wartime Communist District Committee for Kosovo demonstrated a "debilitating penchant for urban terror" that even further alienated Albanians from the Partisan cause.

In Kosovo, this led to a series of separate wars within wars as the Partisan campaign came to a close. Noel Malcolm has written hyperbolically, and without supporting data, that "lingering resistance to Communism was a phenomenon encountered in many parts of Yugoslavia. Nowhere, however, did it last as long as in Kosovo." Still, there is some truth in this statement. Tito and his colleagues needed above all to clear Kosovo of opposition to them, and this opposition was so widespread that the Tito biographer and historian Vladimir Dedijer commented, "Tito's greatest worry at the end of the war and in the first days of peace was Kosovo." Dedijer, basing himself on reports from the field, accepted an estimate that up to 30,000 Kosovar Albanians had risen in arms against the new regime.

Tito's policy in Kosovo revealed hesitation, improvisation, and self–contradiction, qualities generally absent from the personality of the architect of Yugoslav Communism. The most significant measure taken to secure the region was extraordinary: in 1944, Albanian Partisan units were invited into Metohija from Albania proper, to do the work Slav troops could not be expected to complete. This was especially bizarre in light of the earlier, repeated, and stiff rejection by Yugoslav Partisans of Albanian Communist initiatives toward recognition of Kosovar Albanian demands, and Yugoslav Communist insistence that Albanian Partisans active in Western Macedonia withdraw into Albania or face armed attacks by their alleged comrades who happened to be Slavs. Enver Hoxha, installed by the Yugoslavs as head of the Communist network in Albania, expressed no qualms at that point about supine obedience to orders from Tito. But as Banac has written, the Kosovar Albanians greeted "strictly Albanian" Partisan units with "occasional tolerance", rather than enthusiasm. Earlier, Banac notes, Albanian Partisans in Kosovo claimed their enemies included not only rural folk, but also "dogs, shepherds, and even goats", while one source describes an hours-long, pitched battle between Partisans and 2,000 armed and enraged Albanian peasants, which only ended when the attackers realized the Partisans were also Albanian.

Thus, not all those Kosovar Albanians who actively resisted the Partisans were Nazi collaborators, although they were portrayed as such by Communist propagandist and historians. One element of Albanian insurgency in Kosovo was led by a remarkable individual, Gani Kryeziu, and his two brothers, Hasan and Sahit, woshe father had been a leader of the 1912 Kosovo uprising. The Kryezius favored the British, Americans, and other democratic and non-Communist powers in the Allied coalition. At the end of 1943, one of the Kryezius initiated contact with a British agent sent into Kosovo, Peter Kemp, a man of the political right who, curiously enough, had fought for Franco in the Spanish civil war Kemp was presented with a proposal for an independent, insurrectionary movement against the German occupation. Albanian Communist cadres were so fearful of such a possibility that they secretly informed the German Gestapo of Kemp's first meeting with Hasan Kryeziu. Kemp soon agreed to provide support, but he was overruled by his superiors in London, who favored the Partisans.

Still, if the British liaison officers on the ground, could not provide immediate aid to the Kryezius, they depended on them for help. Earlier work with the Kryezius had been carried out by another British agent, Julian Amery, who had also gone to Spain during its war, but as a journalist while A squadron leader in the Royal Air Force, Tony Neel, also established a liaison with Gani Kryeziu, in the Kukës area of north Albania, on the Kosovo border. After six months, British backing, at least in words, was given to the Kryezius' effort, which aimed at liberation of the Albanians from the Axis, but with continued unity of Albania proper and Kosovo. The Kryezius allied with local supporters of the deposed King Zog in Albania, and were joined by another obscure but fascinating figure, the old Albanian Communist, Llazër Fundo.

Fundo had gone to Moscow years before as a supporter of the Comintern, but was apparently denounced there by the Communist writer Sejfulla

Malëshova (who after the second world war would himself be victimized, under Hoxha in Albania, by Stalinist repression). Fundo avoided a trial and execution during the Soviet mass purges of the late 1930s thanks to the intervention of Comintern chief Georgi Dimitrov, his personal friend. He then went to Western Europe, and, like the British agents Kemp and Amery, became involved in the Spanish civil war. Indeed, the Spanish war proved a major influence for many protagonists in Yugoslavia and Albania during the 1940s, as numerous members of Tito's command staff, as well as Enver Hoxha's then-confidante, Mehmet Shehu, had fought in the Soviet-controlled International Brigades there. Miladin Popović, for example, whose name certainly looms large in Kosovo history, was wounded in February 1937 while fighting in Spain and was evacuated from that country in 1938.

Fundo, however, cleaved to the fairly considerable anti-Stalin forces in Spain. He turned up in revolutionary Barcelona, apparently under the pseudonym 'Jovan', alongside the exiled leader of the Greek Archeio-Marxists, Demetrios Yotopoulos, who called himself 'Beta', pronounced 'Vitte', since he considered himself second only to Trotsky, or 'Alpha'. Both men frequented the same circles as George Orwell, associating with the Partit Obrer d'Unificació Marxista, or POUM, and, like Orwell, both were threatened by the Soviet secret police while in Spain. Fundo returned to Albania soon after the beginning of the second world war, and was denounced as a major Trotskyite by the Yugoslav Communists in a letter sent to the newborn Albanian party organization in September 1942.

Fundo was interned by the Italians, and met Gani and Sahit Kryeziu, who were then also in fascist custody. The veteran revolutionary became the personal adviser and translator for the rebel leaders after the Italians left the war and the imprisoned Albanians were freed. Another of the British agents among the Albanian anti-fascists, Reginald Hibbert, comments that the Kosovar Albanian Partisans, led by the semi-literate Fadil Hoxha and Mehmet Hoxha, "were not popular with the predominantly Albanian population of Kosovo and made little headway there. The Kryeziu movement, if it had continued, might have led to a general nationalist uprising of the Kosovars; but this would have been embarrassing and perhaps dangerous… to the Communist leaders of both Yugoslavia and Albania."

At the end of summer 1944 Enver Hoxha's Albanian Partisans entered Kosovo. Although their main responsibility was supposedly to combat the Germans, they attacked the Kryeziu fighters, aggravating existing conflicts in Albania proper between Communists and non-Communists which, even more than in Yugoslavia, had assumed the dimensions of a civil war. Fundo, in the company of two British officers, was captured by Hoxha's followers and beaten to death. Hasan Kryeziu was executed by Tito, while Gani Kryeziu disappeared after being sentenced to forced labor, and Sahit Kryeziu escaped to America.

The roster of Albanian patriots murdered by Tito and Hoxha in Kosovo at that time was not limited to revolutionary nationalists like Hasan Kryeziu or dissident Marxists such as Llazër Fundo. Fr. Lek Luli, an Albanian Franciscan, with two other members of his order, was arrested by Yugoslav Partisans. A British liaison officer, David Smiley, remembered the slender, sensitive Fr. Luli as "very amusing", and a convinced anticommunist "who always carried his tommy gun slung over his cassock". According to Smiley, Fr. Luli was handed over to Mehmet Hoxha, a "notoriously brutal" figure. Torture was applied to Fr. Luli in an effort to force him to disclose information about the relations between the anti-communist leader Abas Kupi and the British. "But the brave little priest refused to divulge any details," Smiley later wrote. "He was flogged, had his fingers broken, and was branded with hot irons. In the end [Mehmet] Hoxha ordered his throat to be cut," and Fr. Luli was buried in an unmarked grave. Lek Luli is recorded in the history of the Albanian Catholic church as the first of its many victims to Communism, which would include two outstanding Albanian patriots spoken of the previous chapter, Fr. Anton Harapi and Mons. Luigj Bumçi.

It is difficult to determine to what degree the fury that would be visited on Albanian Catholics by the Enver Hoxha regime reflected primitive hatred within the personality of Hoxha himself, or an unrestrained attempt to fulfil orders from Belgrade, for the patriotism of the Albanian Catholics, especially the Franciscans and Jesuits, was as fervent as their Christian commitment. In any event, the savagery visited on the Franciscan martyrs of Kosovo had its antecedents in the murder of the outstanding folkorist and compiler of the *kanun* of Lek Dukagjim, Fr. Shtjefën Gjeçovia, (mentioned in the previous chapter), as well as three of his brethren: Frs.L.Paliq, L. Mitroviqi, and B. Llupi, by the Yugoslavs.

The outstanding postwar Albanian Catholic martyr, Fr. Anton Harapi, was not a Kosovar, but came from the area of Lake Shkodra, which is divided between Montenegro and Albania. After being trained in theology in Austria, he became one of many Catholic teachers instructing the young in northern Albania. He was active in relief work during a cholera epidemic in the highest mountain areas in 1916, while the world war raged; he buried the dead and instructed the highlanders in methods of fighting the disease. He often traveled for up to ten hours, on foot, to succor the ill.

During the struggle for Albania's survival in the early 1920s, Fr. Harapi wrote an account of life in the mountains, *Andrra e Pretashit* (Pretashi's

Dream). In the words of an Albanian Catholic historian, professor Michael Marku, therein "the real figure of the Albanian Franciscan priest, intelligent, dedicated to religion and fatherland, philosopher... comes out." After the second world war, Fr. Harapi was killed in Albania during the period of Yugoslav dominance, as a traitor. He told the judges, "If to suffer for the people and with the people and fight for the Faith and Fatherland are considered weakness and treason, then, not only myself but all the Albanian Franciscans deserve the great honor of being shot." He was executed during the night of February 14, 1946 in his 58th year.

Mons. Luigj Bumçi died under Albanian police surveillance 11 months before, aged 73. He had become best known among his countrymen for his defense of Albanian sovereignty over the southern towns of Korça and Gjirokastra in Albanian proper. When at the 1919 Paris Peace Conference, which ended The First World war, the great powers turned these two cities over to Greece, Mons. Bumçi, then serving as bishop of Lezha in northern Albania, organized a delegation that went to Paris in protest of the decision. Informed that the matter had been effectively settled, he later recalled, the mainly Muslim delegates implored him to appeal to Pope Benedict XV. Mons. Bumçi did so, and the pontiff agreed to intercede on the behalf of the Albanians. The two cities were saved for Albania, and in 1921 the Vatican became the first government in Europe to recognize Albania.

The outstanding disciples of Fr. Gjeçovi, folklorists Frs. Bernardin Palaj and Donat Kurti, discussed in chapter II, were also among the victims of the Albanian Communist regime, which above all, aimed at the physical destruction of the Catholic clergy, regardless of the patriotic, educational, and literary services they had rendered in the past. In a particularly ghoulish development, the main work of Frs. Palaj and Kurti, their 1937 second volume in the two-volume *Visaret e Kombit* (The Treasure of the Nation), considered this century's outstanding contribution on traditional oral Albanian literature, was looted for reuse by the Albanian writer and servant of Enver Hoxha, Ismail Kadare, who fully supported the suppression of Albanian Catholic scholarship. Fr. Palaj, also a major poet, was executed in 1946; Fr. Kurti was arrested that year and served 17 years in various labor camps in Albania. He was last heard of by exiled Albanian Catholics in 1969; it was not until the middle of the 1990s that it was learned he had died in 1983, at 80. Fr. Donat Kurti remains one of the greatest Albanian prose writers.

And of course, even Partisans were not exempt from the hecatomb of Communist victims. In a series of incidents that remains alive in the collective memory of Kosovars, at least 4,000 Kosovar Albanian Partisans under the command of Shaban Polluzha refused to assist in the suppression of a renewed uprising against the Yugoslav Partisans, at the end of 1944, directly after the crushing of the Kryezius. Polluzha's situation was extremely confused and tragic, yet he became an immortal hero to Kosovars, who write ballads about him even today. Tito's staff ordered Polluzha's Partisans removed to the Srijem district near Belgrade, but Polluzha insisted they were needed to defend Drenica, the old heartland of Azem Bejta and Shota Galica, where a horrific massacre reminiscent of the worst excesses of the Balkan Wars had occurred. Furthermore, an Albanian Partisan sent to investigate the Drenica affair was shot by Yugoslav Partisans when he attempted to present his report. According to one account, 20,000 fighters joined Polluzha's forces, which were attacked by Yugoslav Partisans, with bloody results.

Fighting in Kosovo did not end until March 1945, after the establishment of martial law; 44 Drenica villages were reported destroyed. Miranda Vickers, whose *Between Serb and Albanian: A History of Kosovo* is hardly a pro-Albanian document, nevertheless cites claims that nearly 50,000 Albanians were massacred in the suppression of the rebellion, with a proliferation of ghastly incidents of mass murder. Thus, she writes that Kosovo "emerged from the war into the new Federal Yugoslavia under siege." Much of the detail of these events remains vague in the historical record, but perhaps because Polluzha's men had been Partisans, and could be assimilated into Titoite ideology, they remain more vivid than the Kryeziu brothers in later Kosovar recollection. Yet their vision was far less ample than that of the Kryezius, since Polluzha and his supporters only acted defensively.

As shown by his services to the Yugoslavs in fighting the Kryezius and liquidating the Catholic intelligentsia, Enver Hoxha was no Albanian patriot. After his usefulness to the Tito forces was deemed to have ended, his Partisan units withdrew from Kosovo; in any event, his own early administration, like the original cadres of the Albanian Communist Party, included numerous Yugoslav advisers in positions of authority. This left resolution of the Kosovo issue, within the new, Communist Yugoslavia, entirely in the hands of Tito and his Slav politburo. The first measures taken by the Tito Communists after they established control over Kosovo were unmistakable in their import: the Kosovo Communist District Committee was abolished and all local organizations were placed under the responsibility of the Serbian leadership. Still, Albanian recalcitrance remained visible, as numerous local Communists resigned their posts and gave up party membership in protest of this action. Then, however, a special commission directed by the Montenegrin Milovan Djilas, number four in the party hierarchy, re-established the district party committee for Kosovo, which was granted official but limited autonomy within in Serbia.

Nevertheless Kosovo remained, a troubled region. Miladin Popović, one of those responsible for the creation of an originally Slavophile Albanian Communist party, was murdered in Prishtina after the war; strangely enough, persistent rumors among Kosovar Albanians hold that he was killed by Tito's secret police because he insisted on granting Kosovar Albanians the full rights they had once been promised, which seems on its face quite too extravagant an exercise in conspiracy theory. Unfortunately, the man who would mainly determine the fate of the Kosovar Albanians for some 20 years and more, after the establishment of Communist Yugoslavia, was a highly Albanophobic Serb, Aleksandar Leka Ranković, who became head of the secret police, known under various acronyms, but mainly as the UDBA, or Administration for State Security. The period became known as the Ranković era, with extremely grim connotations among Kosovar Albanians. And in yet another harbinger of bad times for the populace, the sinister Dr. Vasa Čubrilović, author of the 1937 proposal for 'Expulsion of the Albanians', was appointed minister of agriculture in Tito's first government.

Having graduated from membership in the Sarajevo assassination plot of 1914 to praise for the "double star" Hitler and Stalin 23 years later, made a smooth transition to the Yugoslav Communist hierarchy, Dr. Čubrilović and prepared a new recension of his thesis on the need for expulsion of non-Serb communities from Kosovo and Vojvodina within the new Serb People's Republic, as well as from Montenegro and Macedonia. In this document, titled 'The Problem of Minorities in the New Yugoslavia', he recommended to Tito and his leading cohort that Germans, Hungarians, Albanians, and Romanians should be interned in concentration camps if not immediately deported. Ever attentive to the spirit of his times, and eager that Serbia should always be in the vanguard of new developments, Dr. Čubrilović wrote, "This war and its movement of masses has... created the preliminary psychological mood for expulsions." However, with the accession of Albania, Hungary, and Romania to the Communist bloc alongside Yugoslavia, this prescription could only be applied to the Vojvodina Germans, who were indeed forced to migrate *en masse* to Germany.

From 1944 to 1948 the general trend of Yugoslav policy toward Albanians and even toward Albania as a state was based on a novelty that accommodated both of the traditional goals of Great Serbian ideology, that is, the continued control of Kosovo as well as the desire for incorporation into Yugoslavia of northern Albania and its Adriatic littoral. This was nothing more nor less than the claim that as an application of proletarian internationalism, the brotherhood of peoples, and the liberation of humanity from oppressive borders, Albania should be integrated into Yugoslavia as a seventh member of a socialist federation of people's republics, alongside Slovenia, Croatia, Bosnia-Hercegovina, Serbia, Montenegro, and Macedonia.

The extinction of Albania as a sovereign state was apparently viewed by Communist dictator Enver Hoxha- who after all, was put in power by Tito- as a positive solution to nationalist rivalries in the Balkans, at least in those heady years following the triumph of the Communist Partisans. Inaddition, Tito had designs for the further combination of an enlarged Yugoslavia with Bulgaria, under similar terms. Thus would Serbian imperialism, under the pretext of socialist unification, have attained a fantasy of regional domination undreamed of since the mid-19th century.

These ambitions ran aground for reasons filled with irony.Just before the beginning of the Second World War, a certain Trotsky, speakingfrom his Mexican exile had predicted that the Stalinist conception of socialism in one country, in which the original internationalist impulses of Communism were subordinated to the nationalist goals of Russian imperialism, would inevitably fail. Above all, he argued, with the expansion of Communist rule into other countries, new socialist states would imitate Stalinist Russia in reviving their own nationalist and imperialist programs, which would necessarily conflict with the existing Muscovite control over the international Communist movement. This first occurred in Yugoslavia, though it was later to be repeated most dramatically in China. Although Tito and his comrades eventually adopted a democratic rhetoric in their resistance to Stalin's dictates, the bald truth was that Stalinist Russia could not tolerate a Titoite Great Serbia in the Balkans, particularly one that threatened to effectively absorb Russia's more favored regional ally, Bulgaria. Although Stalin claimed to support realization of a federation of Albania, Yugoslavia, and Bulgaria in the shortest possible time, such declamations were no more than a disinformational tactic.

Thus it was that in 1948 Stalin and Tito broke relations in spectacular fashion, stunning the world, but especially upsetting foreign Communist intellectuals. Thus it was also that Enver Hoxha, for the first time, took forthright action against the threat of Albanian annexation have deleted as makes little sense. Stalin's split with Tito had devastating effects within the Communist bureaucracies of the East European states, as the Stalin loyalists outside Yugoslavia now sought to root out and exterminate any and all sympathizers and possible emulators of Tito's independent Communism. The first such purge came, predictably, in Albania, as Hoxha sought to affirm his party's subordination to Moscow and Stalin, in place of Belgrade and Tito. And Albania now became a major enemy of the Yugoslav state, an outcome with disastrous consequences for ordinary, non-ideological workers and peasants in Kosovo. The indigenous population that had previously been massacred repeatedly for refusing to accept Serbification saw itself labeled anew, in its entirety, as a potential traitor to the state in which it held citizenship. This was a nightmarish fate, for as previously shown, Enver Hoxha had done nothing, and would do nothing in the future, for the Kosovar Albanians; his name was and is cursed among them. To suffer prison and death in Yugoslavia on the charge that they served Hoxha's regime was a cruelty that could hardly be exceeded.

It may therefore be considered something of a minor blessing for the Kosovar Albanians that Tito and his cadre, in the interest of resistance to Soviet pressure, soon had to seriously consider public opinion among the democratic powers of the West, to a degree unheard of in monarchist Serbia and Yugoslavia. The Titoites could not simply expel the Albanians through the mountain passes into Albania proper, as their forefathers (and successors) sought to do, although the Ranković era saw deportation of at least 250,000 Albanians to Turkey. In addition, Tito himself, as a Croat, was by no means bloodthirsty in his attitude toward Albanians or enormously enthusiastic about Great Serbian ideology as a principle of statecraft. His personal drive for power in the Balkans had coincided with the historic aims of Great Serbianism, in such a way as to give new life to it, but he himself was obviously ambivalent about its direct effects on those of his subjects who were not Serbs.

This contradiction was visible in Tito's orders, following the suppression of the Kosovo uprising, and regarding the status of Slav colonists in the region. As a concession to the Albanian population, the colonists were not allowed to regain their homesteads if they had been confiscated from working peasants or political exiles, or if the colonists had served in the police or were absentee landlords. More than 11,000 cases were investigated, and about 6,000 had to give up some or all their holdings. Thousands of Serbs moved to Vojvodina, where they took over property that had formerly belonged to Germans. Nonetheless, Tito ruled Yugoslavia, not just Kosovo, and he could not concern himself in the first instance with the welfare of those living in a poor southern region. That was left, for two decades, to Ranković, the secret police boss, who imposed wholesale repression in Kosovo. Ranković's UDBA was a Serb organism par excellence in a Yugoslav Communist state that never came fully to grips with the heritage of Great Serbian imperialism.

Ranković had always stood in the extreme Stalinist wing of Yugoslav Communism. He had become active in the party in the late 1920s, and was first arrested in 1929, soon after proclamation of the monarchist dictatorship; he emerged as a leader with the generation of Stalinists that rode the wave of purges and murders in Russia and throughout the world that transformed world Communism in the 1930s. The mass trials and executions of Communists in Russia decimated the Yugoslav Communists who were exiled there; the victims included the former Serbian socialist Kosta Novaković. Ivo Banac notes estimates that of some 900 Yugoslav Communists in Russia, 800 were arrested, and only 40 survived the terror.

In 1937, Ranković was one of a group of prominent Communists held in the Yugoslav jail of Srijemska Mitrovica, who undertook to bring the Stalin purges behind the prison walls. These fanatics, led by a rigid and narrow-minded Montenegrin named Petko Miletić, were nicknamed 'Wahhabis' by the other Communist prisoners, after the well-known Islamic fundamentalist movement. It is interesting to note that within Srijemska Mitrovica they formed an alliance with prisoners from the Croat extremist *Ustaša*.

In addition to Miletić and Ranković, the Wahhabis in Srijemska Mitrovica included another Montenegrin of note, the future 'dissident' Milovan Djilas, who would be lauded to the skies throughout the West. Most importantly, however, the Communist Wahhabis launched a campaign of physical assaults against the older and less extreme Communist prisoners. The liquidations practiced in Moscow, in the Spanish civil war, and elsewhere, were necessarily to be repeated in a Yugoslav jail, according to the Wahhabis. This situation led 17 leading Communists to request the authorities to place them in solitary confinement, separated from the majority of their comrades, who enthusiastically backed the Wahhabis as representatives of the new and murderous dispensation emanating from the Kremlin. The situation became so scandalous among Communists that Tito himself, who had become head of the party as a supporter of Stalin, was forced to become involved in the Srijemska Mitrovica war. Of the Wahhabis, only two remained in the temporary leadership established by Tito in 1938: Ranković and Djilas. Both would accompany Tito through the hardships and glories of the Partisan war.

Ranković's Wahhabism, i.e. Stalinism, and his penchant for Great Serbianism made a natural combination. Throughout the decades of his control over UDBA, Kosovar Albanians were routinely arrested and charged with separatism, Stalinism, sabotage, spying, and other crimes, at least some of them imaginary. Possession of weapons, including hunting guns, was deemed a criminal offense, and even reading the official Yugoslav Communist media in the Albanian language was considered suspicious. Indeed, Ranković attempted to reproduce in Kosovo the terrorist regime the Wahhabis had temporarily established in the Srijemska Mitrovica jail years before, or, better, a little ethnic *gulag*, to use the Soviet term that would later gain global currency. His methods were not alleviated by the rise of Khrushchevite reform in Russia, which would logically have ended the temptation for Moscow or Tirana to infiltrate agents into Kosovo against the Titoite system. Ranković's minions investigated Sufis, high Communist officials, writers, and ordinary peasants; that is, anybody who was Albanian and who provided a convenient target by standing out from the majority – and a great many were locked up.

One of the most remarkable of his victims was a young author named Adem Demaçi. He was born in 1936 in Prishtina and first showed literary promise in the early 1950s, when he was a high school student. His work was discovered by the literary editor of the Kosovar Albanian daily, *Rilindja* (Rebirth), Gjon Sinishta, a former Jesuit seminarian, poet and exile from Hoxha's Albania. Demaçi's short story, 'Lustraxhiu' (The Shoe Shiner), won the annual short story contest run by *Rilindja*. Demaçi joined the paper's staff and worked alongside Sinishta until 1956, when Sinishta was arrested; a believing Albanian Catholic was a fairly obvious target for Ranković's personnel, and Sinishta had refused to become a Communist party member.

In 1958 Demaçi published a novel, *Gjarpinjt e Gjakut* (Bloodthirsty Snakes), a depiction of blood feuds among Albanians that is considered his masterpiece. The book became extremely popular among Kosovar Albanians, who appreciated Demaçi as an author "acutely sensitive to the suffering of helpless folk and to social inequality," according to the Albanian American scholar Peter R. Prifti. A Kosovar literary critic, Idriz Lamaj, who edited a definitive edition of the work, perceived in it a serious critique, indeed an exposure and denunciation, not only of violence between Albanians, but of Slav rule in the region. This message was not lost on the Yugoslav authorities. Soon after the book's appearance, Demaçi was arrested for the first time on November 19, 1958, joining his friend and mentor Sinishta in prison. The pair were together in jail three years, and became extremely close, even though Demaçi was a Marxist in conviction and Sinishta a Catholic and opponent of Communism.

Demaçi became the leading symbol of Kosovar Albanian patriotism. After his release in 1961, Demaçi was rearrested in 1964 and 1975. In the latter instance he was tried as the leader of the group of Adem Demaçi. He was tortured, and nearly went blind. His third arrest resulted in a sentence of 15 years. Like the ultimate architect of his torment, Ranković, Demaçi served time in the cells of Srijemska Mitrovica, as well as on the infamous Goli Otok (Naked Island), the most feared of the UDBA's punishment sites. But between his second and third arrests, Ranković fell, and glimmers of hope began to brighten the darkness in which the Kosovar Albanians languished.

The purge of Ranković came in 1966, at a turning point for much of the world. That year saw, in the United States, a dramatic increase in protests against the Vietnam War and the full blooming of the hippie phenomenon, as well as continuing ghetto insurrections in the major American cities along with civil rights demonstrations in the Southern states. In the then Soviet Union, the writers Andrei Sinyavsky and Yuli Danyel emerged as the first open literary dissidents in many decades, and were charged with treason. China underwent the commencement of the Great Proletarian Cultural Revolution with the purge of Peng Zhen and Lo Juiching, and Mao Zedong's swim in the Yangtze River. An outbreak of student and labou rioting in the Netherlands led to the efflorescence of the anarchist Provos, who briefly fascinated Europe in the world. In France, the surrealist poet André Breton, a long-time opponent of Stalinism whose disciples had included a number of close collaborators of Tito, died at 70. In Detroit, Michigan, in utter obscurity, the former prison companion of Adem Demaçi, Gjon Sinishta, who had escaped Yugoslavia, established a modest Albanian Catholic Information Center.

It seems strange to recall, decades later, that at that time the Communist states in power from the Adriatic to the Pacific were considered immutable in their authority, destined to last forever, or, at least, into the far and unpredictable future. Even conservative intellectuals in the West accepted the presumption that Soviet Communism represented a new and enduring social form. Furthermore, attempts to educate the Western public in the realities of Communism were increasingly rejected as Cold War propaganda. In Yugoslavia, it must be said that many people seemed to really think that Tito was somehow immortal, while in Albania Enver Hoxha certainly attempted to build up such a belief. Soon Hoxha, who had allied himself with the Maoist Chinese after their break with Soviet Russia at the beginning of the 1960s, would emulate the Cultural Revolution in Beijing by launching his own febrile attempt to utterly extirpate religion in Albania, declaring the country the first officially atheist state in the world.

Ranković was suddenly fired from his post as secret police boss at a conference called by Tito on the island of Brioni, where the supreme ruler had his vacation complex. A year later, in 1967, the British journalist David Pryce-Jones visited Belgrade and saw Ranković lurking in a bookshop, where his appearance seemed to fully justify his "sinister Beria-like reputation as a torturer… Flabby and expressionless, the man had a putrid color," Pryce-Jones recalled years afterward. Above all, the end of Ranković's career symbolized something fairly remarkable: that Tito, now advanced in years, had decided to make a last effort to curb Great Serbianism within the Communist Yugoslav bureaucracy. Tito ordered a series of measures to put the Kosovar Albanian populace on an equal level, from the standpoint of civil rights, with other Yugoslavs.

In 1968, a year of even greater global radicalism, the Yugoslav socialist constitution was revised to make the autonomous region of Kosovo and autonomous province of Vojvodina (the latter with a large Hungarian population) distinct socio-political communities, which was the political basis for recognition of Slovenia, Croatia, Bosnia-Hercegovina, Serbia, Montenegro, and Macedonia as republics. Vojvodina, it should be noted, had enjoyed far greater local decision-making power than Kosovo, from the beginning of the Titoite commonwealth; but both, while remaining within the territory of Serbia, were now granted most of the functions previously reserved to the constituent republics in the socialist federal state. Calls for a full republic of Kosovo began to be heard among the region's Albanians, and demonstrators soon chanted the phrase aloud.

A Kosovo republic would never be achieved within socialist Yugoslavia, but Tito's government responded to Kosovar Albanian demands by granting the right to fly Skanderbeg's black double-headed eagle on a red field, i.e. the Albanian national flag, and the establishment of an Albanian language University of Kosova, at a level of education previously absent from the region. Albanian participation in the regional party and government increased exponentially; in effect, a Kosovo Republic was being achieved *de facto*, if not *de jure*. In 1974, the Tito reforms culminated in a fuller revision of the Yugoslav constitution, under which Kosovo and Vojvodina were granted nearly-equal status with the federal republics in everything but name. Both would have seats in federal governing bodies parallel (but numerically inferior) to those held by representatives of the lead republics; both could write their own constitutions, although they remained within Serbia.

Tito died in 1980. Many Yugoslav citizens, including not a few Kosovar Albanians, wept. Many were confused, bereft at the idea of life without Tito. The official doctrine of the Yugoslav state held, "After Tito, Tito!" That is, if he could not enjoy physical immortality, his political and social heritage would be preserved. But the exact opposite occurred. Above all, without him the reforms he had instituted in his last years, which benefited Kosovar Albanians, began unraveling. The first serious crisis came in 1981, during the months of March through May, and then in July, in Prishtina, when students and workers demonstrated in large numbers, now demanding that the Socialist Autonomous Region of Kosovo become a full republic. Many chanted the name of Adem Demaçi, still in a prison cell.

Without Tito's restraining hand, the Yugoslav authorities reacted brutally, with police shooting into crowds and tanks patrolling the streets. Kosovo filled up with Yugoslav Army troops. In the entire cycle of protests, according to official statements, nine people were killed by the forces of order, but

Albanian sources held that the figure was far higher. It is interesting to note that while the London *Evening Standard* for April 21, 1981 reported that more than 1,000 might have been killed, and a German journal claimed 2,600 dead, the official Communist press in Hoxha's Albania cited only 129 dead; Hoxha was no more anxious than in the past to rush to the rescue of the Kosovars. Later, Kosovars would complain that Hoxha had encouraged them by words in 1981, but betrayed them in deeds. By the end of the first week of June, more than 1,700 people had been arrested, and by September 9, some 500 had been sentenced to prison. The Yugoslav secret police, returning to the habits typical of the Ranković era, applied the practice of differentiation, which consisted of arrest, interrogation, surveillance, and accumulation of dossiers on virtually the entire active population. By the middle of the 1980s it was estimated that two-thirds of the adult male Albanians in Kosovo had been arrested at least once.

The events of 1981 polarized opinion in Kosovo. Yugoslav officials professed to see a separatist conspiracy behind the demonstrations; numerous Serbs responded hysterically; Albanians increasingly concluded that there was no hope for them ever to attain justice in a South Slav state. Yugoslav journalists perceived economic grievances behind much of the discontent, since even with the constitutional reforms of Tito's last years Kosovo remained poor, with investment low and unemployment and underemployment endemic. In addition, Kosovar Albanians had begun expressing concern over the situation of their kinfolk in neighboring Macedonia and Montenegro, and resentment over statistics showing that half the penal population of the country was Albanian, including, of course, Demaçi, the longest held prisoner in the country.

Indeed, even during the period of reform, from 1974 to 1981, 618 Albanians had been arrested in Yugoslavia on allegations of separatism and nationalism. The post-Tito rulers of Yugoslavia increasingly asserted the existence of a plot by Hoxha, the 'great absent one' in Kosovar history, to unite the region with Albania proper. But such opinions were by no means unanimously held; on September 21, 1981, Vladimir Bakarić, the last surviving member of Tito's top leadership, warned his fellow-Croats that Yugoslav state media handling of the Kosovo situation was becoming a matter of "full-fledged incitement against Albanians". Albanian Catholics in the U.S. charged that Kosovars were second-class citizens and 'the niggers' of Yugoslavia. Émigré commentator Maliq Arifi, writing from New York, described the Kosovo situation in 1982 as "the most striking example of colonialism still left in Europe," and, like others, pointed to economic inequities aggravating the regional problem.

The crisis did not end. As years went by, arrests and trials increased dramatically, along with dismissals and reprimands, most notably of faculty from the University of Kosova. The philosopher Ukshin Hoti, a lecturer at the University, received a sentence of two to eleven years' imprisonment, along with seven academic colleagues, a film maker, and an outstanding attorney (Hoti remains in jail at the time of this writing, in January 2000). The distinguished poet and critic Agim Vinca, the leading Albanologist Rexhep Qosja, the prominent historian Ali Hadri, the philosophy professor Fehmi Agani, and the authropologist Mark Krasniqi were among a group of 47 more educators dismissed from their posts. A generation of Kosovar intellectuals took their places alongside Adem Demaçi, as representatives of the Albanian national conscience.

Serbia began to respond in ways supplemental to the sending of police to Kosovo. A wave of books appeared in Belgrade recounting old allegations of Albanian injustice to Serbs in Kosovo. Soon, according to Noel Malcolm, "What might be called the culture war was... in full swing." A disaster beyond measure was near, nearer than anybody imagined.

* * * * *

Chapter VI:

The Crisis of Yugoslavia, 1985–1989

Kosovo was not the only weak link in Yugoslavia. With the death of Tito in 1980 and the crisis of European communism beginning a half-decade later, Yugoslavia came face to face with all the fault lines of the former Habsburg and Turkish empires. Yugoslavia, soon identified worldwide with Serbian politician Slobodan Milošević, as it had once been wedded to the image of Tito, broke violently into pieces in the 1990s. The first explanation on the lips of most foreign commentators was familiar: 'ancient hatreds', a phrase that quickly became a cliché.

Thus, American and Western European viewers of television news as well as readers of print media were told for the nth time that the Serbs hate the Croats because of what the latter did to them in World War II; or, going further back, that the Serbs hated the Albanians for taking over Kosovo.

As suggested in chapter I of this book, the ancient hatreds argument had certain obvious merits. It would be absurd to deny that the Balkans, like much of Eastern Europe, have remained outside the mainstream of European history, and that their penchant for brutality in politics and war indicates that, in some ways, some of these cultures remain unassimilated to Western values and attitudes. Further, it is clear that violence in the region has a repetitive character, going back even before the Slavic intrusion in the sixth century A.D. We have particularly examined the reality of ethnic rivalry in Kosovo, in contrast to Bosnia-Hercegovina.

In addition to its merits, the ancient hatreds argument had a certain convenience for some of those who embraced it. It assumed, implicitly or explicitly, the moral equivalence of the warring parties, with 'a plague on all your houses' its apparent policy corollary. This view had a natural appeal for those who did not wish to take sides.

But is the presence of ancient hatreds, legendary resentments, and atavistic habits – even those as potent as existed between Albanians and Slavs in Kosovo – really sufficient to explain the extent and intensity of brutality in the Yugoslav wars of the 1990s? This is somewhat akin to blaming Gothic paganism for Nazism. We have outlined the examples of Serbian aggression toward Albanians that foreshadowed the most recent Kosovo crises. Nevertheless, the distance from cultural divergence to mass murder remains a long one for most societies, particularly since the Hitler era, no matter how backward they may have been.

No, these ancient hatreds could not and did not combust spontaneously. The blaze was prepared, lit, and stoked by the Serbian political leadership in a massive assault against its neighbors, Slovenia, Croatia, and Bosnia-Hercegovina, and its subjects, in Kosovo, planned and executed to unite 'Great Serbia' behind its communist rulers. In pursuit of this end, Milošević would effectively revive an authentically fascist style of ethnic incitement, one with a terrifying potential for the destabilization of European — and even international — civil society.

Moreover, there was no equivalence between Milošević and the political leaders he confronted in Slovenia, Croatia, Bosnia-Hercegovina, and, eventually, Kosovo. The Slovenes under ex-communist turned free-marketeer Milan Kučan would consistently act in only one interest: the efficient integration of the former Yugoslav republics into Europe. The late Croatian president Franjo Tuđman, as devious and corrupt a politician as Milošević, kept his country in a kind of banana republic semi-dictatorship, imposed policies leading to human rights violations on its own territory as well as in Bosnia-Hercegovina, and often appeased Milošević. But with all his many faults, Tuđman acted defensively and opportunistically. The Bosnian Muslims, for their part, never engaged in the wholesale human rights violations characteristic of Serbian and Croatian military operations. As we shall see, the Kosovar Albanians maintained a position of non-violence for 10 years before they took up arms, though they faced a constantly rising level of Serbian police and paramilitary atrocities.

As for ancient hatreds, the divergence between West and East, it is all too obvious, has marked the Balkans for 1,500 years. Yugoslavia represented an attempt, probably doomed to failure in any event, to bridge the gap. Laid over the bedrock of ethnic rivalry, however, a network of thoroughly up-to-date grievances was visible, though little noticed outside Yugoslavia. These resentments were perpetuated and exacerbated because of policy issues as current as any in the world. The real, immediate reasons Yugoslavia broke up so horrifically came not from the poetry of long-ago battles, or recitations of wartime atrocities under the Nazis, or from the plotting of German bankers or American militarists, but from the dry and seemingly sterile world of public policy. These reasons involved attitudes toward property and entrepreneurship, the legacy of centralist statism in government, and tax policy.

Yugoslavia at the time of its breakup was marked by the widely disparate levels of readiness among its constituent components for membership in the modern world. Serbia under Milošević lagged far behind the others. The 1990s war and brutality in the Balkans were a product of Milošević's decision to embrace war and brutality as the solution to the problem of Serbia's own backwardness.

In a discussion early in 1999 with several American advisers resident in Bosnia-Hercegovina, a Bosnian Muslim professor of library science, Kemal Bakaršić of the University of Sarajevo, recalled his experiences in that besieged city. Bakaršić was head librarian at the National Museum of Bosnia-Hercegovina. On May 18, 1992, the National and University Library in Sarajevo was shelled by the Serbs; it burned for three days. In the week after, a fine ash like snow fell upon the city. During a similar Serb attack on the Oriental Institute, three months later, tens of thousands of Arabic, Persian, Turkish, Hebrew, and Bosnian manuscripts were destroyed. Bakaršić himself, an expert on the unique cultural artifact known as the *Sarajevo Haggadah,* a Hebrew manuscript created in Spain and brought to Bosnia, evacuated the contents of the National Museum library, which was directly threatened by Serb snipers.

The world condemned the Serbian destruction of the Bosnian libraries as acts of vandalism aimed at destroying the record of the Muslim presence in the Balkans. But Bakaršić's interpretation of this evil was distinctive; he saw it as driven less by ethnic hatred and an instinct for pure destruction than by a specific economic outlook. The Serbs, he said, mainly wanted to destroy the *defterler,* or Ottoman Turkish property registers. The aim of this, according to him, was not merely to wipe out proof that Muslims had once dominated the country, but, even more, to destroy evidence that Serbs had once held property alongside Muslims. "The *defterler* didn't just list the property of Muslims, but of Croats, Serbs, and others, as well," he noted. "They showed that coexistence between the three communities had always existed here. And they showed the extent of Serb property ownership, so that the Serbs were destroying their own history as well as that of the Muslims."

The destruction of Kosovar Albanian property records, along with personal identification and vehicle registration, was also a prominent feature of the 1999 Serbian assault on Kosovo. But while the media universally viewed such actions as an effort to negate the legitimacy of the Albanian presence in Kosovo, they failed to see that behind the burning of property documents lay more than ultranationalism; there was also a historic and cultural attitude toward property in general. Very early in the Yugoslav conflict in the 1990s, some observers did point out the legacy of economic and social disparities between Serbia, on the one hand, and its original victims, Slovenia and Croatia, on the other. But because these differences were elusive, were obscured by the role of Serbia in controlling the Yugoslav economy, and led those who discussed them publicly to be condemned as anti-Serb if not racist, the topic was never pursued as it ought to have been.

Nonetheless, the economic lag between Slovenia and Croatia, to the West, and Serbia, in the East, was the real source of the Yugoslav dilemma. And this gap, whatever its statistical configuration from year to year, grew out of certain long-standing cultural assumptions.

As previously described, Yugoslavia spanned the West-East border delimited in 395 A.D. by the Roman emperor Theodosius. What would become, after the Slavic invasions, the Slovene and Croat lands were included in the Western empire; the much-later Serbia was in Eastern territory. Although the Albanians were 'officially' assigned to the east, the coasts of Montenegro and Albania, as well as Bosnia and Kosovo, along with their inhabitants, essentially remained in the middle, on the borderland.

This cultural split would prove far more significant for the history of the Balkans than the later cleavage between Christian inhabitants and Muslim governors. The areas that became Slovenia and northern Croatia were absorbed into the domain of Charlemagne, fell under the ecclesiastical authority of Rome rather than Byzantium, and were swept (especially Slovenia) by Protestantism as well as the Counter-Reformation. The Croats of the Dalmatian shore came under Venetian rule, and, while distinguishing themselves as mariners and seaborne merchants, also participated in the penetration of the Slavonic world by the Renaissance. Both the Slovenes and Croats were ruled by the Habsburgs; they were briefly conquered and illuminated in the direction of revolutionary romanticism by Napoleon, but they were restored to Vienna and carried into the age of capitalism under the stewardship of Austrian and Hungarian industrialists. At the beginning of the twentieth century, Slovenia and Croatia had both produced wealthy peasant classes, prosperous commercial strata, and a healthy local tradition of trade and investment. Their future evolution as bourgeois nations seemed assured.

The cultural heritage of Serbia could scarcely have been more different. Having fallen under the Byzantine and later Orthodox religious order, Serbia never experienced a Reformation or Counter-Reformation. Essentially landlocked, it never fostered seamanship or foreign commerce. And then came what amounted to a wholesale disaster, at least from the viewpoint of European-style economic development, in the aftermath of the Kosovo battle, and the conquest of Serbia by the Turks. Trade in the Ottoman empire was concentrated on the imperial capital, Constantinople, and the caravan routes to Anatolia, Persia, and central Asia. To the west, the lesser Ottoman trade routes went from Venetian-Croatian Dubrovnik to Sarajevo in Bosnia, and from there, as well as from Shkodra and Durrës in Albania, to Skopje and Salonika in Macedonia. Serbia, aside from Kosovo, which stood astride the Sarajevo-Salonika and Shkodra-Skopje routes, was largely passed by.

Serbia's commerce never developed beyond local trade, and, commensurate with that, a domestic business or investment class emerged only very late. Overall, Serb culture consistently treated warfare as the manly profession, preferable to commercial activity. Milošević himself enunciated this view early in the 1990s in a speech directed against the Slovenes, who had enriched themselves by sub-licensing Western consumer goods for sale to the Yugoslav market. Unlike the Slovenes, Milošević declared defiantly, Serbs were not good at producing things — "but we are good at fighting," he asserted.

This handicap was pointed out, as previously noted, by Ilija Garašanin, father of political Great Serbianianism. Serbia did not begin its break with Ottoman domination until 1804, and for long afterward, its economic character was Asiatic rather than European. In Slovenia and Croatia, and even in the Ottoman remnant of Bosnia, well-established ecclesiastical and political structures promoted the stability and expansion of farming; inherited land remained in the hands of the extended family, which sought to improve and expand its holdings. Although landless peasants emigrated from Slovenia and Croatia in considerable numbers, seeking their fortunes in, among other places, Gold Rush era California and, later, in the mines and factories of Belgium, France, and the American Midwest, those who possessed land held to it tenaciously, and organized associations and parties to defend their interests.

In post-Ottoman Serbia, in contrast, the lack of an effective legal and social framework generated anxiety among the peasants, distrust within families, and ever-smaller division of landholdings among heirs. The Serb peasant defended his interests by maintaining a nuclear family on his diminished property, for which the physical labor of one's wife and children was the only available form of investment. Almost from the beginning of its national independence from the Ottomans, Serbia suffered a crisis in agriculture that continues even today.

Thus, the difference between West and East among Slovenes, Croats, and Serbs, involved a great deal more than the theological argument over the authority of the Bishop of Rome as Pope, or the use of the Cyrillic as opposed to the Latin alphabet. We have already noted the comment of the infamous Dr. Čubrilović that the Albanians were unfortunately "accustomed to the western European notions of private property". For Serbs, property was most often a basis for conflict, either with family members or with landlords (the latter who had lately been Muslims), rather than for personal and collective improvement (except by violent expropriation of the same Muslim landlords). Entrepreneurship involved peddling and market haggling, and was suspect. When capitalism arrived in the Balkans the first time around, toward the end of the past century, the Slovenes and Croats were well-prepared for it. But the Serbian bourgeoisie had arrived late on the historical scene, and its development as a class was also belated.

All of this was visible in embedded attitudes toward property. The burning of property registers was a symbolic expression of Serbianism, expressing not only a radical protest against the long Muslim domination, but also a deep ambivalence about the broader social and legal reality beyond the nuclear family. Not only were Ottoman land records suspect, as an institution of a foreign ruler; all records, all papers, all law outside that of the family became an object of mistrust.

The backwardness of Serbian agriculture, and Serbian hostility to post-traditional concepts of property, aggravated other problems caused by the belated entry of the Serbian bourgeoisie onto the stage of world history – the latter phenomenon having been brilliantly analyzed by the Serb socialists like Kosta Novaković, who wrote of Serbia's "striving to catch up," which would prove an eternal effort. But the irony important to foreigners, as well as Serbs, was that if Serbia had problems dealing with the first era of dramatic capitalist expansion into the Balkans, from 1850 to 1900, such problems were magnified beyond measure at the time of the most recent such expansion, in the 1990s.

Tito's Yugoslavia, through the 1950s, '60s, and '70s, had flourished as the beneficiary of a kind of dual international welfare. Put simply, the Yugoslavs were paid by the Russians, in hard currency, for construction and other sophisticated projects Soviet socialism had failed to master, while the U.S. subsidized the Yugoslav military on the presumption that in a war between the Warsaw Pact and NATO, Yugoslavia would side with the West. Tito himself, a wily Habsburg military officer by professional training, added two policy innovations, unknown to the rest of the communist world, to the mix. He encouraged Yugoslavs in the millions to emigrate — to Germany, Austria, Switzerland, even the U.S. and Australia, and to send as much of their earnings back home as they could. In addition, he threw the country open to foreign tourists, so that families, notably on the Dalmatian coast, could collect millions of *deutschemarks in* room rentals every year.

But the real basis of Yugoslavia's seeming success was dual subsidies from West and East. After the psychological defeat of Moscow by Poland's Solidarity and the Polish pope, John Paul II, in the early 1980s, something curious happened in Eastern Europe. Soviet Russia itself continued for some time on its triumphalist path, convinced that the global correlation of forces favored socialism, and that it could make up for what it might lose in Poland by subverting the American backyard in Nicaragua, Grenada, and El Salvador, as well as by its adventures in Africa and Southeast Asia. Hungary, East Germany, Czechoslovakia, and the other westernmost European communist states underwent, more or less rationally, the slow and steady emergence of a non-communist civil society. Nobody in Moscow, Budapest, East Berlin, or Prague spoke openly of the end of communism, just as nobody did in Washington. But in the former cities, the intelligentsia began hoping, silently, for a closure that had long been inconceivable.

In Yugoslavia, in contrast — particularly in Serbia — the 1980s produced the beginning of a real panic. Tito died in 1980, but few Yugoslavs felt fear, or expressed their fears if they had them, about the internal forces that might lead to the collapse of Yugoslav communism. Titoite communism was the most liberal, most open, most successful Marxist-Leninist regime. The onset of mass anxiety had little to do with immediate problems inside the country and everything to do with the awareness that, although the West had not seemed to notice it and the East would not say it aloud, Russian communism entered its death throes with the Pope's survival of an assassination attempt. Bolshevism was doomed; and with the end of Bolshevism, Yugoslavia's dual international welfare payments would end as well. Russia would no longer need Yugoslavs to build factories and the U.S. would no longer need the Yugoslav Army as a bulwark against a Soviet invasion of Europe.

This realization struck the Serbs with special force because Serbia — in marked contrast to other parts of the former state — had little to bring to the table of what would eventually be called the 'new world order'. Slovenia, for example, would prosper even without support from Washington and Moscow; its local communist leadership had already given up Marxist economics, had integrated Slovenia with the Austrian and Italian economies, and, as previously noted, had made the country a producer of quality consumer goods for the rest of the Yugoslav market. Croatia, too, expected few problems in the absence of foreign aid; it had not only a spectacular and largely unexploited tourist potential, one whose transformation could be expected to fuel prosperity in the same way tourism remade Spain in the 1950s, but also a large *diaspora* that would continue to add to domestic income through *deutschemark* remittances. Even Bosnia-Hercegovina was relatively well-prepared for entry into the new world, thanks to the modernization of its agriculture and its links with the Islamic nations.

But Serbia? Aside from the superficial cultural sophistication of Belgrade, Serbia had very little to offer the new world. While Slovenia was producing computer peripherals and the Croats were planning resort hotels and the Bosnians were getting rich by exporting agricultural products, Serbia's economy rested on the major assets it had possessed since the beginning of monarchist Yugoslavia at the end of World War I: the Yugoslav state bureaucracy, the army, and the police. The only value added to this store of wealth by the Tito era consisted in communist-style state enterprises. And this bad situation was made even worse by certain educational disparities. For while Slovenes and Croats tended to get degrees in engineering, the hard sciences, and medicine, Serbs flocked to careers as state functionaries in the cultural as well as administrative fields. Indeed, Belgrade in 1989 may have had more unemployed structuralist film critics than any other city in the world.

It was raw fear for the future of a statist, centralist Serbia in a free-market world that transformed the Serbian communist organization into an agency of ultra-nationalist incitement to violence. The Slovene communists thoroughly and effectively remade themselves as free-marketeers, and the Croat and Bosnian Muslim communists were prepared to surrender power to elected non-communist parties, because they all knew they had professional, economic, and political options as something other than communist bureaucrats. That is, they were willing to exchange power for property; but for the Serb communists, loss of power meant loss of everything. There was no economic buffer to make the transition easier for them.

The Serb communists could not trust entrepreneurship, which they equated with corruption, and private property rights, which they associated with injustice, as the foundation of their future. Lacking assets in property, they were, again, nothing without power. But as we have seen in the statesmanship of Slobodan Milošević, who came to embody their desperate hopes, they were not much even in possession of power. Although the overall historical project that emerged came to be identified, justifiably, with him above all, Milošević, for his part, was not the inventor, but rather the instrument, of Serbia's response to its crisis, namely the attempt to unite Serbia by launching wars against its Western Yugoslav rivals. The real originators of this reaction, as it turns out, were literary intellectuals, including virtually all of Serbia's former professional dissidents and humanist Marxists.

These included, for example, the novelists Dobrica Ćosić, whose series of leaden narratives of Serbian suffering in World War I amounted to manuals for nationalist indoctrination, and Vuk Drašković. Drašković would later play the dissident card himself, but was originally known for a novel, *Nož* (the Knife), which was really no more than a febrile pamphlet justifying violence against Yugoslav Muslims. Its success as a bestseller in the mid-1980s was one of the first signposts in the direction of hell to appear in the country's common life. The main gambit by this layer of frightened intellectuals, however, was the *Draft Memorandum of the Serbian Academy of Sciences and Arts (SANU)* or *SANU Memorandum*, which was 'leaked' to the press in 1986. The

Belgrade press, once celebrated far and wide for its accuracy and independence in reporting on the Soviet bloc, soon became filled with paranoid propaganda about the threat to the security of the Serb nation of Muslim fundamentalists, Albanian gangsters, and recusant Croat fascists.

The lesson of Serbian history is that political power in the hands of a weak and backward ruling class, one incapable of making itself an effective bourgeoisie, is much more harmful for the general interest than a robust and self-confident bourgeoisie. Had they spent more time in comparative historical study, Western political scientists might have noticed ominous parallels with the case of Yugoslavia, in which the productive and entrepreneurial Slovenes, Croats, and Bosnians were ruled by a parasitical and anti-entrepreneurial Serbia. One such resemblance was to monarchist Yugoslavia up to 1941. But a far more disturbing precedent would have been Spain in 1936, where the industrialized Basque Country and Catalonia groaned under the statist, taxing regime of the economically stunted Castile — a Castile which, like Serbia, had historically exalted military careers over commerce. In Spain, of course, the disparity between the center and the periphery had contributed mightily to the coming of a civil war in which some 2 million people lost their lives.

Serbia also resembled Castile in its Jacobin attitude toward nationality — its persistent belief that all South Slavs, comprising Slovenes, Croats, Bosnians, Montenegrins, and, before 1945, Macedonians, should consider themselves, in their essential being, as Serbs. After 1945, even as Tito broke with Stalin, Serbian communists of the Ranković stripe looked to Stalinism for inspiration in their treatment of, above all, the Kosovar Albanians. Tito, who was half-Croat and half-Slovene, attempted at many turns to limit the power of the Serbian elite in Yugoslav public life. But he allowed Serbia to retain a traditional influence in the army, the police, and the state bureaucracy. After all, so long as Belgrade was the capital of Yugoslavia, no other outcome was very likely.

The lopsided Serbian domination of Yugoslavia, even under Tito, was visible in many places. In 1989, Yugoslavia's army was among the largest in Europe, and its officer corps was 70 percent Serb. Yugoslavia relied on revenues taxed from the more economically productive regions to support its (largely Serbian) central government. Furthermore, every *deutschemark* accumulated by the sale of Slovenian skis or the rental of rooms in Dalmatia had to go through the Belgrade banks, once again providing an opportunity for looting by taxation. In 1991, Milošević rubbed the inequity of the situation into his subjects' faces when the central bank, which had already inflated the Yugoslav national currency almost beyond belief, unilaterally seized all the private foreign currency accounts in the country. It seems almost too obvious to mention that the prospective loss of tax revenue, with the prospect of greater Slovenian, Croatian, and Bosnian autonomy, was as much a stimulus to Milošević and his backers as any ethnic or religious issue.

Serbia's rage at such an eventuality was most visible in its destructive strategy toward the constitution of the Yugoslav Federation. For Serbia never acted to preserve the federation; rather, by refusing to surrender the rotating federal presidency to the moderate (and later anti-Tuđman) Croat Stipe Mesić, in 1991, Serbia forcibly liquidated the federation. This came at a time when Slovenia and Croatia still advocated a looser Yugoslav federation rather than independence, and when the Muslims of Bosnia-Hercegovina, notwithstanding hair-raising Belgrade propaganda about Islamic fundamentalism, were clearly reluctant to consider the breakup of the existing arrangement.

To understand what happened in Yugoslavia, one must imagine a United States in which Maryland and Virginia, because they surround the national capital, tax the rest of the country to support their local budgets; in which only residents of those two states have any chance at a military career, only Virginia and Maryland authors are seriously studied in schools, and only historical figures from those states are publicly praised as national heroes. The consequences for America, one can speculate, would be no less bloody.

A final parallel should be drawn, so obvious as to provoke wonder that it seems to have gone unnoticed among Western policy experts and journalists. Above all, Serbian imperialism in Yugoslavia resembled Russian imperialism, both tsarist and Soviet. As Moscow dealt with the Baltic nations, for example, so did Belgrade view the Slovenes. Certainly, the Great Russian claim to a historical link with Kiev, seat of the first Russian polity, was as legitimate, if not more so, than the Serbian legend about Kosovo. Yet nobody sane, even in Russia, would have tried to justify Stalin's long-ago fantasies of deporting all the Ukrainians from their homeland, much less its application in the 1990s. Serbia, Kosovo, and the Albanians, however, were different. While the West hailed the collapse of the Russian empire, it quailed at that of the Serbian empire; while Kievan Rus was a topic limited to university seminars, "Serbian Kosovo" was a fixture of newspaper columns and television panels, and while the Ukrainians were entitled to independence, the Kosovar Albanians were condemned to suffer. The internal borders of the former U.S.S.R. would count for nothing, with those of the former Yugoslavia sacrosanct.

But why, one might ask, did the Baltic states, Poland, the Czech Republic, Hungary, and Slovenia survive Communism so much better than Russia, Belarus, Ukraine, Slovakia, Romania, Bulgaria, and, of course, Serbia? The first and most obvious explanation is that Nordic (specifically, Scandinavian and German) economic penetration of the former brought about a certain irreversible progress. But that is an explanation freighted with risk for most Western intellectuals, who are loath to appear as defenders of Teutonic imperialism. Capitalist advocate Jeffrey D. Sachs, whose popularity in the former Communist states has proved uneven, commented in 1999 in a disingenuous if not dull-witted manner, "The closer the country is to European Union markets, the more successful and dynamic the transformation. States bordering the EU, such as Poland, Hungary, the Czech Republic, Slovakia, Slovenia, Croatia, and the Baltic states have done much better at attracting foreign direct investment, expanding exports and generally achieving a successful transition. Further away, some of the Balkan states are doing downright poorly [!] And the non-Baltic former Soviet Union is in worse shape still." While we may thank Sachs for having noticed the disparity, his circular argument is comparable to explaining the slavery system in the southern United States by nothing more than geographic closeness to other slave economies.

The second explanation for the discontinuity between the nearer and further regions in central and eastern Europe, and which is nearly as obvious as that of historical influence, involves the role of Catholic and Protestant Christianity in promoting a certain limited, but nonetheless real, pluralism, which seems necessary for the development of enterprise. Greek and Slavonic Orthodoxy, in contrast, fit remarkably well with a totalistic view of nationality, as well as of the state. Orthodox theology posits the nation, the church, and the state as a single organ (much as Lenin viewed the proletariat, the Communist Party, and the workers' state as a single entity) — an outlook that is arguably an impediment to the cultural pluralism and entrepreneurship necessary for success in the modern world. How do we imagine changing such attitudes, held by many millions of people? Greece, the Orthodox exception, is entrepreneurial if not culturally pluralistic; this seems to suggest some alternative outcome is possible. But the Greeks, one also feels compelled to observe, were a maritime and commercial nation a thousand years before they became Orthodox. As the modern Greek poet Nikos Gatsos wrote, "Travellers to India have more to tell you than the Byzantine chroniclers."

The final enigma of the Yugoslav experience has to do with the Serbian view of modernity and of Serbia's own place within it. Serbia has always seen itself as a Balkan vanguard of the civilized, the contemporary, the progressive, and the modern. This conviction was visible no less in its adoption of Soviet socialism than in its embrace of Jacobin nationalism. But it also was an expression of the belated and handicapped development of the Serbian elite, which, as described by Novaković, has always striven too hard to catch up with the world... and has always failed.

When Serbia set up public schools in which all instruction was in Serbian, and from which Kosovar Albanians withdrew their children, the attitude in Belgrade was one of righteous political correctness: "We set up free schools for them — they who don't want to educate their daughters anyway. We offered to teach them the Serbian language, part of the great Slavic family of millions of speakers, but they hewed to their reactionary, traditional culture!" Serbs were flabbergasted that Westerners would side with the "clannish, patriarchal, primitive Albanians" against the modern, urban, sophisticated Serbs. During the Bosnian war, in an apparent paradox, Serb *četniks* were urged to attack Bosnian Muslims with the argument that the Serbs' grandparents had been poor peasants in leather britches and barefoot, while the Muslims' forefathers were rich landlords whose wives wore silk pantaloons and velvet shoes. Progressivism and resentment of private property in Serbia, along with the cult of anti-imperialist national liberation, produced complete impunity in the robbery, rape, and mass murder of the 'backward' communities.

Something necessary for success in the contemporary world was missing in Serbia, and the lack thereof undermined the Yugoslav project from the beginning. That something, which seems absent throughout the Eastern Slavic world, is elusive, and does not have a name that immediately springs to mind.

It was not a matter of a European outlook per se, because we see in Bosnia-Hercegovina and Kosovo that communicants of an 'Eastern' religion, Islam, who hew to Ottoman Turkish, (i.e., Asiatic) as well as, in the Albanian case, Mediterranean cultural traditions, possess it. We could call it, as above, free-market pluralism, tracing it back to the Catholic and Protestant transformations of Europe. But perhaps the best description of this ineffable cultural element was provided 144 years ago by the Russian liberal Aleksandr Herzen, who wrote as follows about the Slavic East, and an earlier encounter with modernity, in his 1855 work, *From the Other Shore:* "The revolution of Peter the Great replaced the obsolete squirearchy of Russia — with a European bureaucracy; everything that could be copied from the Swedish and German laws, everything that could be taken over from the free municipalities of Holland into our half-communal, half-absolutist country, was taken over; but the unwritten, the moral check on power, the instinctive recognition of the rights of man, of the rights of thought, of truth, could not be and were not imported."

What, then, were the specific roles of Kosovo and its Albanian majority in this set of conundrums? The fate of each of the Yugoslav nationalities attacked by Milošević and his crew had to do with the psychological function assigned to each target in the development of Serbian extremism. The Slovenes were viewed as rich, arrogant, traitors who, thanks to the terrain of their country, probably could not be subdued by force of arms, and should better be driven away. The Croats were labeled as monstrous fascists who might not be beaten by arms, but who deserved to be fought as violently as possible, to show that Serbs were not afraid of them – although of all the former Yugoslav nationalities, Croats inspired the greatest fear in Serbs, because in World War II, as in the Yugoslav wars of the 1990s, the Croats demonstrated they could give as good as they got when it came to ethnic terror. The Bosnian Muslims were said to be weak, passive, fatalistic and destined to disappear in any event, which would justify their mass extermination. The Kosovar Albanians were viewed as a subhuman species chiefly known for breeding like vermin, worthy of even more extreme genocidal measures than the Bosnian Muslims. The contrast between the Serb hatred of Bosnian Muslims and absolute disregard for the humanity of Albanians became visible in the terror practiced in each case: proportionate to overall numbers of victims, many more women and children were simply murdered outright by Serb extremists in Kosovo, than in Bosnia-Hercegovina.

Each of these stereotypes served to justify a specific element of the Milošević project for ultranationalist mobilization. Each combined economic and historic resentments – hatred of those better off (Slovenes and Croats), fear of those who had previously killed Serbs (Croats), grievances against former masters (Bosnian Muslims), contempt of minorities in general (again, Bosnian Muslims), and anxiety about alleged 'interlopers' (Albanians). Serbs argued that Bosnian Muslim imams would engage in forcible circumcision of Serbian children, and that Muslim rulers, Bosnian and Albanian, had kidnapped Serbian boys as sexual playthings. Above all, fear of masculine potency – symbolized by the higher birthrate of the Albanians – aggravating the sense of Serbian victimization on the subconscious level.

But of all these targets the Kosovar Albanians were the most useful for the success of the Milošević project. They had been so dehumanized in the eyes of the Serbian masses that it was made virtually impossible to imagine them mounting a serious resistance. If Albanians fought back, according to the Milošević mentality, they would do so through individual terror and crime, not through an organized movement. In addition, it was presumed that they would put their large families first if attacked, and would flee rather than commit themselves to combat. Little or no intermarriage between Serbs and Kosovar Albanians served to rescue Albanians from rejection by Slavs as 'the other', and their otherness was, in any case, definitively established by their non-Slav language and traditions. Albanian cultural isolation would induce the West, it was presumed, to ignore their fate, since the very idea of departments of Albanian studies in British, French, and American universities –

which set the agenda for academic studies worldwide – would have been a source of humour.

Finally, two other aspects of Kosovar Albanian culture sealed their fate as primary targets for the Milošević strategy. Unlike Bosnia and Macedonia, which had considerable Slavic Muslim populations, Kosovar Albanians had not been offered much of a chance to abandon their Islam for communism. Bosnian and Macedonian Muslims were subject to a fairly successful secularization, with the inducement of party membership (available only to atheists) and its concomitant rewards, backed up by such measures as the official suppression of the Sufi orders by the pro-regime *ulema*, or assembly of Muslim scholars, in Bosnia in 1952. But Titoite communism was a mass phenomenon among Bosnians and Macedonians. In contrast, the party never became a major social institution among Kosovar Albanians. It remained an elite body provided with an opportunity to rule over a community that, if it was glad to see Albanians represented in governance, nonetheless retained a deep suspicion of Slav communism. For this reason, Islam did not diminish among Kosovar Albanians; rather, it became strengthened, as an expression of cultural self-defense comparable to the influence of the Catholic Church in Ireland under British rule. For example, in 1945 all *medresas* or Islamic secondary schools had been closed in Kosovo, but in 1951 a primary *medresa* was founded in Prishtina. This institution became Medressah Alauddin, "a symbol of Albanian resistance to Serb domination", according to Kosovo Muslim leader Dr. Rexhep Boja.

In addition, suppression of the Sufi orders was much less successful in Kosovo than in Bosnia, with the result that although the dervish lodges or *teqeve* were publicly closed, Kosovar Sufi disciples continued to meet in private homes. In particular, the purging of the Bektashi order from Kosovar Albanian life was a literal impossibility; as Khrushchev said of Stalin's attempts to wipe out the Ukrainians, there were simply too many of them. The Sufis, and especially the Bektashis, with their reputation for Albanian patriotism going back to the previous century, became a leading element for Kosovar Albanian cultural self-defense. But this very vitality also provided Milošević and his cohort with a high card to play against the Kosovar Albanians in the court of European and American opinion: the spectre of Islam in Europe.

The last weapon at the disposal of Milošević in his targeting of Kosovar Albanians was the widespread belief, inside Yugoslavia and abroad, that Kosovars had overwhelmed the province after World War II by mass emigration from Albania. This was provably false on two bases. First, as previously noted, Kosovo had had an Albanian majority from the beginning of monarchist Yugoslavia, and although this fact was marginally affected by Serb colonization, Serbs had never flocked to Kosovo in such numbers as would have changed it. Further, the Albanian communist regime of Enver Hoxha, after World War II, had made emigration an extremely difficult option. Those who escaped to Kosovo from Hoxhaite Albania were far too few to affect the statistical profile of ethnic groups in the province. Nevertheless, nearly all Serbs, many other Yugoslavs, and numerous foreign observers and commentators assumed that Kosovar Albanians were mainly first generation immigrants to the region, comparable to, say, Central Americans in California, and that they could be easily and justifiably pushed back over the mountains.

Thus the range of targets for Serbian extremism replicated the multiple attack of Hitlerian ideology on the Jews: at the top of society, hatred of the 'rich Jewish exploiters'; at the bottom, obloquy against Jews who allegedly bred out of control while living in an unhygienic environment, and everywhere, slander against the Jew who supposedly seduced Christian women. Resentment of wealth, fear of contagion, and sexual anxiety formed, for Hitler as well as Milošević, a trinity of fascist incitement.

But Hitler also agitated against the radical left, and simultaneous with the revival of Serbian ultranationalism and the emergence of Milošević, there intruded another issue in Yugoslav politics that dramatized the Kosovo situation, although it was largely (and probably deliberately) ignored in Yugoslavia and overlooked in the West. That was the matter of free labor organization in the period of communist decline, and its potential impact on the party-state. Put more simply, there was the threat, most immediately, of a Yugoslav version of the Polish Solidarity movement, and, secondarily, of the resurgence of the old ideal of multi-ethnic unity of the workers, expressed in sincere form by Dimitrije Tucović and his comrades at the time of the first Balkan wars, and turned into a virtual burlesque by the official 'brotherhood and unity' rhetoric of Titoism.

This topic has excited obscure and mainly irrelevant comment by the remnants of Western ultra-leftist radicalism, but it is nonetheless worthy of examination. Polish Solidarity represented a startling and powerful challenge to Sovietism precisely because it rested on the proletarian class that, since Marx, had been viewed by revolutionaries as the most effective engine for wide-scale social change, and because its organization of that class represented so thorough a repudiation of the socialist pretenses of Soviet regimes. Yet the experience of Polish Solidarity turned out to represent an end, rather than a beginning; a last flareup of the once bright light of proletarianism before its complete disappearance from the modern world. Workers as a class had essentially vanished from global economic reality and, above all, from the stage of history; the very existence of such an economic and social category was roundly denied.

Thus Polish Solidarity, although dramatic and glorious, may be said to have represented an expression of Polish economic backwardness rather than of something new. Polish Solidarity also conducted what amounted to a uniquely Polish experiment in Catholic labor organization, made possible by the power of the church in Polish culture, the ethnicity of Pope John Paul II, and the church's modern stance in favor of unions. But in the end, Solidarity was, indeed, entirely unique to Poland; the experience was not repeated anywhere else in the Soviet empire, and it had no real effect – notwithstanding the vaporings of numerous dreamers – on the conservatism of the labor movement in the West.

This, however, was not perceived by communist bureaucrats in Yugoslavia, any more than in then East Germany, Hungary, or Russia itself, in the late 1980s. Polish Solidarity had broken the back of the Warsaw regime and had contributed more than any other factor to the irreversible crisis of the Moscow system. For communists unwilling to give up power, especially in Belgrade, the idea of a new proletarian movement was absolutely terrifying. And when such a possibility briefly became visible in Yugoslavia, it did so in the form of protests by the miners and related workers at Trepça in Kosovo, most of whom were Albanian, but many of whom were Serbian and Montenegrin.

A cycle of strikes at Trepça in 1988, for example, began with a defense of the local Albanian communist leaders against the increasing encroachments of Milošević, and the mass marches, sit-ins, and other demonstrations by the miners were, at least at the beginning, predictably channelled in that direction by the Kosovar Albanian communists. But the miners' movement, as often in the past, soon turned in the direction of radical economic demands, and, lo and behold, threatened to gain the participation and support of Serb and Montenegrin miners. Thus Trepça produced the most frightening spectre of all, from the viewpoint of the Belgrade communist bureaucracy: authentic labour action against the communist state, and across national lines. Real brotherhood and unity could not but have an even more destructive effect on the Yugoslav party-state than the proletarian self-organization of Polish Solidarity had in Warsaw.

Thus it was anything but coincidental that, on April 24, 1987, Milošević, having triumphed within the Serbian communist cadre 10 months before, chose Kosovo as his Nuremberg, as the place from which to issue his call for Serbian rebirth and revenge. There he could invoke the Serbian myth of 1389, while implicitly seeking to frighten the West with 'the Islamic threat'; there he could recruit aggrieved Serbs ready for direct action against their neighbors; there he could head off the possibility of a unified worker movement against the communist elite.

We will not reiterate, here, the biographic details in the rise of Slobodan Milošević, which are recounted in many other volumes. However, the intellectual environment of his rise, and specifically those features drawn from the landscape of Kosovo, need to be reviewed. The soil of Kosovo had been poisoned by deliberate and public Serb agitation beginning in late 1985, when a petition was signed by 2,000 Serbs from Kosovo asserting that they were victims of aggression by immigrants from Albania. There followed more petitioning and similar events, leading to a first climax late in 1986 with the publication of the *SANU Memorandum*, written under the influence of Ćosić, the intellectual godfather of Milošević and author of ethnic sentimentalist novels, and with the notable participation of an internationally admired humanist Marxist and "democratic dissident," Mihajlo Marković.

The *SANU Memorandum* is a document that can really be only described as hallucinated. Serbia, which had dominated and exploited Yugoslavia since its formation in 1918, was presented as an eternal victim of the better developed nations, Slovenes and Croats, and above all, of the noticeably poorer Kosovar Albanians. Yet the rhetoric of the text itself seemed, to most outside observers, anything but obviously inflammatory. In the classic style of communist theses, the *SANU Memorandum*, which may justifiably be called the Mein Kampf of Serbian neofascism, began innocuously, "A slowdown in society's development, economic difficulties, growing social tension and open inter-communal clashes have all given cause for deep concern in our country." The *SANU Memorandum* identified the major problems of Yugoslavia as "laxity and irresponsibility in the workplace, corruption and nepotism, a lack of legal security, bureaucratic high-handedness, flouting of the law, a growing distrust among the people and crass individual and group egoism."

But the document quickly got down to basics. Among the "key issues of Yugoslav reality," it identified "the ambiguous and difficult position of the Serbian people, which has been brought into sharp focus by recent events." Although it included much that was concerned with such seemingly anodyne matters as the efficient integration of the state railroad, and expatiated considerably on such communist ideological shibboleths as "democratic centralism," the *SANU Memorandum* was truly a national-socialist text in the spirit of Hitler – one that demonstrates, to an extraordinary degree, the fundamental sociological identity of fascism and communism. For the *SANU Memorandum* followed the logical of Hitlerian incitement from disquisitions over the failure of the Titoite state to evocation of national vengeance. "The Serbian nation… was not given the right to have its own state," its authors declared, going on to claim that "large sections of the the Serbian people who live in the other republics, unlike the national minorities, do not have the right to use their own language and script, to set up their own political and cultural organizations or to foster the common cultural traditions of their nation."

Most importantly, the *SANU Memorandum* identified a convenient and vulnerable enemy: an "unremitting persecution and expulsion of Serbs from Kosovo" had taken place. "Principles which protect the autonomy of a minority [the ethnic Albanians] are not applied when it came to a minority within a minority [Serbs, Montenegrins, Turks, and Roms in Kosovo]." Serbs, then, were wholesale victims of discrimination, of a kind that would prevent Yugoslavia from being considered "a modern and democratic state". The *SANU Memorandum* did not stop with such mild phrases. In its key section, "The Status of Serbia and the Serbian Nation", its authors referred to "the genocide in Kosovo" – where no governmental measures had been taken against Serbs and no Serbs had yet been killed, except for individuals murdered in ordinary criminal cases. Prior to that gem, the document blamed lagging Serbian economic development, more properly traced to local social factors as well as a dependence on statist economic theory, on Slovenia and Croatia. Its authors insisted, as if in a fever, that Serbs were "the only nation in Yugoslavia without their own state".

The emphasis remained on Kosovo, where, they charged, "The expulsion of the Serbian people... bears dramatic testimony to their historical defeat." An open war between Serbs and Kosovar Albanians had allegedly been underway, without anybody publicly acknowledging it, since 1981, i.e. since the brutal suppression of Albanian demonstrations for equal status of Kosovo as a socialist republic rather than an autonomous province. The single case of a Serb farmer, Đorđe Martinović, who suffered a non-fatal rectal injury in circumstances never fully elucidated, was transformed by the scholars of the Serbian Academy into "unprecedented violence... reminiscent of the darkest days of Turkish impalement" and the basis of Kosovar Albanian secession from Serbia! This "war" was the continuation of the 1944-45 Kosovar Albanian uprising, which was ostensibly "neo-fascist." And of course, since the fascist slur could not be brandished without attacking Croatia, that republic also stood accused of genocidal intentions against Serbs. Never since the time of the Ustaša regime, said the *SANU Memorandum*, had Serbs been so threatened in Croatia as in the mid-1980s.

Unarguably, Serbs had emigrated out of Kosovo since the arrival of the Tito regime after World War II. But the scale of such emigration has never been firmly established, and Serbian extremists further developed a penchant for labelling the low Serbian birth rate, particularly in comparison with Albanian fecundity, as genocide. Many Serbian colonists may have left Kosovo when it became clear that the communist authorities would not provide them with special financial subsidies such as existed in monarchist Yugoslavia. And finally, economic development within Kosovo was extremely slow, and could not be expected to attract very many urban Serbs. But to gauge the full psychosis of the *SANU Memorandum* and its authors, one must imagine, in the U.S., 'white flight' to the suburbs from the inner cities, beginning in the 1960s, described as 'anti-white genocide'. Or suppose that in Britain, members of the National Front did not merely claim that whites are subject to discrimination because of anti-discrimination laws intended to protect non-white minorities, but argued with complete seriousness that non-white immigrants have literally enslaved the majority of whites. Such propaganda in the U.S. or U.K. would gain its proponents no more than laughter, if not a serious opportunity for psychiatric examination. In Serbia, the *SANU Memorandum* was taken as gospel.

Unfortunately, the *SANU Memorandum* had another, key feature that increased its credibility to the Serbian masses as well as making it seem harmless, if not beneficial, to many Western observers. That was the way the text dealt with the history of the Yugoslav Communist party, and specifically, with the party in the context of the Comintern. The authors of the document asserted that an anti-Serb conspiracy had persisted through Tito's rule, but originated in the radicalism of the Comintern, which, as described in chapter IV of this book in its early phase called for the national liberation of the Slovenes, Croats, and Macedonians from Serbian imperialism as well as from a monarchist Yugoslavia supported by anti-Communist white Russian exiles.

The Comintern, for its part, paid little attention to the Kosovar Albanians. Socialist opposition to Serbian imperialism mainly originated, particularly regarding Kosovo, years before the constitution of the Comintern in 1919, with figures of impeccable Serb origin, such as Dimitrije Tucović, for whom a monument had been raised in Belgrade by the Tito regime, Dušan Popović, Dragiša Lapčević, Triša Kaclerović, and Kosta Novaković. This detail was overlooked by the SANU academics. But not by everybody; Slovenian intellectuals scored brilliantly against Milošević by reprinting the writings of the Serb socialists on the reconquest of Kosovo in 1912-13. Still, the paranoia of the SANU 'historians' reached unfathomable depths, as they attempted to bend the real history of Yugoslav Communism to the ideology of Serbian revenge. In later documents, SANU functionaries Kosta Mihailović and Vasilije Krestić declared that Tito was equally evil when he allegedly supported Stalin, by opposing Serbian hegemony in monarchist Yugoslavia, and when he fought Stalin's Serbian acolytes, after World War II. In reality, the Comintern's anti-Yugoslav period largely preceded the Stalin era, and even Stalin himself had never been so devious, nor had Tito; the convolutions of SANU 'theory' responded only to the need to promote 'Serbs all and everywhere', as if to add a new meaning to the 19th century slogan. Serbs were the victims, no matter when or where or how, and Tito, as a Croat, was a natural for the choice of villain.

But the history of Yugoslav Communism and the Comintern was, at that point, a closed book to the great majority of intellectuals, in the West as well as the Soviet empire; closed in every sense, because the great openings of archives, particularly those of the Comintern, which have changed the nature and content of Communist historiography in the past decade, were then still inconceivable. To Serbian intellectuals as well as foreign journalists, the SANU's attack on the history of Yugoslav Communism, and the appeal to national-ism, resembled nothing so much as the spiritual rebirth apparently under-way in Russia itself. The *SANU Memorandum* authors were viewed as figures of conscience not unlike the Soviet dissidents. Perhaps the most grotesque expression of this absurdity came when Branislav Gligorijević's *Kominterna Jugoslovensko i Srpsko Pitanje* (The Comintern in Yugoslavia and the Serb Question), an outstanding example of the falsification of history, ostensibly based on objective research in the Soviet archives, appeared in Belgrade with an epigram from the memoirs of Nadyezhda Mandelshtam, the widow of the greatest of all Soviet dissidents, the poet Osip Mandelshtam, and a distin-guished dissident in her own right.

In one of the most shocking and chilling aspects of the entire phenome-non, many Belgrade intellectuals who had previously been known for their devotion to humanistic Marxism, Western style democracy, and other fads in Yugoslav and global intellectual and political life, participated in writing the *SANU Memorandum* or came out in its support. They included not only the world-renowned 'philosopher' Mihailo Marković but his cosmopolitan col-league Ljubomir Tadić, and many others. This was one of the clearest indi-cators that blood was in the air, with a horrific conflict approaching in Yugoslavia. Indeed, the role of the superficially pro-Western and formerly dis-sident Serb intelligentsia in the 1980s revival of ultra-nationalism was among the most dramatic proofs of the disparity between West and East within Yugoslavia. These men were "poor players, who strutted and fretted their hour upon the stage", acting out a role in emulation of their putative colleagues in the more developed societies, from Croatia to the United States, as their ancestors had sought to imitate the Romantic nationalists who unified Italy and Germany, and later, the European imperialists who plotted the division of the Ottoman empire.

For his part, Trotsky had labelled the Serb journalists at the time of the first Balkan Wars, the "careerist failures and careerist heroes of yesterday", a description that applied exactly to such man as Marković and Tadić. To emphasize once more the warning that had been delivered decades before by Kosta Novaković, Serbia was doomed to disaster yet again, by its retarded elite and their attempts to run ahead of their neighbors. With the end of communism imminent, the followers of new styles among the Belgrade intellectuals gambled that the next fad to sweep the world would be nationalist extremism. They failed to anticipate that only a handful of marginal opportunists and former secret police spies, among intellectuals in Russia, Poland, Hungary, Romania, and Croatia – and nobody respectable in the rest of the world – would similarly shift from modernist dissidence to revived fascism. This situation was perhaps best described by the Bosnian author Jasmin Imamović, in his short story 'Dinner on Mount Kopaonik'. Recalling a visit to Belgrade in the years just before the new round of Balkan wars, he wrote, "I saw a handsome middle-aged man, smartly dressed, university professor type. He had on brand-new Italian shoes, sported an expensive leather jacket, carried a Samsonite briefcase, and wore Ray-Ban sunglasses. A *četnik* hat adorned his head!"

Slovenia, by contrast, produced virtually no nationalist intellectuals. In Croatia, a generation of patriotic writers and political theorists — exemplified by the poet Vlado Gotovac, the publisher Slavko Goldštejn, and the civic activists Marko Veselica and Savka Dabčević-Kučar — had distinguished themselves for their defense of Croatian literary and cultural claims. Gotovac, for example, had nearly been murdered in a Yugoslav prison, and Veselica was an internationally-known human rights figure. But when these Western oriented Croat intellectuals saw Tuđman, whom they had once considered a dissident companion, turn in the direction of nationalist extremism, they took their distance from him and became leaders of the Croatian opposition. No such phenomenon occurred in Serbia, which has yet to produce a repudiation of nationalism among its intellectuals.

Sixty years before, Adolf Hitler had argued that history was not as it appeared, but was controlled by hidden conspiracies. Hitler alleged that he hated capitalism and its system, that the difficulties suffered by the German workers could be traced to their oppression by the Jew, and that peace was denied the German nation by the plutocratic West; all whilst he coldly planned the most extreme dictatorship of the capitalist elite, the utter obliteration of the long-recognized rights of the German labou movement, and wholesale armed aggression against the rest of Europe. As Hitler, to the end, claimed to oppose the capitalists and to defend the workers and peace, so would Milošević assert he was defending Yugoslavia against neo-fascism and secession and rescuing the Serbs from a discrimination unacceptable in contemporary civilization.

But Hitler had never won over the bulk of the German intellectuals. And Milošević benefitted from the evolution of history after Hitler. The German dictator had wasted years in ventures like the 1923 Beer Hall Putsch in Munich, which resulted in a prison sentence. In contrast, Milošević made his move after he had consolidated power within a ruling communist bureaucracy.

His declaration of intentions, at Kosovo Polje on April 24, 1987, has been described by an eyewitness, the journalist Slavko Ćuruvija, who after many a bizarre twist in his career was murdered in Belgrade during the 1999 Kosovo war. As Ćuruvija later recalled, "It was a hot, dusty day. A column of official cars appeared around five in the afternoon. Only minutes before, the street and square in front of the town's Cultural Center had been more or less empty, with a few groups of people standing around in Balkan somnolence even though a meeting had been announced, in which the head of the Serbian communists would meet with representatives of the Kosovo Serbs. Suddenly, as if on order, 15,000 Serbs poured into the square. The column of cars was surrounded. When Milošević got out of the car, the air was broken by booming chants, 'We want freedom! We want freedom!'"

According to Ćuruvija, "The police had to virtually carry Milošević into the run-down Cultural Center," where he was joined by Kosovo Albanian communist leader Azem Vllasi. Thousands pressed into a building intended to accommodate a few hundred. Kosovo province police, both Albanian and Serb, surrounded the structure and, in typical communist style, pulled out their long truncheons and flailed into the crowd. The assembled began throwing stones, and rushed the doors, and the local Serb organizers pulled Milošević outside to quiet the discontented masses. "Then something happened," Ćuruvija wrote, "that I believe defined the future of this man and of the country. By accident, I found myself next to him. He was pale, bewildered. [This is also visible in videos taken at the scene and widely reproduced in documentaries.] The people carried him [along], yelling and pulling at him. We were pressed together when an old Serb, his hair completely gray and his moustache yellow from tobacco, yelled directly at his face, 'They are beating us, President! Don't let them beat us!' The old man was crying and Milošević began trembling."

Within minutes Milošević had been propelled upstairs to the window of the Cultural Center, overlooking the crowd. Ćuruvija later argued that the responsible tack would have been to calm the demonstrators and then to have them name representatives to participate in a discussion. Instead, Milošević uttered words that spelled the end of Yugoslavia and the beginning of the worst suffering undergone by the Kosovar Albanians in decades. Ćuruvija described Milošević as "nervous and improvising" as he gazed out the window. "Looking into the eyes of the old Serb who had appealed to him for help, he cried out to the frenzied crowd, 'Nobody must ever again dare to beat this people!' "

This people meant Serbs, not the Yugoslav people as a whole. Yet, especially abroad, few really understood this declaration. In the succeeding months, Milošević consolidated his hold over power, imposing an extremist writ from Serbia proper, where he was victorious within communist ranks in June 1986, to Vojvodina in 1988, followed by Montenegro in 1989. But Western journalists, exemplified by David Binder of *The New York Times*, saw in these developments a democratization comparable to that in Russia, and portrayed Milošević to the American public as a Yugoslav version of Mikhail Gorbachev.

Furthermore, foreign journalists and policy analysts neglected yet another set of parallels with sinister connotations. The rise of Milošević in Yugoslavia, utilizing the spectre of an Islamic threat to mobilize his constituents, coincided with a relatively successful campaign by Communist Bulgaria to expel or forcibly 'Bulgarize' its Muslim populations, with thousands who considered themselves Turkish in culture sent to Turkey, and thousands more who were purely Slavic Muslims and historically Bulgarian in culture, but who bore Islamic names, compelled to adopt new, 'national' identities. Both of these Balkan assaults on the rights of indigenous Muslims occurred while Moscow faced exceptional difficulties in its attempt to annex Afghanistan, leading one inevitably to consider the possibility that the new orientation, among Orthodox Slav Communists, in favor of extreme nationalism, had its origins in a single plan emanating from the Soviet hierarchy. Such a plan may well have involved a dry run in Bulgaria, followed by 'wet operations' in Yugoslavia, with experimental applications against the Chechens, Azeris, and other Muslim nations within the Soviet empire. In any event, the emergence of an aggressive Slavic Orthodox strategy against Muslims, within the communist states, clearly illustrated the essential symmetry, as Trotsky once put it, of the Stalinist and Hitlerian philosophies of governance.

In mid-1990, Milošević suppressed the Kosovo regional parliament. This action followed the declaration of a state of emergency, in response to new demonstrations by the Kosovar Albanians. At least sixty Albanians had been killed in a foray by Serb special police into Kosovo. Albanian workers, led by the miners, had declared widespread strikes. With the closure of the regional parliament, Albanians were purged from government affairs as well as from employment in state-controlled enterprises. Most Albanian media was shut down. Serb police and the Yugoslav army ruled Kosovo.

Albanians dead by the score, Albanians dismissed from employment, Serb power backed up by the gun and club. The fatal pattern had been re-established in Kosovo. There was no turning back.

* * * * *

Chapter VII:

Non-violent Resistance and a
Parallel Civil Society, 1989-1998

The strategy of Slobodan Milošević and his cenacle, in attempting to obliterate the Albanian social and cultural presence in Kosovo, as well as in supposedly defending Yugoslavia from disintegration, backfired completely and continuously, over the 1990s. It succeeded in only one respect: nationalist propaganda, the failure of Serbia to produce an effective opposition to his regime, and appeasement by the Western powers, which would help him maintain himself at the top of the pyramid. It is startling to imagine that any politician could be so Machiavellian as to anticipate such an outcome. But in the case of Milošević the possibility cannot be excluded. It may very well be that he deliberately set up his nation for disaster in order to remain the last communist dictator in Europe. As the Serb academician Ljubomir Simović commented late in 1999, "Regimes attempt to maintain their hold on power by improving the situation of their country's. Our country is regime attempts to maintain itself in power in a much more original way: by constantly worsening the country's situation."

In the first strategic error in his treatment of the Kosovar Albanians, Milošević government dismissed thousands of them from employment, thus forcing many to emigrate in search of work. For the first time in their history, the Kosovar Albanians acquired a very large *diaspora* community, in which males young and old toiled in various trades, and sent remittances home. This was not, in fact, the only Albanian *diaspora*. Large numbers of workers migrated from Albania proper, after the end of communism there in 1991, to Greece and Italy. But the life of Kosovar emigrants differed substantially from that of Albanians who went to these Mediterranean countries. The latter typically worked in the least attractive kinds of manual labour, earning small incomes and therefore being limited in their ability to fund their own political activities as well as to assist their families at home. In contrast, Kosovars settled in Switzerland, Austria, Germany, Scandinavia, and the United States, where many opened businesses, which flourished. Particularly in the U.S., a considerable number of Kosovar Albanians enjoyed financial success in the post-1989 emigration. With the money they accumulated in restaurants and other enterprises, they contributed heavily to the repressed but resilient Albanian opposition in Kosovo, which, as we shall see, produced an independent and autonomous civil society under the very noses of the Yugoslav authorities – a counter-power unique in political history.

Of course, the Kosovar Albanian *diaspora* was not the first to emerge from Yugoslavia. The Croats in particular had a large community abroad that was willing and sometimes avid to support political movements in the homeland. But the Croat emigration had existed for many decades; in the United States, for example, three distinct waves of workers and peasants had crossed the seas to earn a living. The first, consisting mainly of Dalmatian sailors, fisherman, and small business operators, had come in the early and middle 19th century; many of them settling in California during the Gold Rush. Although sentimental about their national culture, they were seldom active with regard to politics in Croatia, and as their children and grandchildren and great-grandchildren replaced them, Dalmatia and Croatia in general became a dim memory. Most of them were liberal or progressive in politics, and many became Tito loyalists after the Second World War. They had only very limited interest in supporting the foundation of a new Croatian state as Yugoslavia fell apart.

The succeeding generation of Croats who came to the U.S. were often Slavonians, who concentrated in the industrial Midwest where, during the late 19th and early 20th centuries, they worked in the steel, coal, and related heavy industries. They tended toward extreme radicalism in politics, with a large presence in the American Communist Party, and played a considerable role in the growth of industrial unionism in America during the 1930s. They were also notable enthusiasts for Tito. But they, too, lost interest in Croatia as their children assimilated into American life, and their social profile diminished even further when the industries in which they had spent their lives declined, producing the American 'rust belt' and the gentrification of such cities as Pittsburgh, Pennsylvania. They moved to the American suburbs and became indistinguishable from their retired and politically inactive neighbors. They were Yugoslav Croats by tradition, but their involvement with the old country was typically limited to a visit in old age.

A third wave of Croats landed in America after the Second World War, and they were the most troublesome for both the U.S. and Yugoslav governments. These were frequently Hercegovinan *Ustaša* and other politically suspect exiles who hated Yugoslavia and conspired against it, even resorting to terrorist bombings and similar outrages on American soil. Some contributed significantly to the rebirth of Croatia in the 1990s, but their numbers were small. Furthermore, the majority of them, once they had tasted economic wealth in America, also abandoned politics and became lost in the vast American landscape.

Serbs and Montenegrins had emigrated to America following similar patterns, but their embrace of American life was so rapid and profound that they rarely became actively involved in Yugoslav issues, although after the series of new Balkan wars began in 1991, they suddenly surfaced with a fairly well-organized lobby which actively supported Milošević. It also became disconcertingly apparent at that time that Serb and pro-Serb academics, often behind a mask of Yugoslavism, had infiltrated and essentially corrupted the large field of South Slav studies in American universities, as well as the equivalent institutions in Britain, France, and Australia.

Macedonians had a historic emigration in the U.S. which vanished in the American background by the 1960s, while Bosnian Muslims had never emigrated in large numbers, except to Germany where they were sojourners and did not produce a stable community, until the great refugee exodus generated by the 1992-95 war. Albanians had gone to America beginning in the early 20th century, but their numbers remained small, as they clustered in Boston and Detroit; colonies of Italo-Albanians or Arbëresh existed in some American cities but many considered themselves essentially Italian, and had no particular interest in Albania, much less the situation of Albanians in Yugoslavia.

Kosovar Albanian emigration after 1989 differed from these patterns in every respect. They did not remain abroad long enough to produce a mature second generation; they did not develop an identification with the countries in which they lived and worked; and, above all, they did not forget the struggle of their relatives and neighbors at home. If anything, they grew angrier and more militant as, outside Yugoslavia, they experienced a life without brutal anti-Albanian discrimination. They also became educated in political democracy, the use of modern media, and effective methods of lobbying, especially in the U.S. By forcing thousands of them to go to foreign countries, Milošević not only failed to defeat the Kosovar Albanians; he gave them new incentives and new weapons in their resistance.

The second great error of Milošević was bound up with the first. In suppressing the Albanian working and business classes in Kosovo he cut them off from the ideology and habits of state subsidy, bureaucratic lethargy, and dependency that communism had fostered in other parts of Yugoslavia, most notably within his own Serbia. Thus, he forced the Kosovar Albanians to create an effective free-market system that, at least in the realm of small enterprises and individual entrepreneurship even outshone Slovenia. This was certainly an unintended gift, but a gift, nonetheless. Unlike Slovenes, Croats, Bosnians, and others in Yugoslavia, the Kosovar Albanians would never have to wrestle with the hefty challenge of privatization, exept with regard to large enterprises like Trepça that remained in Serb hands. After the NATO intervention of 1999, U.S. Undersecretary of Commerce David Aaron commented, "Ironic as it sounds, there was a blessing in the last 10 years of martial law dictated by Belgrade in which ethnic Albanians were kicked out of managerial and administrative positions by the Serbs. The result was to create thousands of small entrepreneurs – shopkeepers, retail distributors, builders."

The third error of the Serbian power replicated the second, in media and intellectual life. Unlike the rest of the Yugoslav media, the Kosovar Albanian press after 1989 did not have to contend with a legacy of statist economic control and party dictates in journalism. Kosovar Albanian media workers were thus free to adopt techniques and technologies they learned from their relatives who created a thriving Albanian language press in Zurich, New York, and other exile centers. And finally, in dismissing Kosovar Albanian intellectuals from nearly all academic posts, the Serbian regime unwittingly provided the Albanians with a full-fledged and sophisticated political leadership. The outstanding exemplar of this stratum was Ibrahim Rugova, a French trained literary scholar of great ability and sophistication, who was an expert on Pjetër Bogdani, the 17th century Albanian Catholic author. Rugova, the son of a peasant killed by the Tito forces at the end of the Second World War, was in his middle 40s when he founded the Kosova Democratic League, known by its Albanian initials as the LDK, in 1989.

The LDK soon became the main Kosovar political force, both domestically and in the emigration. Rugova rose to head the government of the 'Kosova Republic,' which was declared to be independent of Yugoslavia in 1991 but was recognized only by Albania. Although this development seemed premature to foreign journalists, Kosovar Albanians saw themselves as comparable to the Slovenes and Croats, who successfully declared their independence from Yugoslavia, after numerous attempts to gain a confederal constitution for the crumbling state. Milošević and co. had demanded utter submission to Belgrade, with the only alternative an armed campaign against "secessionists" by the Yugoslav army. The first such assault, in Slovenia in 1991, was rather handily beaten, but the succeeding wars in Croatia and Bosnia-Hercegovina were distinguished by extraordinary cruelties on the part of Yugoslav forces, aided by Serb *četniks*.

Of course, the unintended benefits of Serbian repression were difficult to perceive if one was an ordinary Kosovar Albanian worker dismissed from one's position, or a peasant subject to daily police harassment, and Serb atrocities elsewhere in former Yugoslavia were a deadly harbinger of the fate awaiting Kosovar Albanians. But it soon became clear even to the most remote villagers that something quite remarkable was happening in Kosovo. That is, while the Slovenes and Croats were fighting for their national independence in arms, the Kosovar Albanians had set about creating, on their own, every kind of institution necessary for the functioning of a modern society.

When a Serbophile curriculum was introduced into the Kosovo schools, with the imposition of physical segregation between Serb and Albanian pupils and the dismissal of Albanian teachers, Albanians organized a system of private instruction that came to include thousands of children. After Albanian doctors and nurses were ejected from the Kosovo hospitals, a similarly extensive network of dispensaries was established on private premises, supplementing an existing network of small clinics run by Albanian Catholics. For years, Albanian infants were delivered in private homes. All these activities were co-ordinated by Rugova's 'government,' using a budget derived from a tax collected in the emigration. Most of the humanitarian services were co-ordinated by an alliance of Muslim imams and Catholic priests, while a Christian Democratic party that happened to include a number of prominent Muslims became a lesser element in the Kosovar Albanian political spectrum, alongside the LDK.

And above all, the Rugova 'administration' committed the Kosovars, for a decade, to non-violent, passive protest and resistance.

The miracle of Kosovo, reminiscent of Rev. Martin Luther King, Jr., and of Gandhi before him, excited the admiration of American politicians, including a Republican Senator, Robert Dole. Dole became an advocate for the Kosovars, stimulating some of the most extravagant and entertaining rumors ever to appear in the Serbian press, where it was claimed that the Kansan Dole, from a solid, middle-American background, was actually the child of Albanian Muslims! That Albanian Muslims had never settled in Kansas was a detail irrelevant to the Belgrade propaganda factory, which so assiduously broadcast this absurd fable that many residents of the vanishing Yugoslavia, including not a few Albanians, came to believe it. In any case, joined by a number of other American political figures, many of them Jewish, Dole began a long campaign of criticism directed against Belgrade. The U.S. Congress, although reluctant to entertain support for secession in Slovenia and Croatia, adopted numerous resolutions warning Milošević of the consequences of further repression in Kosovo.

The Belgrade media also railed against the Kosovo Albanians as supposed partisans of the Stalinist communism still in power in Albania proper, without attempting to explain how such a phenomenon would gain the support of American conservative Republicans, as well as of the free-market oriented Slovenes, who, among Yugoslavs, took the initiative in assisting the Kosovar Albanians. Slovene youth organizations collected more than 300,000 signatures on a petition demanding full enforcement of the 1974 constitution granting autonomy to Kosovo and Vojvodina, and contemptuously, as well as effectively, rejected anti-Slovene threats by Milošević.

While bogus charges about the family tree of Bob Dole were effective only within Yugoslavia, disinformation from Belgrade about the alleged Maoist ancestry of the Albanian civic resistance caught on in the West, and kept a tenacious hold on the minds of many journalists and so-called experts. After all, only three Albanians were then known to the world: Enver Hoxha, Mother Teresa, and the actor John Belushi. The latter two had no apparent interest in stirring anti-Yugoslav sentiment, even though the father of Ganxhe Bojaxhiu, the name of Mother Teresa when she was born in Macedonia, was reportedly a victim of the Serbs. Although Hoxha was dead, he had been a prominent Marxist for many years, and his political bent was viewed by Westerners as, at least, contagious among Albanians. In reality, aside from nostalgia for Titoite Communism, the radical leftism of Kosovar Albanians was overwhelmingly fictitious. Although some had the disconcerting habit of defending Stalin for reputedly protecting Albania against Tito, and while the demonstrations of 1981 had been guided by a small group of Leninists, most Kosovars viewed all forms of communist ideology with disaste.

As the Kosovar political scientist Nexhmedin Spahiu has written, Rugova was popularly called a Titoist, and his main rival, the Albanologist Rexhep Qosja, an Enverist, in that the former concentrated on the specific problem of Kosovo, while the latter focused on the broader perspectives of the whole Albanian nation, including the millions living in Albania proper and in Macedonia and Montenegro. Qosja had founded a rival organization to the LDK, titled the United Democratic Movement (LBD) of Kosova. But authentic supporters of either Titoite or Hoxhaite Communism were very thin on the ground in Kosovo. Even those Albanians who had risen in the local Yugoslav Communist structure were motivated by personal ambition and a need for community representation, rather than belief in Marxism. The long domination of Kosovar Albanian politics by Rugova also gave the lie to Serb claims that the Kosovars sought a greater Albania in union with Albania proper. Rugova sought an independent Kosovo, not a merger with a country that was the worst economic disaster area of the Balkans. Spahiu has argued that Kosovo, and not Albania proper, is the true heartland of the Albanian nationalism, writing, "Kosovar national ideology represented the core of the Albanian nation and the original version of the Albanian national ideology."

As before in this dolorous history, it was the Serb side that represented opposition to modern, bourgeois concepts of property and economy. Among the most onerous oppressions inflicted on the Kosovar Albanians was a series of measures that first banned Albanians from purchasing or selling land without obtaining permission from Serb authorities, then cancelled sales of land by Serbs to Albanians. But the greater meaning of all such details was not clear to the Serbian rulers of Kosovo, whose aims were simple: to keep Milošević in power, and the Serbs united, by beating on the Albanians, and as a side effect, to drive as many of the latter out of the region as possible. Since the Mediterranean Albanians could never be assimilated by the Slavic Serbs, they should be liquidated, either by direct physical means or by inducing them to depart according to the recommendations of Drs. Čubrilović and Andrić, six decades before.

Because the conflict between Serbs and Albanians in Kosovo was truly cultural, and not simply political and economic, with cultural shadings, as in Slovenia and Croatia, the Serb authorities made a serious attempt to exterminate the Albanian intellect. In perhaps the single most symbolic such event, the so-called opposition Serb politician Vuk Drašković, who bore major responsibility for the overall outbreak of violent Serb ultra-nationalism, rose in the Serb national assembly in October 1991 to call for the abolition of the Kosova Academy of Sciences and Arts. The measure was adopted. In the same period, the regional university was 'de-Albanized' the University Library's Albanian holdings were purged, with many books in Albanian sent for pulping, and the Provincial Archives were sealed and taken to Belgrade. As noted by the Albanian-American scholar Sami Repishti, "Theaters, art galleries, and cultural associations were also closed. Even sports events were banned to avoid the gathering of Albanian crowds." In the geographical heart of Europe, Serbia had created a situation that uniquely imitated the racist *apartheid* regime that long tormented South Africa.

Nevertheless, under the Serbian lash, the Kosovar Albanians had successfully carried out a unique transition away from communist governance. While the Poles and Hungarians revitalized civic traditions within the existing state, and the Slovenes and Croats created states as a context for the fostering of civil society, the Kosovar Albanians established a civil society as a function of a parastate, which was in reality a resistance movement. Without resort to violence – which all among them then viewed as a suicidal option – they had organized and maintained a free or liberated zone such as revolutionaries and reformers of the past, worldwide, had long dreamed. Unfortunately, these fine points of political science were largely ignored by the rest of the globe.

But' as elsewhere in anti-colonialist struggles, writers and especially poets played a major role in galvanizing the national movement. Rugova and Qosja have already been mentioned, but many other such figures came to prominence as representatives of Albanian aspirations. Repishti has described this as "the coming of age of the intellectuals", in which the mass education created by Titoism made possible the "shedding [of] the overbearing complex

of inferiority, the image of an 'an uneducated and uneducable populace'...
created by vicious and persistent Serbian propaganda for over a century."

The poets and other authors who were read by Kosovar Albanians in those
years have yet to become known outside their own community, except in a
fragmentary way in Croatia and Bosnia, thanks to the general neglect of
Albanian literature in the outer world. But their work is generally distinguished
by delicacy, wit, insight, and an incisive style. Not for them the crafting of
pseudo-populist or ideological verses; rather, they seemed to follow the example of such dissident intellectuals as the Czech Vaclav Havel, who, of course,
went from artistic modernism to the presidency of his country.

The poet, critic, and translator Esad Mekuli (1916-1993) was born in the
town of Plava, in the Gusinje region of Montenegro, which lies within the
Albanian culture area. Mekuli has been called "the father of modern Albanian
poetry in what was once Yugoslavia" by the Albanologist Robert Elsie, and
his influence in Kosovo remains immense. He lived in Peć as a youth, then
studied veterinary medicine at the University of Belgrade, before serving as a
Partisan in the Second World War. After the war, he was the founding editor
of *Jeta e Re* (New Life), which became the leading literary journal in Kosovo,
and was its guiding personality until 1973. Interestingly enough, he was com-
missioned to translate the violently anti-Muslim Montenegrin epic, Njegoš'
Mountain Wreath, into Albanian, in co-operation with the writer Zef Nekaj,
who later emigrated as a political exile to the U.S. He also produced Serbian
translations of many Albanian works.

One of Mekuli's most famous verses asks, "Is it the Albanian's fault that
he lives under this sky/Under this sky, in the land of his ancestors?" But his
best work is psychological and even somewhat surrealist, rather than political. A favorite of many Kosovars is his 1935 poem 'Longing for the
Unattainable,' which begins, "Clouds play high above like lambs on the hills
/while longing for the unattainable is held within me." Here it must be stipulated that Albanian authors, no less than other literary personalities in
Communist Yugoslavia, benefitted from the absence of a strict canon of socialist realism under the Tito regime. Those who lived in Hoxha's Albania were,
of course, by no means so lucky. On the other side of the mountains, writers
were held to the standard articulated by the court novelist Ismail Kadare in a
noted speech in 1977, 'The Literature of Socialist Realism is Developing in
Struggle Against the Bourgeois and Revisionist Pressure.' Kadare declared, "In
their spirit, in their content, even in their style and intonation, many of the
works of the present day decadent bourgeois literature are reminiscent of the
Bible, the New Testament, Qur'an, the Talmud, and other tattered remnants
of the Dark Ages." Given such attitudes in Tirana, it is no wonder that Kosovar

Albanians preferred to consider themselves 'Titoists', as in the case of Rugova, rather than 'Enverists'.

Indeed, Kosovo produced a far more developed modern literature in Albanian than Albania proper, at least until the end of communism in the latter territory, in 1991. Elsie notes that in the closing decades of the century up to 70 percent of book publication in Kosovo was poetry. Other outstanding poets included four whose first books appeared in 1961: Din Mehmeti (1932–1999), born in a village near Gjakova, and one of the first victims of the Serb terror in response to the NATO intervention, Fahredin Gunga (1936–), from Mitrovica, Adem Gajtani (1935–), born in Podujeva, and Ali Podrimja (1942–), also from Gjakova. Podrimja, in particular, became well-known throughout Yugoslavia, and even internationally; Elsie described him as "the most typical representative of modern Albanian verse in Kosovo". If Esad Mekuli was the T.S. Eliot of the Kosovars, Podrimja was their Allen Ginsberg. With biting sarcasm, in a poem published years before the catharsis of 1998–99, he answered the question posed a generation before him by Mekuli:

> "It is the Albanian's fault
> Who sketches his own face under the moon
> And breaks windows and stirs up muddy water
> Who speaks Albanian, who eats Albanian, who shits Albanian
>
> It is the Albanian's fault
> The Albanian is the one at fault
> For all my undoings
>
> And for my broken tooth
> And for my frozen laugh
> So therefore: BULLET"

The list of major poets could be extended to include Azem Shkreli, Rrahman Dedaj, Mirko Gashi, and Sabri Hamiti, as well as the writer considered by many of his contemporaries to be the most talented and significant, Beqir Musliu. Born in Gjilan in 1945, Musliu has followed a rigorously surrealist line, with works like 'The Hidden Pagoda' beginning, "Someone has built a pagoda at the top of the Accursed Mountains," the latter a reference to the range that delineates the border of Montenegro, Albania, and Kosovo.

With the spread of war in former Yugoslavia, it was inevitable that the unexpected images included in many Kosovar Albanian poets' works would take on a new meaning. The flight of thousands of Serbs from Croatia after the army of Franjo Tuđman recovered the Krajina region, in 1995, exacerbated the situation in Kosovo, as numerous refugees were resettled as colonists there, often against their wishes. In addition, one of the worst Serb terrorists to operate in the Croatian and Bosnian wars, a babyfaced former secret police thug and gangster named Željko Ražnjatović, who called himself 'Arkan' moved his base of activities to Kosovo, from where he was 'elected' to the Belgrade parliament. Meanwhile, Adem Demaçi, who had been freed in 1990, had established a Council for the Defense of Human Rights and Freedoms (KMDLNJ) that painstakingly chronicled the continuing attacks of the Serb authorities on Albanians; he also set up a Kosova Parliamentary Party. But Demaçi was not an exclusivist Albanian nationalist; he advocated a regional federation, which he dubbed "Balkania".

In 1993, Demaçi addressed one of many appeals to U.S president Bill Clinton, calling for intervention in the Bosnian war. He wrote, "Mr. President, in the name of innocent children, the disabled elderly, and the peace-loving Albanian nation – which has been enslaved by brutal and hegemonistic 'Great Serbian' policies for over 80 years – in the name of innocent Muslim people who, through fire and steel, have been driven from their homes, whose sons are being executed as if they were nothing more than ants, whose daughters are being raped in the most bestial manner, and in the name of all peace-loving and just peoples throughout the Balkans, I ask you not allow an inert international bureaucracy to perpetuate the injustice being brought against small and defenseless nations. Do not to allow our souls to be burdened by new sins."

Unfortunately, when the U.S. and NATO finally acted to stop the war in Bosnia-Hercegovina, late in 1995, no justice was forthcoming in Kosovo. The Dayton agreement, which ended the Bosnian combat, left the Serbs in control of considerable territory within that scarred land, faithfully expressing the international stance of moral equivalence between Milošević and his victims. Kosovo went unmentioned at Dayton; worse, Milošević suddenly enjoyed favor as a key figure in the maintenance of peace in Bosnia-Hercegovina.

Kosovar Albanians were not prepared to submit forever to an international community that evidently considered them expendable; in addition, voices began to be heard criticizing Rugova and the LDK for their failure to go beyond a situation in which Serbs continued killing and imprisoning Albanians. When the crisis of the non-violent line began, it came, unsurprisingly, in Drenica, the region that had produced the greatest *kaçak* heroes, Azem Bejta and Shota Galica, as well as the rebel Partisan Shaban Polluzha. It took the form of the Kosova Liberation Army, known in Albanian as *Ushtria Çlirimtare i Kosovës* or UÇK (pronounced 'oocheka'), which carried out its first attacks on Serb police in 1996.

Many strange assertions would be made about the UÇK in the succeeding period. Coming out of nowhere, and asserting bold opposition to the pacifist line pursued by Rugova, the movement was first believed by many people inside Kosovo as well as those outside to be an agency of provocation created by the Serbs to justify repression. Foreign journalists, recycling propaganda out of Belgrade, and themselves knowing neither the Albanian language nor Albanian history, least of all Kosovar Albanian history, ascribed Hoxhaite origins to the UÇK, a curious claim considering that Hoxha had died in 1985, eleven years before its emergence. In addition, as we have discussed, Hoxha had done nothing to free Kosovo from Yugoslavia, and was not viewed favorably by Kosovar Albanians.

But Belgrade had played this tune so long and loudly that foreigners naturally sang along; and the spectre of Hoxhaism *redux* in the ranks of UÇK would soon be supplemented by further shopworn items from the storehouse of Serbian disinformation. Although Muslim fundamentalism had never existed in Kosovo, that label was attached to the movement; later came charges that UÇK was a front for Albanian drug dealers. It should be noted that when the Nicaraguan *contras* were similarly accused, the claim was based on the real cases of Nicaraguan cocaine dealers who had been tried, convicted, and were serving time in various prisons. No Albanian drug dealers were ever named as being linked with UÇK, although Albanian drug dealing did exist in Albania, Italy, Turkey, and Switzerland.

Eventually, charges against UÇK included allegations that their forebears had been Nazi collaborators, or in a flight of fancy purveyed by *New York Times* scribe Chris Hedges, "rightist *kaçaks*", a phenomenon previously unknown. Again, no names were ever produced to substantiate such assertions. Although Adem Demaçi, the permanent revolutionary romantic, would join UÇK as its political representative, the truth was that its leaders were unknowns. Uncertainty over who UÇK was and what it represented was only one feature in a landscape of increasing tension beginning in 1995. In scattered incidents at least 50 people were killed by one side or the other over the next two years. Arkan regularly postured before Serbian and global media about Kosovo, producing frequent alarms among Balkan observers. Then, late in 1997 beefy Serb police descended, clubs in hand, on a peaceful march of Albanian students in Prishtina demanding restoration of their access to the university. Anyone regularly watching Belgrade television could see the crisis was intensifying. Serbian media were filled with not-very-subtle tales about Albanian mafia and alleged Albanian mistreatment of Kosovo Serbs.

In January 1998, an armed attack on a Serb police station and the killing of a Serb official on a highway followed a raid on the Kosovar Albanian village of Prekaz i Poshtëm. At first, the Serbian press reported that the assault on the police station had been carried out by "unidentified persons", seemingly indicating an unwillingness to admit to a certain vulnerability, and Serb authorities denied that intercommunal fighting had occurred. Rather, they said, two Albanian factions had engaged in a gun battle. However, the conflict had actually begun on January 21 when Serb police tried to enter Prekaz i Poshtëm for the first time since 1992. According to the Serb opposition weekly *Vreme*, they had set up a forward post in a factory yard, then sneaked into the village itself, at midnight. But they were greeted with gunfire from the family compound of Adem Jashari, a well-known local personality. Adem Jashari had participated in all the main Kosovar Albanian demonstrations since 1968, but he had fled to the nearby hills in 1991 after receiving a 20 year jail sentence, and remained there until the day of his death in 1998. In hiding, he organized the first unit of the as yet unnamed UÇK. Two girls from the Jashari family, Selveti and Iliriana, were in the house with their grandfather, Shaban Jashari, when it was attacked and they initiated the armed action; both young women were wounded. Adem and his brother Hamza Jashari, hearing the shots, rushed to the scene and drove the police away with further gunfire. The body of an Albanian factory worker was later found nearby. In the wake of the incident, the Serbs imposed a *de facto* military curfew throughout Drenica.

The funerals of the two dead men - the Serb official killed on the road, mourned by 10,000 Serbs and Montenegrins, and the Albanian factory worker from Prekaz i Poshtëm, attended by 20,000 Albanians – marked the end of the era of non-violence in the Kosovar Albanian resistance. Next 'Serb forces carried out summary executions and massacres in Likoshan near Gllogoc and Qirez in the Skenderaj district, on February 28. These villages were hit by coordinated operations over 24 hours, involving large numbers of masked Serb police, paramilitaries, and soldiers. One family, the Ahmetajs, saw their menfolk executed one by one.

Then, most dramatically, came the destruction of the Jashari family compound and the murder of nearly all its residents, including women and children, beginning at 5:00 a.m., March 5, 1998. According to popular accounts, a spy had seen Adem Jashari enter the home. Forty-six Albanians were killed, including 20 from the family of Shaban Jashari; 15 of the victims were children between the ages of 7 and 16, and 17 of them were female. Their corpses were seized by the police and they were denied a Muslim funeral. Adem Jashari, said to have sung Albanian songs while shooting back from the inferno of his house, became the great symbolic hero of the UCK. Soon songs were composed and sung about him.

But the story of his father Shaban, as related by the Kosovar Albanian bal-
ladeer Naim Berisha in his 'Song of the Jasharis', not only reveals an authentic
Albanian hero, it also explains the real history of the UÇK fighters, who were
slandered abroad as Islamists, Maoists, drug dealers, and the offspring of Nazi
collaborators. Shaban Jashari had served in the dissident Partisan forces of Shaban
Polluzha fifty years before. In 1947, he witnessed a Serb massacre of 5,000
Albanians in Drenica. Soon after that, Shaban's father Murat Jashari sheltered
two members of the Albanian anti-communist movement Balli Kombëtar, which
had almost no following in Kosovo, in his home. A secret policeman from
Albania, Mal Sadiku, threatened to kill Shaban Jashari because his father had
protected the two Ballists. Shaban challenged them to go ahead and shoot him,
but a volunteer officer saved him. Later, Shaban worked for four years as a teacher,
but his opposition to the authorities led to the loss of his job and an ultimatum
to leave Kosovo, which he rejected. When his son Adem went into the hills,
Shaban was so severely beaten by the Serb police he lost an eye. After five decades
of continuous struggle this family of freedom fighters was exterminated in 1998,
save only for one teenaged girl who survived the massacre and three sons who
had been sent abroad in anticipation of just such an outcome.

Between late February and March 9 at least 50 more people, and as many
as 80, were killed, with dozens reported missing; the victims were mostly
Albanian. But massacres proliferated. The world press reported the outbreak
of war in Kosovo, but by all accounts, the Serb campaign was a pogrom, an
orgy of killing, intended to thrill the Serbs by once more venting their frus-
trations with the universe of difficulties into which they had been lured. The
ruling circle in Belgrade had come to include Milošević's charming wife
Mirjana Milošević, who posed as a kind of late-blooming hippie, proclaiming peace and love between peoples as leader of the Yugoslav United Left, a
mafia operation disguised as a political party. Milošević would soon incor-
porate the deranged Vojislav Šešelj, a jumped-up version of Arkan, and the
despicable Drašković into his leadership group. But Milošević was clearly running the Kosovo operation directly, even more than he ran the Slovenian,
Croatian, and Bosnian wars. And it was obvious that the Belgrade offensive
in Kosovo followed a plan that had been worked out long before.

The hand of Belgrade's oppression struck at all levels of Kosovar Albanian
society. Veton Surroi, editor-in-chief of the Albanianlanguage daily *Koha Ditore*,
was beaten up in his newsroom, while a photographer, Fatos Berisha, was
thrown out of a secondstorey window in the paper's building. Four staffers from
Rilindja, the main Albanianlanguage daily – Avni Spahiu, editor-in-chief,
Mehmet Gjata, editor, and reporters Rexhep Demiri and Flamure Selimi-Lahu
– were also abused by Serb police. Ibrahim Osmani, a stringer for the Voice of

America and Agence France Press, was assaulted, and Chris Wenner, a British television cameraman, was very seriously injured by Serb extremists. Worldwide protest was forthcoming from journalists' unions, and the International Federation of Journalists, from its Brussels headquarters, declared, "It is shocking that we are witnessing the type of media attacks which took place at the beginning of the war in Bosnia... The charge of terrorism [against the Albanians] is commonly used window dressing when the authorities want to stop information to the public which might undermine government support." At the end of March, a group of so-called peace workers from the U.S., who had journeyed to Kosovo to teach non-violence – both an unnecessary and increasingly irrelevant task – but who mainly promoted the theory of moral equivalence between the Serbs and their victims, discovered that the Serbs were less than appreciative of their refined approach. They were arrested and jailed, with the heads of the males compulsorily shaved, and were then deported to Macedonia.

In the end, the pious declarations of media watchdogs and humanitarian tourists for peace counted for little in the face of Serb brutality. The contest over Kosovo had come down to an unavoidable choice between hard men: on one side, Milošević and his minions; on the other, UÇK. Supporters of the latter set up a network in the émigré community, Homeland Calling (*Vendlindja Thërret* in), which openly solicited funds from Zurich to The Bronx. By March 9, U.S. Secretary of State Madeleine Albright had prevailed on the Contact Group, consisting of the U.S., Britain, France, Germany, Russia, and Italy, to express concern over the latest round of aggression by Belgrade. But at that point the Contact Group would agree to little more than a weapons embargo against rump Yugoslavia, which now consisted only of Serbia and Montenegro. The main concern of the so-called international community appeared to be to keep Milošević on board as a supporter of the Dayton agreement.

In Kosovo the time of terror had descended in full measure. Kosovo is a flat plain, with few mountains or forests in which to hide, unlike Bosnia. Belgrade filled the terrain with tanks, manned by oversized men armed with the most sophisticated weapons. These forces ranged across the countryside killing anybody and levelling anything they chose as targets. The rest 1998 was nightmarish for Kosovar Albanians. Notwithstanding the rhetoric it purveyed in the diaspora, UÇK could, in the final reckoning of things, do little to protect its constituents. Major massacres continued, occurring at Poklet i Ri at the end of May were 11 died and in the Junik district near the Albanian border, which 70 years before had been a safe haven for *kaçaks;* there at least 60 were killed, many more were wounded, and the corpses were removed by police, with the identities of the dead unknown. In a new development, Serb military claimed more dead than Albanian sources, clearly intending to inspire further terror.

On July 19, 1998, the first pitched battle between Serb forces and UÇK took place in the town of Rahovec, which became the Gernika of the Kosovar Albanian resistance. Open fighting in the streets culminated in a Serb assault on the Helveti-Karabashi Sufi lodge in the town, known as the Sheh Myhedini *teqe*, in which hundreds of terrified residents had gathered. The leader of the *teqe*, Myhedin Shehu, was killed along with many of those who had sought refuge therein. At Rahovec, up to 150 Albanians died; within two days the Serbs had buried the victims in two mass graves in Prizren. In August and September mass executions were recorded in Ranca (11 people killed, eight of them children), Galica near Vushtrri (14 dead, mainly young men), and Golluboc (eight child victims), while in Abria e Epërme, a whole family, the Deliajs, was wiped out, totaling 22 people. The only survivor of that incident, an infant of three months, Diturie Deliaj, was found alive beneath her mother's corpse. The child died a month later.

By the end of the year a half million Albanians had fled their homes. They began to pour across the borders of Kosovo, into Montenegro, Macedonia, and Bosnia-Hercegovina. From the beginning of the crisis, peaceful protests took place across Kosovo, but participants were attacked by police and civilian Serbs. The Serb authorities ordered Albanians out of their homes and apartments, and dismissed those who had jobs. Medical personnel and aid workers were killed, beaten, and disappeared. The Kosovar Albanians were fighting for their lives; but where was UÇK? Its effectiveness as a military force was clearly limited. Unlike the Slovenian, Croatian and Bosnian armies, in the earlier Yugoslav wars, UÇK could not organize an effective defense.

According to the annual report of Demaçi's Council for the Defense of Human Rights and Freedoms, in 1998, 1,934 Albanians were murdered, 818 were wounded, 3,758 were tortured, with 1,047 cases of severe mistreatment, and 799 missing; the victims included 913 women and 439 children. Burned, destroyed, and looted settlements totaled 450; 41,538 houses and 1,995 businesses were wrecked. Thousands were living in gullies and on unprotected hillsides, in the cold of a severe winter. And then came Reçak.

The atrocity at Reçak occurred on January 15, 1999. Serb civilians, military, police, and paramilitaries descended on the village, followed by Serb infantry. Forty five victims were slaughtered, then mutilated, their eyes torn out, ears sliced away, and their internal organs removed. The head of one old man was cut off. Serb authorities seized the corpses and prevented their burial. U.S. diplomat William Walker appeared at the scene and angrily denounced the Serbs. The Serbs forbade human rights investigator Louise Arbour from visiting the site, turning her back at the Macedonian border. Two weeks later, the Serbs demonstrated their understanding of the situation: at Rogova near Gjakova, on January 29, 26 Albanians were killed, most of them while fleeing in all directions, after Serb special police and military units, at 5:30 a.m., surrounded the village.

These massacres did not have the effect the Serbian authorities intended: the Albanians were not intimidated. Since the death of the Jasharis almost a year before, a great excitement had seized the Kosovar Albanians, and especially young males. The moment had come to stand once and for all, or lose one's honor forever. Thousands tried to enlist in UÇK, but were turned away, sent back to their homes to await a call. For many the call never came; UÇK, to repeat, was not the efficient force its pretensions might have suggested. Many Kosovar Albanians would later conclude that the real spirit of UÇK, and its best as well as its first commander, had perished in the flames of the Jashari compound early in 1998.

Meanwhile, the music rose like a windstorm. Songs about Adem Jashari and his family were composed and sung everywhere, recorded on cassettes and compact discs, some accompanied by the çiftelija, a two-stringed instrument, and in other traditional styles, others set to a background of electronic effects. They represented a style of protest music, or revolutionary balladry, that would have been startling to foreign audiences, if they had been heard by them. The songs were edgy, excited, and very energetic. The composer Xhemil Saliu recorded a song, 'Voice of the Çiçaviça Mountains' with a beat as infectious as any found in technopop, but, at the same time, electrifying in its patriotism. Many heroes have come from Çiçaviça, he sang, reciting the names of Shota and Azem Galica, the "hero of heroes" Shaban Polluzha, and others, but at the heart of our days stands Adem Jashari, the first UÇK commander… the massacre at Reçak did not frighten us, for the blood of the martyrs makes the heroes stronger!

But how would the world respond? A photograph by Wade Goddard of Sygma, appeared in The New York Times on Thursday, October 8, 1998. It expressed the pathos of Kosovo in unforgettable terms. In that image, a girl, her hair cropped short, sat in a wheelchair, surrounded by trees.

The caption read, "Thousands of ethnic Albanians have fled to Kosovo's forests after Serbian attacks. A paralyzed girl sat in a refugee camp south of Stimlje [Shtimje] yesterday."

The girl was identified in the next day's Times: Elfije Kadriaj, 13, "paralyzed most of her life from an early illness". She was placed in her wheelchair and pushed into the woods by her brother Rexhep, 16. The Times reported, "Today, Elfije sat in her wheelchair under a tree on the edge of a tractor-trailer refugee camp as raindrops sprinkled on her."

Her head was bowed as she sat, paralyzed, in the shelter of the forest.

The world seemed paralyzed in its response to the Serb terror. Elfije waited, "raindrops sprinkling on her", for the world's paralysis to end.

The great Russian dissident poet Osip Mandelshtam wrote of living "in the black velvet of the Soviet night, in the velvet of worldwide emptiness". In the velvet of worldwide emptiness, Elfije Kadrije, 13, sat in her wheelchair, waiting. Waiting for UÇK, waiting for the world, waiting...

* * * * *

Chapter VIII:

1999 – Intervention and Its Aftermath

On February 6, 1999 negotiations between Serb and Albanian representatives, sponsored by the Contact Group, began at a French castle called Rambouillet. Six weeks later, on March 19, the Rambouillet talks ended. The Albanian delegates, with occasional hesitations from UÇK representatives, had signed a document agreeing to a process administered by the international powers, under which the basic human rights of their community would be restored, while Kosovo would remain under Yugoslav (and Serbian) sovereignty.

The Serb delegates had treated the entire matter with utter contempt, drinking all night and loudly singing *četnik* songs. What, after all, had they to worry about? So far their luck had held; the world had treated Albanian babies as unworthy of defense against mass murder. The leading Belgrade statesman, Milošević, had declined to make the trip to France. The head of their delegation, a certain Milutinović, capered and mugged like a circus clown. The Serbs had had quite a good time.

Across the globe, Albanians and their friends asked one another, will anything really happen? The U.S. had warned the Serbs that flouting the Rambouillet parley would result in bombing. But Croatia had bled for four years, with the rest of the world doing nothing to save its people; Bosnia-Hercegovina had been similarly crippled. Albanians compared themselves to the Jewish victims of the Holocaust, in that the world had treated them as distant, exotic, and not very desirable as neighbours or friends. Who knew anything about them? Who cared?

But on the night of March 24, fleets of bombing planes revved up their powerful engines and filled the skies over the Balkans. Residents of Sarajevo heard the sound and rushed to their roofs, seeing nothing, because in addition to the darkness, most of the aircraft were protected by advanced technology, or flew too high to be detected. But they could be heard. Croatians went wild with delight; Bosnians were more restrained, since the moment had come a bit late for them. But it had finally come. The old conscience of the democracies, the spirit that had defeated Hitlerism, that had saved South Korea, and upon which inspiration the North Atlantic Treaty Organization was founded, had finally asserted itself. The first objectives were airports in Kosovo, at Belgrade, and in Montenegro. In Prishtina, Albanians neglected their own safety to watch the bombs fall, dazed and amazed.

The Kosovo intervention was a war of theories and images. Narcissistic American media treated the action as an internal matter having more to do with the prior scandals involving President Clinton than with Milošević. The latter individual acted with supreme self-confident, blandly asserting that his people had nothing to fear. The Serbs, or so the disinformational propaganda went, had secret weapons developed by the long-dead scientist Nikola Tesla, which would shield them from Western bombs. Or the West would fold up and back away after a few of its personnel were killed by the brave Serbs. Or the Russians would come and save them. Bizarrely enough, although the Tesla rumors were ignored outside Serbia and its network of supporters, many Western journalists bought into the remaining claims. The Serbs would never surrender, it was said. And the Russians would never allow their Orthodox Slav brethren to be subdued.

Unfortunately, the self-proclaimed experts of the punditocracy, who immediately effected a coup in the U.S. media, had never read Serbian history and did not know that one of the chief characteristics of Serb armies had always been a high rate of desertion. And nobody in the West ever found out that fewer than 10 percent of Russians favored involvement in the Kosovo war. Callow Russians who attempted to enlist as soldiers of fortune at the Yugoslav Embassy in Moscow found that the diplomats therein welcomed them, then demanded that the volunteers pay in hard currency for visas giving them the right to fight, as well as for their transportation. Those who got to the front discovered that Serb troops were overjoyed to see them, because they believed the Russians would be the first into battle, leaving the hardy Serb heroes to concentrate on such matters as locating decent liquor for themselves. The Russians also found out that they were expected to pay for their own food, on top of the fees they had previously handed over, if they wanted anything edible.

Russian recruitment for combat in the Balkans ended abruptly when H.E. Ravil Gainutdin, the Grand Mufti of the Kazan Tatars, announced that Russian Muslims would solicit volunteers to fight on the Albanian side. The spectacle of Russian citizens of differing faiths killing each other far away did not brighten the breakfast chatter of Boris Yeltsin and his advisers. Of course, there had always been those who said that if a few Chechens had shown up in the ranks of the UÇK, thousands of Serbs would have run, not walked, all the way to Siberia, if not Korea… but that is another story.

The American pundits, and the British newscasters who used the opportunity to try to outshine their Yankee counterparts in egregious objections to the war, did not bother with such issues. They were much too busy posturing as experts on the military capacities of their own countries. Some American conservative journalists, mainly women, decided that whatever the merits of the effort, Clinton was personally unfit to win the campaign, since he had cheated on his wife and lied about it. That the American leaders in the Second World War, President Franklin Roosevelt and General Eisenhower, had both been accused of adultery (long after the fighting, it must be said) was overlooked. Querulous BBC journalists decided Kosovo would be NATO's Vietnam, and that their mission as reporters was to pick holes in the information they were furnished. That journalists had more access to sensitive information in this war than in any other in history failed to impress them.

It was soon universally asserted among the Anglo-Saxons that the war could not be won without the use of ground troops, and that no war had ever been won by bombing alone. The subtext of these allegations was that the West was cowardly about sacrificing its own. That was indeed true; but that truth did not imply the foregoing arguments. U.S. President Bill Clinton and British Prime Minister Tony Blair did not, luckily for the Kosovar Albanians, depend on the wisecracking guests on American talk shows and the impertinent behavior of BBC presenters as a basis for NATO strategy. Incredibly enough, both men knew quite a bit of what they were about. But the U.S. and British media interviewed and quoted many 'experts' that thought otherwise. The Center for Media and Public Affairs, in the U.S., reported unblushingly after the hostilities ended that "more than two out of three sources cited in coverage of the Kosovo campaign opposed it".

At the close of the first week the Serbs responded to the NATO offensive with their typical delicacy: they attempted the wholesale eviction and deportation of the Kosovar Albanians. What had been a steady flow of refugees across the borders of the neighboring states, mainly Albania and Macedonia, now became a flood. And this eventuality changed everything.

Certain aspects of the Kosovo intervention had much to do with direct television coverage, beyond the obsession of commentators with the previouslynoted policy clichés. Because foreign television reporters were absent when the atrocities began in Croatia and Bosnia-Hercegovina, the real horror of the wars in those countries had never been brought home to the foreign public. In contrast, the massacres in Kosovo had been reported quite adequately, almost from the beginning. This also had a curious effect in that certain sectors of Western opinion acted as if the Kosovo conflict were entirely novel. Many canards laid to rest by serious journalists in the Croatian and Bosnian conflicts were now revived, spread their wings, and flew again. One of these was the claim that the good Serbs, staunch supporters of the allies in the Second World War, were fighting anti-Jewish Muslim extremists, the Palestinians of the Balkans.

This invention was well on its way to poisoning American Jewish attitudes about the intervention, when the videos arrived showing the thousands of Kosovar Albanians pushed into railroad trains and forcibly conveyed to the borders of the country. That settled that for the Jews, including the vast majority in Israel. Belgrade would not get a break in that quarter, and rabbis across America began demanding that, indeed, ground troops should be sent in as rapidly as possible, to prevent a new Holocaust. Israel even took in some thousands of Albanian Muslim refugees, and Jews worldwide finally learned about the protection of their coreligionists under the Albanian *besa* extended to them in the Second World War. Unfortunately, there were no authentic Kosovar Jews to bear witness to the situation; the Sephardic synagogue of Prishtina was among several structures in the historic city center – including a 16th century mosque - that had been demolished in the mid-1950s, to be replaced by government offices and hotels, typical of the Marxist era. A 'Prishtina Jewish community' was invented by the Belgrade authorities, but existed purely for propaganda purposes.

Especially in America, factions pro and con lined up in utterly bizarre ways. Leftists who hated NATO much more than they hated fascism defended the Belgrade clique for standing up to the new world order; conservatives who recalled Churchill and others like him two generations past called for increased bombing of Belgrade. Most of the latter-day American Trotskyists had never read Trotsky, and they decided that Milošević made a splendid comrade. (Some, but not all, of the British Trotskyists had read the old man, and their reaction was notably saner, although many of their local comrades also became Belgradophiles.) Most neo-Nazis considered ethnic cleansing a delightful concept, and so cities like San Francisco, California, saw demonstrations in which ultra-leftists were joined by extreme Jew baiters. Lonely hearts had finally found their own.

But the most remarkable aspect of the American debate over the Kosovo intervention consisted in the revival of a largely-forgotten element in U.S.'s political history – the pre-1941 alliance of pro-Nazis and mainstream Republican isolationists, who stood alongside the Communist Party, USA, and other anti-war socialists and pacifists. That alliance was, in large part, a local American expression of the Stalin-Hitler pact that had been signed in August 1939, and which led directly to the Nazi invasion of Poland.

In the Kosovo instance, we saw anti-intervention forces ranging from Noam Chomsky, Edward Said, and the editors of *The Nation* magazine on the left; to Republican presidential contenders including Pat Buchanan, Republican John Kasich and Senator James Inhofe on the right. In 1940, the arrangement was similar: in place of Chomsky and Said, such radicals as the socialist leader Norman Thomas and the editor of the pacifist *The Nation* Oswald Garrison Villard. Instead of Buchanan and company, there were Senator Robert A. Taft and aviator Charles Lindbergh, whose words to the America First Committee in Des Moines, Iowa in September 1941, that pressure for war was emanating from "the British, the Jewish and the Roosevelt administration", suggested the less than veiled threat that were war to come, it would become quite tough for Jews in the United States.

As for Taft, he reiterated the common view of the non-interventionists, that Republicans did not believe that "Hitler presents such a threat to the trade or safety of the United States as requires the sacrifice of several million American boys on the battlefields of the world." Writing shortly before Pearl Harbor, Taft argued that the war party was composed of "the business community of the cities, the newspaper and magazine writers, the radio and movie commentators, the communists and the university intelligentsia." Sounding much like the communists before the Nazi invasion of Russia, Taft opposed "risking the lives of five million American boys in an imperialistic war for the domination of Europe...and the supposed 'manifest destiny' of America."

Similarly, in 1999 some on the right argued – for example, the conservative columnist Mona Charyn - that "it's a bit more difficult to justify asking for sacrifice when the United States has no interests at stake and is merely chasing an impossible dream of world harmony." And Charyn was joined in opposition to the bombing of Belgrade by the editors of *The Nation*, who were more afraid of potential threats to the world from American power than from an alienated and nuclear-armed Russia.

In many ways, the alliance against the Kosovo action may be viewed as a local projection of the 'red-brown' alliance of post-1989 Leninists and anti-Semites in the Russian Communist Party, and the parallel coalition of fascists, leftists, and socialists that happened to rule Belgrade. Milošević had assembled a ruling group, let us again note, by uniting his own ex-Communist cadres with the so-called 'Yugoslav Left' under his wife Mirjana, on one side, and with the murderous followers of Šešelj, on the other.

This Belgrade bloc was anything but secure. Long before 1999, the authentic *četnik* nationalists obeyed Milošević but hated him for his ideology, his corruption, and his prior failures, and, besides, they were fearful that they would be purged by the ex-communists. Many political philosophers viewed Bolshevism and fascism as two expressions of the same totalitarianism; certainly, the anti-Semitic policies of the Moscow regime had a great deal in common with those of the Nazis. But as the fall of communism pushed the former Soviet communists into the arms of Russian neo-Nazis, so the decision of the Western democracies to restrain Milošević by force in Kosovo stimulated the recreation of the anti-democratic front of 1939-41.

Moral equivalence was not, then, a great deal different from what it is today. Just as Chomsky and Said declared that American power is the world's real enemy, and echoed Yugoslav propaganda, the socialist Thomas, the New York intellectuals grouped around *Partisan Review,* and Trotskyists like the writer Dwight Macdonald argued that, in the end, American imperialism was as much a world menace as the fascism of the Axis. Some among them argued that in opposing Nazism, America would itself become a fascist state - a theme repeated often by the likes of Republicans such as Taft and other conservative non-interventionists. And just as Pat Buchanan today thunders about betrayal of the ordinary American by internationalists, the America Firsters of 1940 argued that the American people were being led to war to serve global financial interests.

Both Buchanan, with his poisonous attacks on Israel, and the America Firsters, who applauded wildly when Lindbergh assailed the Jews, use such terms as 'internationalist' to cover an appeal to the crudest kind of anti-Semitism. Anti-Jewish prejudices are a constant factor in organizing against the democracies. In the current incarnation of the anti-democracy campaign, Arab opponents of peace in the Middle East supported Yugoslavia out of conditioned-reflex anti-Americanism. They ironically put themselves not only in the same company as Milošević, the mass murderer of Balkan Muslims, but also of Ariel Sharon, who saw the spectre of Islamic fundamentalism in the misery of the Albanian refugees, and who argued that an independent Kosovo might become part of a "Greater Albania" that would serveas a center of Muslim terrorism against Israel. Sharon went to Russia to meet Prime Minister Yevgeny Primakov, in front of whom he condemned the NATO bombing of Belgrade.

Similarly, in 1940, formerly-leftist Irish nationalists in Brooklyn who hated British imperialism served as the storm-troopers of the Christian Front, assaulting Jews in the streets of New York, while the Nationalist Party of Puerto Rico, supported by liberals and leftists, gloried in regular promotion by Radio Berlin and Radio Tokyo for its campaigns against American imperialism. These alignments have a way of exposing the real psychology behind ideologies. While leftists claim to defend multi-culturalism and to oppose ethnic oppression, they forgot all about those concerns when it came to Yugoslavia, because loyalty to anti-Americanism is more important to them than consistency in their views.

As George Orwell wrote, "There is a minority of intellectual pacifists whose real 'though unadmitted' motive appears to be hatred of western democracy and admiration of totalitarianism. Pacifist propaganda usually boils down to saying that one side is as bad as the other, but if one looks closely at the writings of younger intellectual pacifists, one finds that they do not by any means express impartial disapproval but are directed almost entirely against Britain and the United States… After the fall of France, the French pacifists, faced by a real choice which their English colleagues have not had to make, mostly went over to the Nazis…. All in all it is difficult not to feel that pacifism, as it appears among a section of the intelligentsia, is secretly inspired by an admiration for power and successful cruelty."

Of course, the main example of such twisting and turning – what we would today call spin – came in 1939-41 from the Communist Party of the U.S., which had distinguished itself for the fanaticism of its post-1935 Popular Front anti-fascism but suddenly discovered that 'imperialist war' was the greater enemy, out of nothing other than loyalty to the Soviet state. During that period, the communists outdid themselves in their efforts to convince their Nazi allies, both in Berlin and in the U.S., of their sincere affection for them. Herbert Romerstein has noted that the most anti-Semitic of Karl Marx's works, *Herr Vogt* -- in which Marx engaged in such banter as describing the German socialist Ferdinand Lassalle as "using his Jewish nose to pick up dung from the gutter to throw at his enemies" – was only published in communist Russia once, in 1941.

It must be said that similar ironies afflict open, ideological fascists and racists today. Of course, most of them, exemplified by Le Pen in France, love "ethnic cleansing," and rushed to support the Serbs. During the 1991-92 war in Croatia, however, the fascist movements were split, with some rallying to the Croats in memory of the *Ustaša* regime. One might wish that the ideological left was as divided on Yugoslavia as the fascists, but in fact most of the left lined up automatically with Belgrade.

Here is Noam Chomsky fantasizing on Kosovo: "There is no serious doubt that the NATO bombings further undermine what remains of the fragile structure of international law. The U.S. made that entirely clear in the discussions leading to the NATO decision. Apart from the UK [by now, about as much of an independent actor as Ukraine was in the pre-Gorbachev years], NATO countries were sceptical of U.S. policy, and were particularly annoyed by Secretary of State Albright's 'sabre-rattling.' Today, the more closely one approaches the conflicted region, the greater the opposition to Washington's insistence on force, even within NATO [Greece and Italy]."

And Edward Said denounced "the misguided and totally hopeless goal of humbling, and perhaps even destroying Milošević's regime". According to this enemy of Israel and the West, "All Serbs feel that their country is attacked unjustly, and that the cowardly war from the air has made them feel persecuted. Besides, not even the Kosovo Albanians believe that the air campaign is about independence for Kosovo or about saving Albanian lives: that is a total illusion." Of course, Said never explained how he presumed to judge the mental state of "All Serbs" and "the Kosovo Albanians". But Said is not a Muslim Palestinian, but a Christian; perhaps he felt a special affinity, for that reason, with the Christian Orthodox Serbs. After all, it was not that long ago that it was revealed that relief funds donated by Scandinavian governments to the Syrian Orthodox Church, for assistance to Palestinian refugees, had ended up fuelling the Serb war machine.

In May 1941, only weeks before Hitler brusquely ended his alliance with Stalin, *The Communist*, official ideological organ of the Communist Party of the U.S.A., included some remarkable gems. In 'Zionism and the Imperialist War,' by Paul Novick, editor of the Yiddish Communist daily *Morgen Freiheit*, we find a discourse that uncannily reproduces the arguments of Said: "It is not true that 'every Jew' is praying 'for the victory of the British Empire [against Hitler],' or that Jews generally are engaged in that pursuit. It is most emphatically not the case. Certainly, Jews in the United States, even conservative Jews, are least of all worried about the fate of the British Empire... the Zionist leaders seek to draw the Jewish people into the imperialist war... The destruction of the scourge of fascism in Germany would hardly be welcomed by the Zionist leadership... The Zionist leaders have no objection to extending a war which will bring untold suffering to millions of Jews in Europe... Zionist leadership is gratified by the thought of asking for compensation... Contrary to the wishes and interests of the Jewish people in the United States as well as Palestine, Zionist leadership is trumpeting for war... Zionism represents a dangerous instrument for dragging the Jewish people into the war and thereby for aiding the forces working to drag America into the war."

Thus Novick echoed the slanders of Hitler and Lindbergh: the Jews wanted war. Just as the Edward Said and Noam Chomsky accused NATO, not Milošević, of causing the expulsion of the Albanians from Kosovo, so Novick in 1939 claimed the incipient Holocaust was caused by the Zionists and Western imperialists, rather than by Hitler. As Orwell put it, "One has to belong to the intelligentsia to believe things like that: no ordinary man could be such a fool."

Such parallels may be no coincidence, as Soviet propagandists used to say. The London *Daily Telegraph* of April 4, 1999 reported, "When the Russian Prime Minister Yevgeny Primakov visited Slobodan Milošević in Belgrade last week, he took with him the head of Russian Foreign Intelligence and the chief of Russian Military Intelligence. Primakov's message to Milosevic was clear: 'All our agents in NATO HQ in Brussels, and also in Washington, London, Paris, Rome, Albania and Macedonia, are at your disposal to a man.' "

The *Telegraph* continued, "Intelligence is the main area in which Russia has been helping and will continue to help Serbia. And indeed, Russia does not have the capacity to digest the mountains of intelligence data that it receives from its networks; but it can sift through the information, and pass on what is relevant to Belgrade.

"In addition, Moscow will also be able to place at Milošević's disposal all the relevant information collected by its third espionage organisation, FAPSI [signals intelligence] which monitors satellite, computer, radio and telephone communications. The intelligence contribution is just one of many ways in which the Russians can help the Serbs... Neither [country] was able to create a free market economy; both are attempting to formulate a new ideology -- a hideous mixture of extreme nationalism and primitive socialism. Milošević and Primakov are former high-ranking Communist Party apparatchiks. Now, it seems, the quarrels of the Tito-Stalin period have been conveniently forgotten... But much more important for Russia is to save Serbia as an ally [and to weaken the position of the West]. To this end Russia will continue its active political, diplomatic and propaganda backing for Yugoslavia," the *Telegraph* concluded.

NATO bombing of Milošević's media garnered the Balkan butcher a new friend, in a surprising and, for Belgrade, highly gratifying manner. A certain Aidan White, of Irish origin, exercised responsibility as the head of the International Federation of Journalists, which, not long before, had eloquently protested Serb atrocities against Kosovar Albanian newspaper workers. But White's perspective was badly affected by his anti-Americanism, as well as his short memory, and perhaps by the legacy of Irish neutrality in the Second World War, when Dublin was the only non-Axis capital to proclaim official mourning at the suicide of Hitler. In any event, White was a champion humanitarian tourist, and with NATO striking at Radio Television Serbia (RTS), he hied himself forthwith to Belgrade, where he issued press releases in the full embrace of the local propaganda machine. White became the chief defender of Serbian media in the international journalists' movement, and proved that he had several things in common with Milošević.

While Milošević believed he alone represented Serbia, Aidan White believed that he alone represented the world's journalists. Like Milošević, White proclaimed that RTS was an authentic journalistic enterprise. But most importantly, like Milošević, White had a peculiar concept of journalistic accuracy. In the name of IFJ, White asserted far and wide that the NATO raid on RTS and the other Belgrade propaganda outlets was condemned virtually unanimously by the international journalistic profession. This was, simply, false, as White knew very well. Nobody in the ranks of the Independent Union of Professional Journalists of Bosnia-Hercegovina, the Association of

Journalists of Bosnia-Hercegovina, the Professional Journalists' Trade Union of Bosnia-Hercegovina, or the Alliance of Kosovar Journalists – all of whom White and his staff had frequently visited, and claimed to want to help – supported his position.

Some advocates of this posture asserted that reporters who considered Milošević a fascist and his media illegitimate did so because their strings were being pulled by the Clinton administration or NATO. But in certain cases, it was clearly the other way around: the author of the present narrative first wrote on the probability that the Serbs would massacre the Albanians in Kosovo in the *San Francisco Chronicle* in 1987, 12 years before the intervention, when NATO was completely indifferent to such issues and Clinton an obscure American governor. Certain foreign journalists had watched RTS for hundreds of hours, and, in describing Milošević as monstrous and his media as fascist criminals, were reporting, not offering an opinion.

During the Bosnian war Aidan White repeatedly went to Sarajevo, presenting himself as a friend of the embattled journalists there. Bosnian reporter Mensur Čamo wrote about the bombing of RTS, in the May 2, 1999 issue of the Sarajevo newsmagazine *Svijet:* "It is not true that the people at RTS were journalists and media professionals; the people from RTS long, long ago lost any right to call themselves that… [NATO] was doing something that in my view it was absolutely obliged to do." White would also offer the argument that bombing Milošević's media meant "we have to contemplate the potentially tragic consequences of targeting the media… worldwide", but he was years late, with moral consequences even worse than those of NATO's tardiness in finally intervening. As also noted by Čamo, the killing of journalists "just because they were journalists" had begun in the Balkans in 1991 with the assassination of Slovene and Croatian reporters by Serb terrorists, and continued through the decade with the deliberate murder of numerous Bosnian and Kosovar Albanian reporters and editors by Milošević's gangsters.

Months after the end of the NATO intervention, new controversy about the bombing of RTS, in which 16 people had been killed, erupted in Belgrade, underscoring the unwise nature of Aidan White's stunt. "In the regime media, the dead [in the bombing] were immediately declared journalists, even though none of them were," wrote Vlado Mares, a Belgrade correspondent for the Institute for War and Peace Reporting. "The aim seemed to be to stir up the press, primarily, in fact, the foreign press, who are known to be sensitive to the killing of journalists." But the relatives of the dead, Mares, and others discovered some remarkable aspects of the incident. How was it, they asked, that people were present in the RTS building after air raid sirens had sounded, and given that RTS was a known target? The offices of two other media outlets for Milošević propaganda, TV Pink, and Radio Kosava, were empty when the building they were in - which also housed the headquarters of Milošević's Socialist Party of Serbia - was bombed. Television Novi Sad was also destroyed, but the building was empty.

It transpired that two top bosses at RTS, Dragoljub Milanović and Milorad Komrakov, had barred the night shift workers from leaving the RTS building, even though the pair had departed at 2 a.m., just before the bombing. Aidan White, purporting to lead an international grouping of journalists' unions, might have much more appropriately condemned the RTS management, than NATO, for the deaths of the 16 workers. RTS was not, in any case, loved by ordinary Serbs. It was even said that Yugoslav soldiers rejoiced on hearing news of the NATO strike at RTS.

But in Serbia, Montenegro, and Kosovo, the bombs had continued falling. The Belgrade regime's economic infrastructure was rapidly being obliterated, and its military was better at intimidating Albanian families than at real war, so its master manipulators mobilized the human resources they knew best how to exploit, i.e. the civilian populace. Free rock concerts were held to boost morale. Serbs proclaimed national unity in the face of an alleged aggression, pinned paper targets on themselves, and began holding demonstrations on bridges, making sure they did so, in most cases, when there was little probability they would be bombed. In addition, it soon became obvious that Belgrade was being warned of imminent attacks on specific sites by a spy or spies in the NATO high command, as the *Daily Telegraph* had warned.

Finally, however, NATO won a smashing military victory, complicated only by the deviousness and antics of Russian politicians, diplomats, and commanders in the Balkans, who all seemed bent on proving that Moscow still represented a major world power. As revealed by American national security expert Zbigniew Brzezinski, months after the war was over, Belgrade's sudden surrender, which came in June 1999, had been much influenced by Russian pressure; but the Russians had also conspired to establish a separate Russian occupation zone, in co-ordination with the Serbs, on the northeast Kosovo border with Serbia proper. This would have constituted a partitioning of Kosovo and the establishment of a Serbian Republic comparable to that Dayton had left in place after the Bosnian armistice.

The Russians in Bosnia-Hercegovina even dispatched a force to race across Serbia and seize the Prishtina airport. That the larger plan for a Russo-Serb zone was not carried out was a consequence of courage and fortitude on the part of Bulgaria, which refused to grant their erstwhile patrons passage of up to 7,000 Russian troops. Bulgaria took its new association with the Western democracies quite seriously, and permission for Russian planes to enter

Bulgarian airspace was denied until the Russians submitted fully to NATO authority in Kosovo. Thus the gambit failed. The occupation of Kosovo by a new military force known as KFOR or Kosovo Forces was fully controlled by NATO, and even the problems at the Prishtina airport were resolved soon enough.

But if NATO had indeed won brilliantly in the military area, some aspects of the triumph were murky, to say the least. First, from the perspective of many Kosovar Albanians, UÇK had failed. The *guerrilla* force had faced serious problems throughout the war: the boycott on weapons to it by the Western powers, being the most significant. Finally, its contribution to the NATO intervention consisted of little more than service as target spotters for the bombing fleet. But Kosovar Albanians were unimpressed. Almost as soon as the intervention ended, with UÇK leader Hashim Thaçi preening as supreme hero, voices were heard demanding to know where UÇK had been when Serb police evicted people from their homes and killed their relatives.

Why had UÇK permitted the deportations to be organized without obstacle? Why had they not impeded the destruction of identity papers and property records? Why had they done nothing to protect leaders like the poet Din Mehmeti and the academic Fehmi Agani, both of whom were murdered, or to assist other intellectuals forced to hide in basements, such as the journalist Baton Haxhiu? Why had they let thousands of young men be led away to prison in Serbia? Why had they not at least distributed small arms, which were extremely plentiful in Albania, and organized defense groups among the civilian populace? The question was repeated incessantly: where had they been? The grim answer was, hiding in the countryside, according to many Kosovars.

Disgusted patriots who themselves had joined the organization or sent their sons and daughters into its ranks now warned that UÇK had been infiltrated by Serb spies all along. They pointed out that an UÇK uniform could be bought for 100 *deutschemarks,* and that anybody could put one on and claim to be a hero… and at least one UÇK leader later used this unfortunate fact to explain away crimes apparently carried out by UÇK members. Within weeks of NATO's triumph the UÇK were seizing homes, businesses, and vehicles illegally, or at least immorally, since there was no law in Kosovo. And ordinary Albanians insisted that Hashim Thaçi and his crowd, who soon formed a 'government' were nobodies, with no past and no ability to rule. The revolution, as so many times and in so many places before, had been betrayed.

Ibrahim Rugova had become somewhat unpopular among Kosovar Albanians saresult of his unfortunate appearances on Belgrade television during the intervention, in which he said nothing aloud. Western chatterboxes, including reporters, depicted him as fully discredited, and asserted confidently that Thaçi was the only important figure in Kosovar Albanian politics after the intervention. But this judgement, like so many others, reflected utter ignorance of Kosovar Albanian society, for Rugova had qualities that Kosovar Albanians considered quite preferable to the handsome profile of Thaçi; Rugova was a serious intellectual, and Kosovars had grown to know him well, regardless of his errors. If he had a fault, it was naïveté, not corruption and ignorance, which many Albanians saw in Thaçi and his group.

A figure that, tragically, was justifiably relegated to history was that of Adem Demaçi, who had become a political spokesman for UÇK but had not accumulated real authority either with the fighters or with the public. Kosovars felt he had changed his mind too many times; nobody really knew what he thought or would think next. Nevertheless, he was alone among the Kosovar Albanian leaders in refusing to leave Prishtina for the duration of the conflict. In an interview with the Serb opposition weekly *Vreme*, published on June 26, 1999, he reminisced with characteristic dry wit, "I didn't have too much trouble. I was stopped several times in the street. Only once, I think that was on May 25, I was taken to a police station. There were threats, they said some very nasty things. At one moment I asked them: 'Do you have guns?' Of course, they said. Then I told them: 'Kill me, but do not insult me.' Later a commander showed up. He was more polite. One of those who had insulted me at first even proposed to have a 'friendly' conversation. Of course, after all those insults, I refused. In the police station, some even wanted to discuss politics. I explained to them that there is only one person in their country to whom I could talk about politics. Their boss understood that. He said: 'All 12 million Serbs are Slobodan Milošević.' I replied: 'In that case, I do not have time to talk to that many people. ' "

Demaçi had announced his departure from political activity, but his essential humanism had remained undiluted by the atrocities he had seen. "Albanians were not threatened by ordinary Serbs," he declared. "Those people were mobilized, they had to accept that. How can you refuse if you're going to be sent to a prison? What is important is that most of them did not support this war. They had to fight." Since an exodus of Serbs from Kosovo had begun almost as soon as the ceasefire was in place, Demaçi was questioned as to his views about a common life between Serbs and Albanians in the future.

"There are several types of people among those who are leaving now," Demaçi explained. "Some were involved in the crimes committed in Kosovo and are aware that they cannot live here any more. They are followed by the members of their families. There are ordinary people who are frightened. They are afraid of revenge because Albanians are returning to their homes and finding destroyed homes and numerous mass graves. Because of that these people are leaving for Serbia, although they are completely innocent. Those who had huge privileges here are also leaving. They were bought by the regime. In Belgrade, or any other city in Serbia, people of that sort could not live in three or four room apartments. Here, they even had a chance to say, as blackmail, 'If I do not get such and such an apartment and a job, I am going to Serbia. ' They were close to the regime. Such people know that they will lose their privileges and they want to leave. I personally hope that a large number of Serbs will come back. There are examples that people in some villages around Prishtina still live together. During the war, they did not bother each other. That is encouraging."

Amazingly, the old prisoner's vision of the region's overall solution remained unchanged; he continued to favor a Balkan federation, or 'Balkania: 'A confederation would be even better than [Kosovo] independence. If we gain independence, the problems with Serbs and Montenegrins remain, and it is questionable how independence will be achieved. In a confederation, there are no such problems. From here, you could go to Belgrade, people from Belgrade could come here. No one would feel isolated. That would be a better solution for our Albanians who live in Presheva and Bujanovc in Serbia or in parts of Montenegro. We would remain in the same state. That is a common interest... it is impossible to talk about the unification of Europe and keep the Balkans outside such [a concept of] integration."

Demaçi was apparently matched, in his devotion to reconciliation and co-existence, by a figure from the Serb side: Hieromonk Sava Janjić, the Serbian Orthodox deputy abbot of the Dečani monastery. In the July 18, 1999 issue of *NIN* (Weekly Illustrated News), published in Belgrade, he candidly described the Serb policy toward Albanians as one of "the systematic deportation of the Albanian population, extermination of their identity, and destruction of cultural heritage". He blamed Milošević and his regime alone for "the current mass murders, slaughter, and revenge rapes" by Albanians against Kosovo Serbs that he described after the NATO intervention ended.

Fr. Sava later became well-known as the 'cybermonk' directing an Internet information center from the monastery of Gračanica, five miles outside Prishtina, on a main highway. With the passage of months, and the revival of mass demonstrations against Milošević in Belgrade, Fr. Sava appeared to be the only prominent individual representing a legitimate alternative to the regime. Obviously, given the role of the Orthodox clergy as a key institution of Serbian society, a man in his position would have some credibility.

157

Interviewed at Gračanica in October, Fr. Sava spoke from a besieged redoubt. British KFOR troops surrounded the village, which was exclusively Serbian; by then all the remaining Serbs in Kosovo had withdrawn into 'compact areas'. In one respect, Fr. Sava had not changed. He still referred to Milošević with such phrases as "the cancer of Europe", accusing him of "holding the entire Balkans hostage".

But in contrast with Adem Demaçi, who explicitly foreswore Albanian nationalism, Fr. Sava was said by many foreign observers to have lent himself to extreme Serb propaganda. He authored a preface to a glossy brochure issued by the Serbian Orthodox Diocese of Raška and Prizren with the unsubtle title *Crucified Kosovo*, listing 52 Serbian Orthodox monasteries and churches that had been vandalized or destroyed by Albanians after the KFOR entry into the territory. Therein, he charged the existence of "a systematic strategy... to annihilate once forever [sic] all traces of Serb and Christian culture in Kosovo".

However, it seems much more probable that local Albanians, often villagers, carried out these acts in isolation, in outrage at the suffering they, their relatives, and their neighbors underwent in the period before and during the NATO intervention. Shaykh Xhemali Shehu of the Rifa'i Sufi *teqe*, or lodge, in Prizren, who had fled to the U.S. during the war, noted: "During all the centuries we Muslims lived in Kosovo, how is it that all the Serb monasteries were left intact? We could have destroyed all of them, but because we followed *Qur'an* which recognizes the sacred in past traditions, we respected the Serb holy sites."

Indeed, Albanian Muslims rejected any intolerance or fanaticism toward other faiths. In an interview with the historian Andras Riedlmayer, H.E. Rexhep Boja, president of the Islamic Community of Kosovo, commented on the postwar influx of Islamic fundamentalists. "There are people who come here and want to tell us how we ought to do things," he said. "We have been Muslims for more than 600 years and we do not need to be told what Islam is. We have our own history and tradition here, our own Islamic culture and architecture. We would like to rebuild our community and to rebuild our mosques, but we want to do it our way."

According to a September 9, 1999, news release by the Saudi Joint Relief Committee for Kosovo, out of 4,087,353 Saudi riyals spent by the SJRCK on the ground in Kosovo, nearly half was spent to sponsor 388 religious 'propagators,' i.e. missionaries, with the intent of converting Kosovars to the Saudis' own fundamentalist Wahhabi sect of Islam. Another SR581,250 went toward the reconstuction of 37 mosques, and SR222,150 was spent on two schools. The remaining SR1,374,453 went for all other activities, including overhead and administration.

The amount of money involved was fairly modest (SR4,000,000 is less than £300,000 or less than half a million US dollars), except when one considers that the Saudis had only been on the scene in Kosovo for a litte over two months at that point. It was characteristic that a greater proportion of Saudi aid was spent on Wahhabi 'propagators' and on mosque-building, as opposed to broader humanitarian needs.

The same news release boasted of Saudi aid to Bosnia-Hercegovina over the previous five years, including the building the 150 mosques. But the Saudi-built mosques were unpopular with Muslim believers in Bosnia, because their architectural features were dictated by the narrow vision of Wahhabi fundamentalism, which execrates the Ottoman style of mosque decoration. Several notable mosques in Sarajevo, seriously damaged by Serbian artillery and rocket attacks, were rebuilt without their original decorations, so that, for example, the exquisitelybeautiful Imperial Mosque, which before the war had a layout that seemed to invite one to enter, was transformed into a structure that was externally not very different from a parking garage in a Western city.

Another Islamic 'aid' group, based in the United Arab Emirates, promised residents of Vushtrri that they would build them new mosques, which they claimed would be bigger, better, and "more Islamic", if they would first demolish the Ottoman-era gravestones of their Muslim Albanian ancestors, since Wahhabism violently opposes the veneration of the dead. The Saudis seemed intent on completing the work of cultural vandalism the Serbs had initiated, but in the name of Islam.

At the end of 1999, the Kosovapress News Agency, universally considered the media arm of the former UÇK, issued an extremely strong comment against the infilration of Wahhabi and other Arab missionaries into Kosovo.

Issued on December 29, the statement decleared, "For more than a century civilized countries have separated religion from the state... [However], we now see attempts not only in Kosovo but everywhere Albanians live to introduce religion into public schools... Supplemental courses for children have been set up by foreign Islamic organizations who hide behind assistance programs. Some radio stations, such as Radio Iliria in Vitia, now offer nightly broadcasts in Arabic, which nobody understands and which lead many to ask, are we in an Arab country?

"It is time for Albanian mosques to be separated from Arab connections and for Islam to be developed on the basis of Albanian culture and customs. We ask the same regarding the Albanian Catholic church, that it function independently from outside influence, as well as the Albanian Orthodox church."

It would be interesting, to say the least, to know the reaction of the numerous 'reporters' 'scholars' and 'experts' who expatiated at length on the alleged Islamic fundamentalism of the UÇK to such statements.

With the coming of real war in Kosovo, destruction of holy sites presented one of the worst features of the conflict. After the onset of the NATO bombing, mosques were used by Serb forces to shelter tanks. In the Serb attack on the town of Drenoc near Malisheva on May 30, 1999, the local mosque was heavily damaged. In Gjilan on June 16, a grenade thrown at the mosque injured 16 children. The main city mosque in Vushtrri, the Xhamia e Çarshit, was entirely demolished, leaving not one stone standing. In the surroundings of Peć, 34 mosques were vandalized.

Documentation was painstakingly assembled by Dr. Boja's office, on the vandalism of Albanian Islamic sacred structures. In an interview, he stated that 209 mosques were damaged or destroyed (one third of all those in Kosovo), the homes of 150 imams were devastated, 30 imams were killed, 15 were missing or in prison after the intervention, and up to four Sufi *teqes* were wrecked.

Dr. Boja's own office in Prishtina was sacked by Serbs and the community records obliterated, in a blaze set on June 13 by Serb police, that burned all day, with the flames visible on worldwide television screens as a backdrop to the entry of British soldiers into the city. The documentary collection held by Dr. Boja's community had originally been established as an Ottoman provincial archive for the records of religious endowments or *awqaf*, along with Islamic clerical and educational documents. The catalogue of the collection was also destroyed; only a section of materials, comprising about 20 percent of the whole, moved to the state archives years in the past, was saved. Six regional archives of the Kosovo Islamic Community, in Peć, Gjakova, Skenderaj, Gllogovc, Suhareka, and Lipjan, were also destroyed. And in line with Serb ideology throughout the years, great attention was paid to the systematic obliteration of property deeds and similar items.

Riedlmayer found the worst destruction of Islamic library resources in Gjakova, where on March 24, the first night of NATO bombing, Serb media had falsely reported an air raid on the city. Midnight saw Serb police and terrorists killing the town's residents out of hand, on their own doorsteps; the Serb forces then set fire to the historic center of the city. The Hadum Mosque, built in the 16th century, was torched, along with the library of Hadum Sylejman Efendi, from the 18th century. Hundreds of manuscripts and some 1,300 rare books were reduced to ashes, including the oldest known manuscript of an Albanian *Mevlid* text, in praise of the birth of the prophet Muhammad, by the poet Ali Ulqini.

Elsewhere in Gjakova, the Axhize Baba Bektashi *teqe*, the largest and oldest in the city, was burned in May, with the loss of 2,000 rare books and more than 250 manuscripts, including a 12th century manuscript in Persian. One of the Bektashis told Riedlmayer, "Five hundred years of Bektashi history and culture in this area perished in the flames when this *teqe* was destroyed." Even the computerized catalogue was devastated.

In Peć, the 17th century Kurshumli Mosque, constructed by the Albanian grand vizier of the Ottoman empire, Merre Husein Pasha, was left an empty shell, with its roof collapsed, and the library of the Atik *medresa* was burned, with 2,000 books and around 100 manuscripts destroyed. Riedlmayer also found sites where all that remained of mosques were bulldozed, empty lots.

Albanian Catholic churches were also vandalized. Riedlmayer learned that Serb officers had installed anti-aircraft radar in the steeple of St. Anthony's Catholic church in Prishtina, after ejecting the priest and nuns; NATO bombing of the radar, and therefore of the church and surrounding houses, would have been labelled an atrocity. According to the priest, he watched as a dentist's office only yards from his window, behind a bakery across the street, was used as a rape center by Serb terrorists. Cars pulled up filled with screaming women throughout the day and night, the priest said.

The Serbian Orthodox compilation *Crucified Kosovo* began with the charge that on July 17, 1999, after the arrival of German KFOR troops in the area, Albanian extremists dynamited the Svete Trojice monastery in Mushtishta near Suhareka. The monastery was constructed in the 14th century and included a library of medieval books. In addition, according to this Serbian source, the Presvete Bogorodice church in Mushtishta, erected in 1315, was wrecked and looted by Albanians in June, with the residence of the priest set afire. However, a reportage in the Serbian newspaper *Nezavisna Svetlost* (Independent Enlightenment) for July 31, 1999, indicated the monastery's destruction had heen a reprisal for the murder of the Albanian imam and burning of the entire Albanian village nearby.

To cite other examples, the Sv. Marka Koriškog monastery, built in 1467, the Sv. Uroša monastery and the Uspenja Presvete Bogorodice church in Šarenik, constructed at the end of the 14th century, and the Sv. Stefana church in Nerodime, also dating from that time, were blown up. These were but a few items on the long list.

It was difficult to fully determine the seriousness of damage in every case. For example, the Dević monastery in the Drenica region, built by Đurađ Branković around 1434, was clearly one of the most important Orthodox sacred monuments in Kosovo. According to *Crucified Kosovo*, "At the end of June 1999, immediately after the retreat of the Yugoslav security forces from

Kosovo and arrival of the French KFOR troops, the monastery was attacked and occupied by the Albanian extremists belonging to the KLA... For three days they systematically robbed, desecrated, and devastated this sacred place. The nuns were maltreated and some of them were badly injured."

But Serbs seeking to make such cases known to the world suffered more than one handicap to their credibility. Aside from the global bad image of Serbs and Serb media after the attempted mass expulsion of the Kosovar Albanians, the Orthodox authorities, during the NATO intervention, had falsely claimed major damage to historic monasteries and churches by NATO bombs.

Of course, holy sites for all three faiths in Kosovo were also saved. Gračanica, the center of Sava Janjić's 'cyberministry' offered one example. One of the most famous Sufi centers in Kosovo, the Sheh Mehmed Sezai Qadiri *teqe*, sits beneath the minaret of the Great Mosque (Xhamia e Madhe) and the Ottoman clock tower in the center of Prishtina. It is maintained by Fatime Shehu, the daughter of Shaykh Sezai, the last Sufi shaykh in the city, who died in 1947. Shaykh Sezai was a Kosovar patriot known for his opposition to the forced expulsion of Albanians to Turkey as well as for his mystical dedication. During the intervention "the *teqe* was surrounded by Serb police, and seven houses nearby were burned down, but the *teqe* was never attacked", according to the shaykh's daughter. She pointed out that the *teqe* once included 500 dervishes but that the community has been in decline over the past half century. Within its grounds is a *turbe* or mausoleum, with four tombs dating back two centuries.

In the destruction of both Orthodox and Islamic holy sites in Kosovo, it was notable how many were recently constructed. Vandalism seemed in numerous cases to have been motivated more by political than religious feelings. Četniks and Albanians alike resented the erection of structures that for each side seemed to represent the encroachment of the other. For the Serbs, the proliferation of new mosques reminded them that the Albanian population continued expanding, and might inevitably overwhelm them, in Kosovo as well as in Serbia at large. For the Albanians, the building of new Orthodox churches was seen as symbolic of Serb political domination. Thus it is unsurprising that among the 52 Orthodox sites reported damaged, we find several consecrated in recent years, such as the Crkva Svete Trojice church near Vushtrri and the Začeća Sv. Jovana Preteče church near Peć, both built in 1998. Albanian Catholic sites, on the other hand, were assaulted by Serbs purely out of ethnic and sectarian hatred.

It is remarkable, after all this, to find that Shaykh Xhemali of Prizren refused to condemn the Serbs as a people. "For years we lived with them peacefully," he insisted. "In fact, quite a few Serbs converted to Islam and became members of the Rifa'i Order after having witnessed our *zikr* 'that is the Sufi meditation ritual of remembrance of God'. But it would seem to require all the profound wisdom of the greatest Sufis and the holiest Christian theologians to bring religious peace to Kosovo.

Sava Janjić, for his part, had a personal background and intellectual history that might have suited him for this profound mission. He was, surprisingly, the product of a mixed marriage; his mother was Croatian, his father Serb. He was not baptized, although his parents were not communists, the usual explanation in such cases in Yugoslavia. He was born in 1966 in Dubrovnik, the historic Dalmatian center of fine arts, liberal philosophy, antifascism, and, in recent times, extreme dislike for Croatian quasi-dictator Franjo Tuđman. Although Croats and Serbs have long competed in claiming Dubrovnik for themselves, with the Croat argument enjoying by far the greater weight, Fr. Sava could be considered an outstanding representative of Dubrovnik Serbdom.

He grew up in the Hercegovinan town of Trebinje – whose beautiful mosques were all destroyed by Serbs during the Bosnian war – but his family was never nationalist. "I never saw myself in ethnically exclusive terms," he said rather shyly, when interviewed. His Serbian grandmother took him to the Orthodox church and his Croatian grandmother to the Catholic mass. His best friends in school were Bosnian Muslims. He became religious, and turned to a monastic life, in a manner that would be extremely familiar to thousands, if not millions of people in the West; feeling his life was empty, he first investigated Zen Buddhism and Japanese poetry and then went to Mount Athos, the Orthodox 'monastic republic' in Greece. The seeker had found a home.

Thus, the most committed opponent of Milošević in Serbia and the veritable conscience of Serbs in Kosovo was a mystic, who said his activism was an extension of his quest for spiritual freedom. His religious belief was clearly intense, and although he favored interfaith dialogue, which in Kosovo in 1999 seemed even more utopian than the overthrow of Milošević, he insisted it must be dialogue, respecting boundaries, it must be serious, and it must be carried out by believers. He rejected the 'guitar and group hug ecumenism' popular in America and Britain.

But there was something infinitely tragic about Fr. Sava. He asserted that religion was not the basis of the Kosovo conflict, and regretted that Serbs were no more religious than their Albanian neighbors. "Bishop Artemije [Radosavljević], my superior, spoke out against Milošević here for years, and nobody listened to him," he lamented. Fr. Sava could not expect, in the final reckoning of things, to realize his stated aim of freeing Serbia from darkness and seeing a revival of mixed villages in Kosovo, with churches and mosques in the same towns, as in the past.

For Fr. Sava himself was a man of the past, not the present or future. Not the past fantasized by Serbs, of Orthodox power in centuries gone by, but of the hippie and New Age excitements of the '60s and '70s, the time when he was born and grew up. It was absurd to imagine such an individual, no matter how appealing he was, representing most Serbian Orthodox church leaders. When he declared that "the majority of Serbian Orthodox bishops did not see Kosovo in political terms," he was simply deluding himself and lending himself to the attempt to delude his listeners. The Serbian Orthodox Church, unlike Catholic clerics, especially in Bosnia, and Islamic leaders throughout the Balkans, completely abandoned the commitment of their faith to peace, when Milošević's minions began the march to war. While the Bosnian Franciscans stood up against the attempt by Tuđman to participate in a permanent division of Bosnia-Hercegovina, while the Islamic *ulema* met regularly in Sarajevo with Catholic and Jewish representatives, the Serb Orthodox clergy typically blessed those who set out to cut the throats, burn the houses, and murder the children of their non-Serb neighbours.

Holy sites were not the only cultural monuments subjected to wholesale vandalism. A source close to UÇK claimed that during the war 64 Albanian libraries in Kosovo were burned, with destruction of more than 260,000 books. In addition, library staff and their families were attacked, and at least six library workers were killed by Serb police and soldiers. In the wake of the hostilities, Kosovar Albanian academic librarians pointed out that six major towns were left without libraries of any kind: Klina, Podujeva, Rahovec, Malisheva, Skenderaj, and Shtime. In the larger Podujeva district, 13 libraries had operated before the war; three remained afterward. Many more libraries in Kosovo were seriously damaged, including those in Peć, Gjakova, and Deçan, which are historical centers of Albanian as well as non-Albanian culture. It was to the credit of UÇK that it concerned itself with such matters, and that those associated with it appealed for financial aid to the affected municipal authorities. But it was utter fantasy to imagine that the international community that had taken over administration of Kosovo would address such problems.

Sava Janjić was also wrong when he claimed that the vandalism against Serbian holy sites in Kosovo represented a 'systematic' phenomenon, even in response to the clearlysystematic attempt to eliminate Albanian libraries. In Kosovo in late 1999, with the active intervention concluded, nothing was systematic, least of all the foreign administration set up by KFOR with the assistance of the Organization for Security and Cooperation in Europe (OSCE). This led to the second great gap in the NATO victory. Although NATO leaders promised that in Kosovo they would not repeat the mistakes they had made in Bosnia-Hercegovina, in reality they could not help doing so. They had settled into a pattern of colonial governorship in the Balkans with which they could not break; analysis of this would require a separate book.

By far, the area of the worst incompetence and misadventure by OSCE and the other foreigners engaged in ruling Bosnia-Hercegovina involved their dealing with domestic journalists. After four years of peace in that country, one became used to the common repetition of certain clichés about this topic, typically heard from the mouths of foreigners: first, that Bosnian media were responsible for the coming of the war; second, that Bosnian media needed to learn professionalism from foreigners; third, that without control of Bosnian media by foreign agencies and their local surrogates, conflict was destined to erupt there again.

In reality, war in Bosnia-Hercegovina was neither caused, nor prolonged, nor even aggravated, in most cases, by Bosnian media workers. And although, unfortunately, some foreigners did not seem to understand it, the Bosnian war did not 'erupt' . That war was a coldly planned aggression by Belgrade. In the preparation and launching of that aggression, Serbian media played a major role, as the instigator and agitator of ethnic resentments. But Bosnian media carried out no such activities. Bosnian media, until the actual beginning of atrocities at the tragic Bajram of the Christian year 1992, were characterized by fairness, neutrality, and a sincere attempt to defend the multi-ethnic traditions of Bosnia-Hercegovina against Belgrade's subversion.

This statement does not apply to Bosnian Muslim journalists alone. Many Croats and Serbs working for Bosnian media defended civic principles and cultural co-existence. Furthermore, the aggressor did not need local media to carry out the criminal plan developed in Belgrade; the existing organizational structure inherited from the communist bureaucracy, placed in the hands of Serbian extremists, along with the invasion by hordes of četniks from across the Drina River, and, most importantly, the withdrawal of Yugoslav troops from Croatia through Bosnia, facilitated the aggression.

The četnik terror began in Bosnia-Hercegovina without requiring a local repetition of the intensive political conditioning and co-ordination developed from Belgrade and most notably applied in the Croatian case. The murderers, rapists, and vandals who attacked such cities as Bijeljina, Zvornik, Foča, Banja Luka, and so many others did not need newspapers or even radio or television to direct them, although a number of Serbian journalists served as propagandists and similar media functionaries in Pale and Banja Luka, as did

Croats in Western Hercegovina, once their masters had occupied the territories on which they pursued their evil projects.

Furthermore, once the war began in earnest in Bosnia-Hercegovina, the majority of Bosnian print, radio, and television journalists served heroically on the front lines of the defense of their country. The whole world learned that the Sarajevo daily *Oslobođenje* (Liberations), kept publishing throughout the siege of Sarajevo, even after its famous skyscraper was destroyed. But many other such stories also deserve the attention of historians: above all, the role of the independent television and radio Studio 99, continuing work throughout the conflict, even after its broadcasting tower was blown up, and the activity of the weekly *Ljiljan*, which gave heart to Bosnian Muslim exiles and friends of Bosnia-Hercegovina abroad.

Thus, it was a despicable lie to treat the majority of Bosnian journalists as anything other than models for their colleagues everywhere, in their activities during the war there. Nevertheless, one heard many times, in Washington, Brussels, and elsewhere, that Bosnian media workers needed to be educated or indoctrinated in professional methods, standards, and ethics. Many discussions dealt with funding of such presumptuous, arrogant projects. However, no such instruction was needed by Bosnian media workers, least of all by people from the United States and Britain. Bosnian media workers had little to learn from foreign journalists, who rather, needed to learn from Bosnian media workers.

What does the term journalistic professionalism mean? It means self-respect. It means that reporters and editors refuse to lie, to serve the ends of propaganda, to incite violence, to accept bribes in reporting news. It also means understanding the risks of the profession, and not flinching or holding back when required to report from war zones or the scenes of riots or crimes, fires or natural disasters. It means being unafraid to face critics. And for reporters as working writers, it means always striving for accuracy and clarity, avoiding self-importance and excessive self-indulgence.

But as others have said, the professional objectivity of journalists does not mean neutrality. Media workers cannot refuse to defend their city, nation, country, religious community, and the human rights of victims. No journalist can be expected to grant some special consideration or understanding to a criminal like Slobodan Milošević, on the pretext of neutrality. Objectivity means reporting the truth about criminal politics, about war crimes, about fascism and Stalinism, about terror, about genocide. It does not mean asking a Muslim reporter to treat *četniks* sympathetically, any more than one would ask a Jewish reporter in New York to treat Nazis sympathetically.

By these standards we can not only praise most journalists in the Republic of Bosnia-Hercegovina; such journalists have demonstrated the highest level of professionalism anywhere in the world.

American journalists believe in a concept of free expression that we call 'the seamless garment'. This means extending to all the right to speak and write as he or she sees fit, without censorship or prior restraint. Of course, as a great American jurist once said, there cannot be a right to shout "Fire!" in a crowded theatre. If the spoken or written opinions of an individual constitute fighting words that lead to physical conflict, that individual should be held responsible before the law. That is why there was no contradiction between support for the NATO bombing of Radio Television Serbia during the hostilities and a demand for complete press freedom. RTS, aside from its history as a propaganda agency that forfeited the right to consideration as a journalistic institution, was the voice of NATO's enemy in wartime; it was fair game. On the other hand, while, according to real journalists, it was acceptable from the viewpoint of press freedom for NATO to bomb RTS, it was unacceptable to force Serbian media in the Bosnian 'Serb Republic' to broadcast pro-NATO news bulletins. To bomb a wartime enemy is one thing; to compel pro-enemy media in a third country to follow a particular line is another. In the absence of real conflict, spoken or written statements alone should not be censored or otherwise restricted.

While this principle might have been objectionable to some Bosnians who suffered at the hands of terrorists during the war there, as well as Albanians in Kosovo, it was far more difficult to accept on the part of foreign functionaries in Bosnia-Hercegovina or Kosovo. Put simply, most of these bureaucrats, who were charged with responsibility for developing local media, did not understand or accept the American concept of free expression. They were mainly Western and Northern Europeans whose own governments regulate media, and they could not comprehend the idea of unregulated media. Some of them, however, were also Americans who, having gone to the Balkans, forgot their constitutional heritage and came to see themselves more as members of the international community than as Americans.

Among these folk, who were granted the immense responsibility of guiding local media, there was also another problem: few, if any, were journalists. One who regularly offered opinions on the state of Bosnian media to the Bosnian public, was a former British military medical officer. Another, with the impressive title of 'senior media adviser' to the OSCE, and whose duties involved the structuring of the media in Bosnia, had a doctorate in psychology. Many Bosnians were at a complete loss to understand what professional qualification made such individuals fit to lay down rules for journalists.

167

Neither of them would, certainly, have trusted a journalist to treat their medical or psychological complaints. Why, then, should Bosnian media workers trust either of them to administer media? If such was necessary, it should have been done by journalists, not by nurses.

But it was not necessary. Even the least reputable media in Bosnia–Hercegovina were no worse than anywhere else in the former socialist countries, and some were considerably better; nor were they inferior to media in the U.S. and Britain, to cite the examples usually held up by foreign functionaries for local imitation. And no Bosnian media workers of any tendency, including Serbs in Banja Luka and Croats in West Mostar, were either capable of 'or interested in' starting a new war. Thus, foreigners had no business interfering in Bosnian media. They should have found other places to practice surgery and psychology; they needed to cease experimenting with Bosnia-Hercegovina as if they were so many Dr. Frankensteins. Perhaps the true heart of all these problems was that those charged with such heavy responsibilities were incompetent to carry them out, lacked imagination, and therefore improvised. But it was unacceptable to allow foreigners to improvise and experiment with the lives of Bosnians and Hercegovinans.

Another foreign official in Sarajevo, whose job involved licensing and punishing television broadcasters, declared that the mission of such bureaucrats in Bosnia-Hercegovina consisted in separating media from political parties and in suppressing nationalism in media and politics. But one should not propose two sets of standards for these issues. It was specious to claim, on the pretext of the 1992-95 war, that in Germany, Austria, Sweden, Norway, or the United States political parties might own or influence newspapers, but not in Bosnia-Hercegovina. And it was certainly unacceptable to say that in Ireland or Catalonia nationalist movements must be dealt with through negotiation, dialogue, and incentives to civic participation, and that in America national or social minorities might advocate for their rights, but not in Bosnia-Hercegovina. No sane person would argue against the freedom of Jews to denounce Nazis and the Holocaust, or that of people of color in the U.S. and Britain to assail colonialism and racism. But Bosnian Muslims were legally sanctioned for using terms like *četnik* and 'genocide' in their schools and media.

A severe criticism of the plans developed by the international community for media control in Kosovo was contained in an open letter sent on August 13, 1999 to United Nations Secretary General Kofi Annan and OSCE chairman Knut Vollebaek, by James H. Ottaway, Jr., chairman of the World Press Freedom Committee. The letter declared, "It is with great dismay that the WPFC learns of plans for a media control system in Kosovo. Despite the negative impact of similar measures taken by the Independent Media Commission in Bosnia, the OSCE – with the blessing of the United Nations - appears intent on imposing prescriptions on the once free and independent news media of Kosovo... As an organization committed to a free press and free flow of news everywhere, we must object to the establishment by OSCE of a so-called Media Affairs Department, which would write codes of practice... and 'monitor compliance and establish enforcement mechanisms. '

"From the outset of allied decisions to create a media control system in Bosnia, the World Press Freedom Committee and others have warned that this would serve as a dangerous precedent for UN operations elsewhere – specifically, in Kosovo. This has now proven to be the case, despite widespread warnings that the controversial and inconclusive Bosnia experience should not be repeated in Kosovo.

"Such plans, unfortunately, do not advance the independence of news media – a stated goal of the allied groups working through the United Nations in Kosovo. Such provisions for regulation are, in fact, in conflict with the principles of democracy and freedom that the United Nations is pledged to uphold.

"Prior to Kosovo's catastrophic... war, a free press functioned there. While financial assistance would be welcome for rebuilding printing houses and broadcasting facilities, foreign direction in how to operate them is neither needed nor desirable. It could, in fact, defeat the purpose of helping independent media to flourish once again in Kosovo."

Predictably, then, on October 13, 1999, the United Nations Interim Administration in Kosovo, known as UNMIK, which in Albanian could be pronounced to mean either 'I am a friend' *(unë mik)* or 'enemy' *(anmik)*, scolded the locals for abuse of freedom of speech. Although UNMIK correctly condemned "incitement of violence," it also assailed "offenses, insults, and personal attacks", which, in the U.S. and Britain, are purely matters of civil law. These abuses, by looking-glass logic, were deemed "an assault on the freedom of the press". The situation was not promising for the Albanian media in Kosovo; but unlike that in Bosnia-Hercegovina, which often had to dance to the foreigners' tunes, because it was impoverished, heavily subsidized or in some cases was even managed by foreigners, Albanian media was robustly independent and was paid for by the *diaspora,* as well as by local advertising.

This was dramatized in November 1999 when Agron Bajrami, from the Kosovar Albanian daily *Koha Ditore,* used the German newspaper *Frankfurter Allgemeine Zeitung* as a forum to blast the OSCE mission in Kosovo for its attitudes toward domestic journalists. Bajrami complained that Daan Everts, OSCE spokesman, insisted Kosovar Albanian media workers agree to a code of conduct applicable to their work; but the code was written by foreign media

advisers rather than Kosovar journalists. Bajrami also pointed out the ignorance in which many foreign functionaries in Kosovo pursued their activities;
for example, *Koha Ditore* had been labeled an UÇK-controlled newspaper the
very week that UCK representatives virulently attacked its main editors, including Veton Surroi, for criticizing alleged UÇK complicity in the mass expulsion of Kosovo Serbs.

On November 28, which is Albanian Flag Day and a national holiday for
the entire Albanian community worldwide, yet another questionable incident occurred, at Radio Gjilan in the town of the same name. At about 4:20
p.m., the station was broadcasting *Marshi i UÇK-së* (The UÇK March), a stirring but not very provocative ballad sung by the extremely popular singer Arif
Vladi. An American soldier, who was never identified, entered the station
premises and ordered that, per the decision of his commander, the broadcast
be terminated for the infraction of circulating nationalist propaganda.
Arguments with the staff led the American to, it was alleged, rip out the wiring,
leaving the station without power.

Whatever the authority or immediate actions of the unknown American,
nine staffers at the station were then arrested and held from about 5:35 p.m.
to 2:15 a.m. the next day. Radio Gjilan did not broadcast for several days afterward.

That Kosovar Albanians would allow any foreigners to prevent them from
describing their ordeal over a century as an attempt at genocide, or from broadcasting patriotic songs on a national holiday, was beyond the realm of possibility. And any such effort was liable to have unpleasant results. The so-
called international community should have grasped that the problem with
media in the Yugoslav wars was to be found in Serbia, not among Bosnians
or Kosovar Albanians. But the international community was cowardly about
restraining Milošević on his own territory, or for that matter, Tuđman in
Zagreb; prostrate, wounded, bleeding Bosnia-Hercegovina and Kosovo were
much easier to interfere with.

But ordinary Kosovar Albanians had other, more immediate things to
think about; by October 1999, they were so disillusioned with the policies of
Hashim Thaçi and his UÇK government that they wanted the foreigners to
immediately hold elections. Polls predicted that Thaçi would lose four to one
in a presidential vote, and that he would likely be beaten by Rugova, who the
international community and foreign journalists had so long dismissed as a
squeezed lemon.

The international community manifested little or no capacity to learn
from their mistakes. But Albanians seemed exactly the opposite. They had
learned a great deal from the calvary we have described in this narrative.

Certainly, the same attempted genocide – which is what it was, without question – had been repeated in cyclical fashion for decades. But the absurdities and moral failures of the international community were also cyclical and repeated.

An instructive example may be drawn from the life of the Catholic priest and Albanian national poet, Fr. Gjergj Fishta, whose epic poem *Lahuta e Malcís* (The Mountain Lute) was the first book printed in 'free Kosova.' In 1913, he founded *Hylli i Drítës* (The Morning Star), a Catholic periodical, in Shkodra; it became, without doubt, the most important single publication in all of Albanian cultural history. Shkodra was then occupied by foreign troops and administered by British governors. In July 1914, *Hylli i Drítës* published Fr. Fishta's classic essay 'A Dishonest 20th Century Comedy', in which he criticized the international authorities who spent their time having fun and did nothing to protect or improve the lives of the Albanians. The magazine was ordered closed, and the British governor of Shkodra, Colonel G. Philips, sentenced Fr. Fishta in absentia to 20 months' exile on the island of Malta. But Fr. Fishta escaped the town, remaining in hiding in the mountains for two years.

This incident would have loud echoes for broadcasters and other journalists in Sarajevo in 1999, fined and censured by foreign officials who could not read or understand what the putative offenders said and wrote. In the worst care, Sarajevo media workers saw the heroic newspaper *Oslobodenje* subjected to crude attempts at its suppression by American 'advisers'.

In addition, of course, the foreign doctrine of moral equivalence between Serb aggressors and their victims was applied at full bore in Kosovo, where OSCE kept hundreds of Serbs on its staff and daily stressed that protecting them was among their main priorities. The new colonial governors of Kosovo seemed wedded to a principle that could best be described as 'aid blackmail', under which no real economic help would flow into the region until Albanians proved they had forgiven the Serbs. This was the logical explanation for long delays in the transmission of funds to Kosovo officials, which resulted in frequent power outages, as one of several examples of the general lack of services for the local inhabitants.

In October 1999, taxi drivers charged 50 *deutschemarks* for a round trip from Prishtina to Mitrovica, the industrial city in the north of Kosovo, so long as it was made clear they would not stay more than an hour or so and would not be asked to leave the Albanian zone; Mitrovica was divided. They were reluctant to go anywhere near the Ibar River, the border between the Serb and Albanian districts. "It's very dangerous," they said. The road proceeds past Milosheva, named for Miloš Kobilić, the legendary slayer of Sultan Murat.

The sultan's *turbe* is also nearby, and the road showed the marks of the war, often disappearing in a detour through a field or narrowing to one lane.

Mitrovica had become a symbol as potent in its own way as the *turbe* of Sultan Murat, which Turkish leader Suleyman Demirel came to visit. On Friday, October 15, 1999, an Albanian student demonstration at the Ibar River borderline, which had been planned for weeks, finally occurred. Thousands of young Albanians, with a few who were very young and quite a few who were long past college age, demanded to cross the bridge. The position of the students was easy to understand: the main university buildings are on the other side, in Serbian territory. The demonstration became extremely turbulent, with French troops and police repeatedly firing stun grenades into the crowd. Four of the French 'peacekeepers' were wounded, as well as some 22 Albanians, including a 12 year-old boy; 100 Albanians required treatment of their eyes, with two sent to hospital in Prishtina.

In an outcome that surprised foreign journalists as well as others, including Serbs, the commotion ended when members of the new Kosovo Protection Corps (TMK in Albanian), which was set up under foreign sponsorship and which Serbs charged was no more than the UÇK in new uniforms, arrived and drove the protestors away. However, several days later representatives of KFOR flatly denied that they had asked the TMK for assistance in suppressing the demonstration.

Bernard Kouchner, the chief foreign administrator in Kosovo, was celebrating the award, the same Friday, of the Nobel Peace Prize to the organization of which he was a co-founder, Doctors Without Borders, when news of the clash arrived. Certain Western cynics, who perceive, in the politics of the Nobel Prizes, efforts to glorify those in need of support for failing or controversial humanitarian projects, suggested the prize represented an attempt to divert attention from the apparent failures of Kouchner's Kosovo mission. Kouchner himself was suitably modest. The Mitrovica demonstration showed he and his colleagues in Doctors Without Borders face "a lot of challenges", he averred. "Mitrovica is calm now as the demonstration is over. But we are facing a very difficult and very symbolic situation. My feeling is that we have not reached at all the point of reconciliation [between Serbs and Albanians]", he confessed in one of the greatest understatements of all time. His solution, however, was an ambiguous one: "co-existence".

Did co-existence in Mitrovica mean persistence of division between two zones, or an attempt to re-establish a mixed town? Serb media and some international outsiders, including the International Crisis Group, equated divided Mitrovica with the wounded Hercegovina town of Mostar; the Belgrade weekly *Vreme* called the Kosovo city "Mostar on the Ibar". There were similarities between the two cities, but there were also significant differences. Perhaps the most striking aspect in common was that Western administration in both places has become deeply confused by the incompetence of the French, who found themselves in the middle of a Croatian riot when they tried to disarm people in West Mostar a day or so before they faced outraged Albanians in Mitrovica. The latter viewed the French unequivocally as the best friends of the *četniks*, regardless of how many peace prizes were awarded to Kouchner and his friends.

One major difference between Mostar and Mitrovica was that in the latter the Albanians were clearly bent on regaining control of the northern sector by mass action if not by arms. "My mother had to leave her home there," said Zana I., a former university professor. "We want our homes back. And my husband's uncle was killed there by Serbs. He was an old man with a shop. They came and began breaking his windows, and since he spoke Serbian perfectly, he went out and asked what they were doing. They struck him on the head and he died within eight hours."

The later behavior of the Serb inhabitants of the northern sector did not help. In the confrontation on October 15, Serbs on the other side of the river egged on the assembled Albanians by chanting *četniks* slogans, and Mitrovica was a center of agitation for the formation of a separate Serbian Protection Corps, even though TMK included some Serbs, Bosnian Muslims, and a Turk in its training mission in France. Within days Kosovar Albanian opinion was stirred anew by reports that the notorious Šešelj had been seen in the Treš hotel at Zvečan, "under the noses of KFOR", in the words of the Albanian daily *Bota Sot* (World Today). The next day KFOR refused to comment on a report that it had arrested a group of armed members of the Kosovo Serb Protection Corps near the Mitrovica cemetery, supposedly coming from Zvečan. In November, the Belgrade 'independent' newspaper *Danas* (Today) reported enthusiastically that Serb employees at the hospital in Mitrovica were "under pressure by the representatives of the international community... to, in the name of multi-ethnicity, accept the return of ethnic Albanian colleagues," but that these humane Serbs had "rejected an offer of foreign currency assistance from local administrator Martin Garrod." They were paid, they proudly affirmed, small but regular salaries by the Serbian government.

One parallel between Mitrovica and Mostar, and for that matter between both those cities and Sarajevo, Banja Luka, Prishtina, and Belgrade, was the intersection of ethnic conflict and economic discontent. Simultaneously with Albanian student protests in Mitrovica over access to the university, Albanian high school teachers in the town threatened to strike for back pay.

A final point was made by the Albanian newspaper *Fakti* (Fact), published in Macedonia, in an editorial reprinted in Kosovo. For Albanians, "Mitrovica will be the place where it is shown whether or not NATO won a full victory." Within this commonsense statement a universe of meaning was hidden, that was all but unknown and incomprehensible to the foreign authorities in Kosovo, from Bernard Kouchner down.

For Albanians, a portrait of history in Kosovo is a portrait of an enemy. Not of a Serb or other human foe; but of history itself as the adversary. With their Illyrian language and Mediterranean customs, they had long defied history. In their best interest, one could only hope and pray that, with the turn of the millennium, history as they knew it had finally come to an end.

* * * * *

Bibliography

Abiva, Huseyin, 'A Brief History of Sufism in the Balkans: The Ottoman Era,' *The Muslim Magazine* (Mountain View, Calif.), Summer 1999.

Abiva, Huseyin, 'Shaykh Xhemali Shehu, Sufi Master of Kosova,' *The Muslim Magazine*, ibid.

Alba, Víctor, and Stephen Schwartz, *Spanish Marxism vs. Soviet Communism: A History of the P.O.U.M.*, New Brunswick and London, Transaction Books, 1988.

Andrić, Ivo, 'Report on Albania in 1939,' v. Pavić, Radovan, 'Greater Serbia from 1844 to 1990/91,' in Čović, Bože.

Anzulović, Branimir, *Heavenly Serbia: From Myth to Genocide*, New York and London, New York University Press, 1999.

Arifaj, Maliq, 'The Albanian Kosovar Youth in the Free World: Memorandum,' *Albanian Catholic Bulletin* (San Francisco), 1983.

Attias, Moshe ben Rafael (Zeki-Effendi), 'La historia de los Judíos de Bosna,' *La Alborada* (Sarajevo), May 24, 1901, cited in Nezirović, q.v.

Banac, Ivo, 'In Memory of Milan Šufflay,' *Albanian Catholic Bulletin* (San Francisco), 1994.

Banac, Ivo, *The National Question in Yugoslavia*, Ithaca and London, Cornell University Press, 1991 ed.

Banac, Ivo, *With Stalin Against Tito*, Ithaca and London, Cornell University Press, 1988.

Bartl, Peter, 'Kosova and Macedonia As Reflected in Ecclesiastical Reports,' in Pipa and Repishti, q.v.

Bataković, Dušan, *The Kosovo Chronicles*, Belgrade, Plato, 1992.

Boja, Rexhep, 'Medressah Alanddin, A Tribute to Albanian Resistance,' *The Muslim Magazine* (Mountain View, Calif.), Summer 1999.

Camaj, Martin, 'Foreword,' in Kanuni, q.v.

Carnegie Endowment for International Peace, *Report of the International Commission To Inquire into the Causes and Conduct of the Balkan Wars,* Washington, Carnegie Endowment, 1993 [reprint of 1914 ed. as *The Other Balkan Wars.*]

Čizmić, Ivan, 'Political Activities of Croatian Immigrants in the U.S.A. and Creation of an Independent Croatia,' in Ravlić, Aleksander, ed., *Southeastern Europe 1918-1995, An International Symposium, Vol. II,* Zagreb, Croatian Information Centre, 1999.

Council for the Defense of Human Rights and Freedoms, Annual Report for 1998, Monthly Report for January 1999, Prishtina.

Čović, Bože, ed., *Roots of Serbian Aggression,* Debates/Documents/ Cartographic Reviews, Zagreb, AGM, 1993.

Crnjanski (Tsernianski), Miloš, *Migrations,* London, Harvill, 1994.

Čubrilović, Vasa, 'Deportation of the Albanians,' in Čović, q.v.

Čubrilović, Vasa, 'Manjinski problem u novoj Jugoslaviji,' (1944 document), v. Cohen, Philip J., *The World War II and Contemporary Chetniks,* Zagreb, CERES, 1997, and Vickers, Miranda, q.v.

Ćuruvija, Slavko and Ivan Torov, 'The March to War (1980-1990),' in Udovički and Ridgeway, q.v.

Demaçi, Adem, *Gjarpijt e Gjakut dhe Novela Tjera,* v. Prifti, Peter R.

Djilas, Milovan, *Njegoš: Poet, Prince, Bishop,* New York, Harcourt, Brace & World, 1966.

Ducellier, Alain, 'Genesis and Failure of the Albanian State in the Fourteenth and Fifteenth Century,' in Pipa and Repishti, q.v.

Durham, Edith, Works cited in Freundlich, q.v., and in Pipa and Repishti, q.v.

Elazar, Samuel L., *El Romancero Judeo-Español/Jevrejsko-Španjolski Romancero,* ed. Muhamed Nezirović, Sarajevo, Svjetlost, 1987.

Elsie, Robert, ed.and tr., *An Elusive Eagle Soars: Anthology of Modern Albanian Poetry*, London and Boston, Forest Books, 1993.

Finn, Peter, 'Support Dwindles for Kosovo Rebels,' *Washington Post*, October 17, 1999.

Fishta, Gjergj, *Lahuta e Malcís*, Prishtina, Buzuku & Dija, 1999.

Fitchett, Joseph, 'New Challenge for Kosovo: Reconstruction,' *International Herald Tribune* (Paris), September 23, 1999.

Freundlich, Leo, *Albania's Golgotha*, Hans Peter Rullmann, ed., tr. by S.S. Juka and Steve Tomkin, *Hrvatska Domovina* supplement, *That Was Yugoslavia* (Hamburg), No. 10-12, 1992.

Garašanin, Ilija, 'Nachertanie,' in Čović, q.v.

Gjergji, Lush, 'Calvary in Kosova: Albanian Catholics in the Former Yugoslavia,' *Albanian Catholic Bulletin* (San Francisco), 1994.

Gligorijević, Branislav, *Kominterna Jugoslovensko i Srpsko Pitanje*, Beograd, Institut za Savremenu Istoriju, 1992.

Goldstein, Slavko, *Jews in Yugoslavia*, Zagreb, Muzejski Prostor, 1989.

Imamović, Jasmin, in Topčić, Željko, q.v.

Ivanov, Ivan Dželetović, *Jevreji Kosova i Metohije*, Beograd, Panpublik, 1988.

Hibbert, Reginald, *Albania's National Liberation Struggle: The Bitter Victory*, New York, St. Martin's Press, 1991.

Hull, Geoffrey, 'A Tour Through the Albanian Vocabulary,' *Albanian Catholic Bulletin* (San Francisco), 1994.

Janjić, Fr. Sava, *Crucified Kosovo*, Raška and Prizren Orthodox Diocese of Serbian Orthodox Church, Belgrade, 1999.

Kadare, Ismail, 'The Literature of Socialist Realism is Developing in

Struggle Against the Bourgeois and Revisionist Pressure,' *Albania Today* (Tirana), No. 3, 1977.

Kanuni i Lekë Dukagjinit/The Code of Lekë Dukagjini, Shtjefën Gjeçov, ed., tr. with an introduction by Leonard Fox, New York, Gjonlekaj Publishing Co., n.d. [reprint of 1989 ed.].

Kaplan, Robert, *Balkan Ghosts: A Journey Through History*, New York, St. Martin's Press, 1993.

The Koran, tr. by N.J. Dawood, London, Penguin, 1990.

Laffan, R.G.D., *The Serbs*, New York, Dorset Press, 1989 reprint.

Lewis, Flora, 'Russia in Kosovo Came Too Close For Comfort,' Paris, *International Herald Tribune*, October 1, 1999.

Lord, Albert B., 'The Battle of Kosovo in Albanian and Serbocroatian Oral Epic Songs,' in Pipa and Repishti, q.v.

Malaj, Vinçenc, O.F.M., 'The Activity of the Franciscans of the Dubrovnik Province Among Albanian Catholics,' tr. by Anto Knezević, *Albanian Catholic Bulletin* (San Francisco), 1994.

Malcolm, Noel, *Kosovo: A Short History*, New York, HarperCollins, 1999 ed.

Mares, Vlado, 'Sacrificed for Serbia?,' London, Institute for War and Peace Reporting, October 29, 1999.

Mertus, Julie, *Kosovo: How Myths and Truths Started a War*, Berkeley, University of California Press, 1999.

Mihailović, Kosta and Vasilije Krestić, *Memorandum of the Serbian Academy of Sciences and Arts (with) Answers to Criticisms*, Belgrade, Presidency of the Serbian Academy of Sciences and Arts, 1995.

Mobarak, Melhem M., 'Pashko Vasa: Governor of Lebanon,' *Albanian Catholic Bulletin* (San Francisco), 1989.

Nedić, Milan Ð., *Srpska Vojska na Albanskoj Golgoti*, Beograd, Štamparska Radionica Min. Voj. I Mornarice, 1937.

Nekaj, Zef V., Review of Dukagjini, Pal, *Jeta dhe Veprat e Gjergj Fishtes*, Albanian Catholic Bulletin (San Francisco), 1993.

Nezirović, Muhamed, 'La Istoria de los Žudios de Bosnia de Moše (Rafael) Atias (Zeki-Efendi),' in *Actas del IV Congreso Internacional de Historia de La Lengua Española*, La Rioja, 1997.

Norris, H.T., *Islam in the Balkans*, London, Hurst & Co., 1993.

Novaković, Kosta, 'The Colonization and Serbianization of Kosovo,' *Liria Kombëtare* (Geneva), July 13, 1931 (translated and republished in the Internet).

Ottaway, James H., Jr., 'Plans for a Media Control System in Kosovo,' *Pa Cenzurë/Uncensored* (London), Autumn 1999.

Pandolfi, Anne, 'Kosovo, Gulf War Coverage Compared,' *San Francisco Examiner*, July 20, 1999.

Pipa, Arshi, 'Serbo-Croatian and Albanian Frontier Epic Cycles,' in Pipa and Repishti, q.v.

Pipa, Arshi and Sami Repishti, eds., *Studies on Kosova*, Boulder, Colo., East European Monographs, 1984.

Podrimja, Ali and Sabri Hamiti, *Dega e Pikëlluar/The Sad Branch*, Rilindja, Prishtina, 1984.

Prifti, Peter R., 'Review of Demaçi, Adem, Gjarpijt e *Gjakut dhe Novela Tjera*,' *Albanian Catholic Bulletin* (San Francisco), 1984.

Pryce-Jones, David, 'Remembering Milovan Djilas,' *The New Criterion* (New York), October 1999.

Pulaha, Selami, 'On the Autochthony of Albanians in Kosova and the Postulated Massive Serb Migration at the End of the XVIIth Century,' *International Journal of Albanian Studies* (Internet publication), Spring 1998.

Rance, Didier, Albanie, *Ils Ont Voulu Tuer Dieu*, Mareil-Marly (France), Aide a l'Église en Détresse, n.d.

Repishti, Sami, 'Albanians in Kosova: From Heroic Warfare to Peaceful Resistance', *Albanian Catholic Bulletin* (San Francisco), 1993.

Repishti, Sami, 'Albanians in Yugoslavia: The Struggle for National Affirmation', *Albanian Catholic Bulletin* (San Francisco), 1982.

Riedlmayer, Andras, 'Kosovo: The Destruction of Cultural Heritage', published on the Internet by the Kosova Task Force USA, at www.justiceforall.org, 1999.

Roatcap, Adela Spindler, *Raymond Duncan: Printer-Expatriate-Eccentric Artist*, San Francisco, The Book Club of California, 1991.

Sachs, Jeffrey D., 'Taking Stock of the Transition', *Central European Economic Review* (Brussels), November 1999.

Sarner, Harvey, *Rescue in Albania*, Cathedral City, Calif., Brunswick Press, 1997.

Schwartz, Stephen, 'Ante Ciliga (1898-1992): Život na Povijesnim Raskrižjima', *Društvena Istraživanja* (Zagreb), Nr. 2-3, 1995.

Shestani, Zef, 'The Vatican and Albania', *Albanian Catholic Bulletin* (San Francisco), 1989.

Silajdžić, Haris, *Albanski Nacionalni Pokret*, Sarajevo, Bosanska Knjiga, 1995.

Sinishta, Gjon, ed., *The Fulfilled Promise*, Santa Clara, Calif., n.p., 1976.

Smiley, David, *Albanian Assignment*, London, Chatto & Windus, 1984.

Spahiu, Nexhmedin, *Serbian Tendencies for the Partitioning of Kosova*, Budapest, Central European University, 1999.

Španija 1936-1939, Vol. V, Beograd, Vojnoizdavački zavod, 1971.

'Sultan Murat and Miloš Kobilić,' legend recounted by Naim Berisha, Gladno Polje (Rakovica-Sarajevo), Bosnia, September 3, 1999.

Topčić, Željko, ed. *Forgotten Country, Vol. 2, War Prose in Bosnia-Hercegovina*, Association of Writers of Bosnia-Hercegovina, Sarajevo, 1997.

Translations from the contemporary Serbian press (*NIN, Vreme,* 1998–99), v. Internet publication at www.cdsp.neu/info/students/ marko, used with great gratitude.

Trotsky, Leon, *The Balkan Wars 1912-13*, Monad Press, New York, 1980.

Trotsky, Leon, *The Bolsheviki and World Peace*, Boni and Liveright, New York, 1918.

Tucović, Dimitrije, et. al., *Srbija i Albanci, Pregled Politike Srbije Prema Albancima od 1878 do 1914 Godine*, published by Časopis za kritiko znanosti, Ljubljana, 1989.

Udovički, Jasminka and James Ridgeway, eds., *Yugoslavia's Ethnic Nightmare*, New York, Lawrence Hill Books, 1995.

Unsigned, 'Adem Demaçi–Longest Held Political Prisoner in Yugoslavia,' *Albanian Catholic Bulletin* (San Francisco), 1985.

Unsigned, 'He is a muezzin and a teacher,' Kosovapress (Prishtina), December 29, 1999.

Unsigned, 'The Arbitrary KFOR Intervention in the Radio-Program of Gjilan,' Kosovapress (Prishtina), December 1, 1999.

Unsigned, 'KTC Condemns Abuse of Freedom of Speech,' *UNMIK News*, Prishtina, 13 October 1999.

Unsigned, 'The Radio-Gjilan is Still Closed,' Kosovoapress (Prishtina), December 3, 1999.

Unsigned, 'A Remembrance of Pjetër Bogdani on the 300th [Anniversary] of His Death,' *Albanian Catholic Bulletin* (San Francisco), 1989.

Unsigned, 'The State of the National Libraries in Kosova,' Kosovapress (Prishtina), November 7, 1999.

Vickers, Miranda, *Between Serb and Albanian: A History of Kosovo*, London, Hurst & Co., 1998.

Visaret e Kombit, 2 vols., Vol. I ed. by Gurakuqi, Karl and Filip Fishta, Vol. II ed. by Palaj, At Bernardin and At Donat Kurti, Prishtina, Rilindja, 1996.

Zickel, Raymond and Walter R. Iwaskiw, *Albania: A Country Study*, Washington, Library of Congress, 1994 ed.

* * * * *

The author's thanks for research and translation assistance go above all to Naim and Rukije Berisha, without whom this book could not have been realized in its final form, as well as Idriz Berisha, Ray Frost, Zana Ibrani, Čedo Kapor, Katerina Mijatović, Vjosa Mujko, Professor Muhamed Nezirović of the University of Sarajevo, Laura Peterson, Boris Petrovčić and Sheh Zymer Salihi. Professor Sami Repishti of Adelphi University, Professor Robert J. Donia of the University of Michigan, Professor Robert D. English of The Johns Hopkins University, and Branka Magaš of the Bosnian Institute in London, graciously read the manuscript; their assistance was indispensable. My friend, the historian Ronald Radosh, was generous with his research on isolationism in the U. S. at the beginning of the second world war.

Special thanks are also due Dr. James Lyon, Sarajevo, and Amb. Brian Hopkinson, Prishtina, both of the International Crisis Group; Kemal Muftić, executive director of BHPress, Sarajevo, and Slobodan Stajić, foreign editor of *Oslobođenje*, Sarajevo. And finally, salaams to Kadrush Hoti.

INDEX